Somewhere on the
MOUNTAIN

THOMAS BECK

authorHOUSE®

AuthorHouse™
1663 Liberty Drive
Bloomington, IN 47403
www.authorhouse.com
Phone: 1 (800) 839-8640

Published by AuthorHouse 03/29/2019

ISBN: 978-1-5462-6960-1 (sc)
ISBN: 978-1-5462-6958-8 (hc)
ISBN: 978-1-5462-6959-5 (e)

Library of Congress Control Number: 2018913842

Print information available on the last page.

Foreword

For me, growing up in the 1950's wasn't very pleasant. I didn't have a normal childhood like a lot of kids. My story deals with an event that happened to me when I was a teenager in 1957. Something which I thought that would really be neat.

Dedicated to the Memory of
Allan Cavender

"He reached out to the stars, and far too soon, touched the clouds."

Part

I

My problems really began when my mother placed me, and my little brother in the care of the Bryan family. I had just turned eight, and my brother, six.

She had some reasons to do this, one of which was that she was working at a bar, and it was easier than looking for a babysitter. At the time, my dad was overseas serving in Korea. This was in the summer of 1951.

I hated the Bryan family. I became very neurotic while staying with them. You never knew what to expect from the old man or his wife, Eunice. They would compliment you at times, and then turn around, and give you a hard, cold slap across the face the next, and beatings weren't uncommon. That was when I first learned not to cry when getting a whipping. Old Man Bryan believed that if you did something wrong, and deserved a beating, then you should take it – crying was for babies.

That included the times he would bend me over in the bathroom, and cornhole me. I was lucky that he was hung like a ground squirrel, or else he could've really hurt me. I never told anyone about those incidents because I was scared to death of him. I didn't think anyone would've believed me anyway.

The Bryans had three kids. A girl Billy's age, and two boys. One was twelve, and the younger boy was the same age as me. They both liked to pick on me, and oh, how I hated it there.

After we lived with them for about five months, our mother died suddenly. This was in November of 1951. Billy, and I weren't allowed to go to her funeral for some reason, although we were taken to the mortuary for a private viewing.

After she died, our father came back from Korea, and I thought he would take us to live with him. But to my dismay, he decided to leave us with the Bryan family. We wound up staying with them for over 2½ years. I felt like we were doomed to live with them forever.

However, fate finally stepped in.

One night, the old man was coming home after he'd drank a few beers, and he blew a stoplight, and his car was T-boned, and he was killed instantly.

I sat very solemnly at his funeral, and listened to the pastor talk about how Old Man Bryan had been taken from us while in the prime of his life.

I was just glad he was gone. At long last, I wouldn't have to put up with his slapping me one minute, and then the next he's taking me into the bathroom, and screwing me in the ass, all the while, talking nice, and softly.

After his funeral, I heard Eunice telling someone that she didn't want to babysit other people's kids anymore, and I could have jumped for joy. For surely now, my dad would let us live with him.

But my father had other plans. He decided to put us in a boarding school for single-parent children, and wards of the courts.

I was now 10, and Billy was 8. We would be with kids much like ourselves, and we'd be properly cared for, and supervised.

At least that's what our dad was told.

Part

2

I t was an unusually, mild, sunny Sunday afternoon in January of 1954, when our father drove us up to a two-story, red brick building call the "Home." It sat on a lot near the downtown part of the city, and a chain link fence surrounded the premises. There was close twenty five kids there, ranging in the age from five to sixteen. The Home was run by an older couple known as Uncle Harry, and "Aunt" Alice.

While Dad got our suitcases out of the trunk, I felt a sense of dread. When we visited the Home before, it had seemed like a great lark. I'd been impressed with the large playground; the big, dining room, and the dormitories with their rows of beds, neatly spaced apart.

But, the best thing was that they had a television, and that's what had sold me. And anything had to be better than staying with the Bryan's.

But now, I wondered if this was such a good idea after all. There was a dark, haunting presence about the place, and I had a sense of foreboding, like something bad was going to happen here but what, I didn't know. I'd never experienced these kinds of feelings before, and it scared me. I tried to shake them off, and Dad seemed to sense my fear, and anxiety.

"Come on now," he said. "There's nothing to be afraid of. You guys will be fine."

"I'm okay," I told him uncertainly.

We walked up to the steps of the spacious, roofed, front porch which was supported by big, white, wooden columns. There were fancy, frosted panes of glass in the front door, as well as the whole entryway itself.

My father rang the bell, and after a couple of moments, Uncle Harry opened the door, and smiled.

"There you are. Please come in," he said.

We walked into the lobby of the Home which Uncle Harry used as his office. Along one wall, was an old-fashioned roll top desk, and a couple of chairs. On the other side of the desk was a door that led into his living quarters.

Directly across from his desk, on the other wall was a long, wooden bench. Next to it were two multi-paned, windowed doors that went into the library of the Home. There was a large, wooden table, and chairs in the center of the room, and along the walls were some soft chairs, a couch, a piano, and of course, to my delight, lots of books.

I loved to read. When I read a good book, I could get lost in the words, and shut out the real world for awhile. I planned on spending some time in there. On the wall at the far end of the office was a doorway that led into the main part of the Home. Looking at it now made me nervous. I knew that once I passed through that door, I'd be stuck here, and there'd be no going back.

The walls of the office were decorated with some old photos, including one of the "camp" in the mountains.

When we first visited the Home, Uncle Harry had told us about it, and how every summer was spent there hiking, fishing, and swimming. That'd really sounded great to me, and was another reason I thought I'd like it here.

But summer was a long ways off now.

Uncle Harry motioned us to sit on the big, high-backed, bench, then seated himself in a wooden, swivel chair, in front of his desk. He was a large, balding man in his mid-fifties. He wore wire-rimmed, bifocal glasses, and appeared to be very grandfatherly in manner.

"Well," he began. "It's Tommy and … uh, Bill is it?"

My brother nodded.

"Well, Tommy and Bill," he began again. "I hope you'll like staying here. Your father has told me a lot about you two. For instance, Tommy, I know that you wet the bed."

I squirmed in embarrassment and he gave me a sympathetic look.

"There's nothing to be ashamed of," he said. "We have several boys here who have the same problem."

He smiled and his next words surprised me.

"I use to wet the bed myself when I was a child."

"Did you really sir?" I asked in surprise.

"Yes I did," he answered. "But eventually I grew out of it just as you will. As I said, there's nothing to be ashamed of. It happens to a lot of children."

Here I felt like I was the only one with this problem and now a grown man had admitted that he used to wet the bed just like me. And I wouldn't be the only bedwetter either. There were other kids here with the same problem. That helped ease my mind a little.

"Now, I think you should know that some of the boys here can be a little mean and ornery," he said. After saying that, he saw the look of concern on the faces of Billy, and I, and he tried to be reassuring. "I wouldn't worry too much about that." He told us. "But if anyone bullies you, and puts his hands on you, don't be afraid to tell me or my two assistants, Mr. Bucholz or Mr. Greene."

Dad seemed more curious than concerned when he asked Uncle Harry if there was a lot of bullying that went on. He believed in settling things with his fists, and he wanted Billy, and I to be like him. My dad wasn't afraid of anything … but I was! I couldn't speak for Billy, but I'm pretty sure he was too.

"Oh, sometimes," Uncle Harry replied then smiled. "You know how boys are."

"Yea," my dad laughed. "I know what you mean."

I failed to see the humor in what was being said. There wasn't anything funny about being slapped, punched, or kicked by a bully.

Uncle Harry went over a few rules with Billy and I, and then asked us if we had any questions. We didn't.

"Well," Uncle Harry said and stood up. "I'll get Mr. Greene. He's in charge of our younger boys. I'll be right back."

He left the office and we got up from the bench. I felt scared, and put my arms around Dad's waist, and hugged him tight.

"I wish we could stay with you," I told him, and close to tears. "I love you Daddy."

Billy just stood there watching us, but I could tell he felt the same way. Dad looked down at me, and seemed uncomfortable. I know he didn't like emotional displays.

"We've already gone over this now," he said kindly. "This was what you kids wanted. You seemed to like this place when we were here before, so what's the problem? I think this is the best way to go right now. I can't work, and watch you, and Billy at the same time. They'll take good care of you boys here, and I won't have to worry about you."

About that time, Uncle Harry appeared in the doorway with a young, dark-haired man with glasses, who looked to be in his early twenties, and I remembered him from before.

"Mr. Janicek" (Jana-check) Uncle Harry said formally. "You remember Mr. Greene. You met him when you toured our facility before. He'll be in charge of your sons."

Dad greeted him and they shook hands.

"Now, Uncle Harry said. "If you boys will go with him, he'll get you squared away."

"I'll see you guys next weekend," Dad promised, and gave us each a hug.

Now that the moment had arrived, my heart was racing with fear, and uncertainty of the unknown. Mr. Greene picked up our suitcases, and walked over to the door leading out of the office, and Billy, and I followed.

Just when we got there, I turned to wave goodbye to Dad, but he was already engaged in conversation with Uncle Harry, and he didn't see me.

When we passed through the doorway, there was another door directly across from us that led out into the large kitchen, and dining room area. In the space between the two doors, was a closet to one side, and on the other was a carpeted staircase that went up to the second floor.

It was reserved for Uncle Harry, and the counselors, and we kids weren't allowed to use it, unless in case of emergency.

We crossed the dining room, and came to yet another door, and we entered the darkened television room. It was large, and squared, and the TV sat off to one side when you walked in, and there were several rows of metal, folding chairs set up in front of the set.

When I saw the flickering, black, and white screen, some of my cares and woes went away. At least I'd be able to watch it while I was staying here, which was something I really enjoyed.

Some kids were doing that, and they glanced over at us curiously when we walked in, and then just as quickly it seemed, turned back to the show they were watching.

There wasn't a back door in the Home, and once we were inside, Mr. Greene turned, and led my brother, and I past the chairs towards a door on the wall directly across the room from the television.

That one led us into a big, washroom where a long, tub-like basin sat in the center of the room. A long, thin water pipe fed six faucets, and a drinking fountain. At the very, far end was a small bathroom.

Directly across from us as we came in, was another door with a window in it. This was the doorway that led out to the yard of the Home. There we're a couple of windows on the wall behind the washbasin, and the light was a shock to the eyes having just come from the shaded TV room.

When we entered, there was a short wall off to the side, and once we went around it, we came to two stairwells.

The closest one went down, and the other up. On the wall next to the farthest stairway, was a door that went into the rear of the kitchen.

It was apparent that the home hadn't been built completely square, and you could really tell that when you reached this part of the building. Three windows across from the staircases, you could see that the kitchen, and second floor area extended to clear out past this end by a good 15 or 20 feet.

Mr. Greene led us up the far stairwell, and we followed. The staircase was made of concrete, and our feet swished, and echoed on the steps.

After we reached the second floor, I could see off to one side, a short, darkened passageway that I remembered went to one of the dormitories. The far end of it was brightened by the open doorway of the room.

Mr. Greene, in the meantime, kept going down the long, hallway ahead of us. I say crooked, because about halfway along, the walls suddenly jutted out about 5 feet, and the door of the storage closet faced us. It was reserved for linen, cleaning supplies, etc.

The wall on the other side jogged over also, and there was a big, bathroom further down, the hall and beyond that, the front stairwell. On the other side of it, facing us, was the doorway to another dorm, and next to it it was a room for the other counselor.

When we got as far as the closet, Mr. Greene turned, and Billy, and I followed him inside the entrance to a large dormitory. It was a long, wide room with a row of single beds on the far wall. The door was in the center of the entryway, and there were a few bunk beds on either side of it.

Over on the outside wall, the bright, afternoon sun was shining through several windows onto the old, yellowed linoleum floor. I could hear some kids playing outside in the yard beneath them.

We were in the "Middle Dorm," which was the largest of the three dormitories in the home. It was reserved for the younger kids like Billy, and I.

The other dorms were called the "Front," and "Back," and of course were for the older boys.

Each dorm had recessed, wall lockers with wooden doors, and Mr. Greene walked up to a couple of empty ones, and set our suitcases down.

"These will be your locker's," he explained. "I'm sure you'll be glad to get out of those jackets now that you've got a place to put them. You don't need them on a day like today."

Both Billy, and I were wearing our winter coats, and he was right. It was rather warm, and I shed mine, as did Billy.

Then he took a roll of white tape from his pocket, and tore off a strip, after which he looked at me. He seemed like a nice guy, and that helped soothe my anxiety.

"I'm sorry," he said apologetically. "What's your name again."

"Tommy, sir"

"No I mean your last name."

"Janicek, sir," I told him.

"You don't have to call me 'sir.' Just call me John," he explained kindly.

The Bryan's had taught us that children should always address their elders as "sir" or "ma'am." They had backed this up with a slap across the face if we didn't.

"Oh. Okay."

"You'll have to spell your last name for me."

"Oh. It's J-a-n-i-c-e-k."

"What nationality is that?" He asked, curiously.

"Czechoslovakian, sir, uh I mean John," I replied.

"That's what I thought," he said. "I'm German myself."

He took a strip of tape, and placed it on the locker door. After producing a pen, he asked me spell my name again, and then he wrote "T. Janicek" on the tape. He did the same thing with Billy's locker which was next to mine.

"Did you guys bring locks?" He asked.

"Yes si …, yes our dad got us each one." I answered.

"Well be sure to keep it locked. Because if you don't, and somebody swipes something you value, we're not responsible. It's up to you to see that your locker stays locked. Okay?" He told us.

Billy and I both nodded and then Mr. Greene pointed at the bunk bed closest to our lockers.

"Those are your bunks. I'll get some bedding, and then you guys will have to make them up."

He walked out, and Billy, and I begin unpacking our suitcases, and putting our coats, clothes, and possessions in our lockers. I took out a small box, and put it under a couple of pair of jeans at the bottom of the locker. Inside was a St. Christopher Medallion, and chain my mother had given me a couple months before she died. The thought that someone might steal it alarmed me. I'd had a hard enough time just keeping the Bryan boys from taking the medal.

One of the Bryan boys had tried to take it from me one time, but I raised such a fuss, his mom told him to leave me be. After that, I kept the medallion hidden, and now would have to do the same thing here. And make sure that I kept my locker locked up tight.

Billy had one too, but I'd never seen him wear it, or show it off. He was a very quiet, secretive, and a solitary child. His hair was brown, like mine, but curly, and his round, cherubic, face, was peppered with freckles. But the most striking thing about Billy, were his eyes. I took after my dad's baby blues, but Billy had our mom's deep, brown, soulful, sad eyes. The kind that really bothered me, whenever I mistreated him. He would look at me like, he couldn't believe I was being mean to him. We weren't very close, and I never really knew what he was thinking, one minute to the next. But I loved him anyway. I just didn't know how to show it.

Where I was loud, outgoing, and a show off, Billy was one of those kids that you never really noticed, or paid much attention to. He was there, but he never had much to say, and was always on the fringes of whatever was going on. My brother never showed a lot of emotion, and pretty much stayed to himself. He wasn't in the habit of sharing things with people, and especially not with me, because he knew I'd blab it all over the place. I'm sure he he had mom's gift to him safely hidden away.

Mr. Greene came in holding some blankets, and sheets, and laid them at the foot of the bottom bunk. Then he looked over at me.

"I assume you know you're going to be sleeping on the bottom?" He said.

"Yessir," I told him, and then cringed.

"Please call me John," he reminded me.

"Oh … okay … John."

"Well the reason I'm asking is because I know you wet the bed and I don't think your brother would want to be in the bottom bunk, when you had an accident," he joked. "He might get a bath!"

He chuckled, but when he saw how embarrassed I was, he quickly apologized. Billy hadn't laughed, and he just stood there, with a blank look on his face.

"I'm sorry Tommy," Mr. Greene said. "I shouldn't have teased you."

"It's okay." I was touched by his sincerity, and I liked him.

"Well," he said. "We better get busy."

He pulled out a rubber sheet, and pinned it to the mattress with safety pins, then after stretching it out, did the same thing on the other side. Then he looked up at me.

"Every time you have an accident you need to strip your bed, and hang your sheets in the clothesline out back," he explained.

"Oh okay," I replied.

I couldn't look him in the eyes, and I felt very uncomfortable. Wetting the bed was something I had no control over, and I tried not to think about it. I didn't like to be reminded.

"As soon as you kids are done, come and get me, and we'll get your suitcases stored downstairs. My room's right across the hall," he told us.

He left, and Billy, and I finished storing the rest of our belongings. When I was through unpacking, I put the lock on the door, and snapped it shut. The solid, chunk, or steel meeting steel, gave me a satisfying, strong, sense of security. Nobody was going to get in there now. I put the key in my pocket, then walked over to my bed, and grabbed a sheet and began to spread it out, so I could fold it under the mattress.

Billy came over, and did the same with the top bunk, and when I was done with my bed, I helped him finish making his.

When we were ready, I carried our empty suitcases out the door, and walked over to Mr. Green's room. It was across the hall from the utility closet in the opposite direction.

He was sitting at a small desk, reading a paperback book, and he looked up at us in the doorway, and smiled.

"Did you guys get everything squared away?" he asked, and turned his book over, then stood up.

"Yessir," I said, absent-mindedly.

"Please, it's John," he told me again.

"Oh, … sorry."

"Don't be sorry," he replied. "That's an admirable quality you have, but I would rather that you called me by my name."

"Uh, okay … John." I answered.

"That's more like it," he said with a smile.

He took the suitcases, and we walked back down the hallway to the stairwell, which we descended to the first floor again. Then we turned, and went down the other set of stairs that led to the basement. When we got to the bottom we turned and walked through a doorway into the recreation room. There was a ping pong table on one side, and a pool table further down. There were both in use.

There were a couple of kids about my age, playing ping pong, and over at the pool table, three older boys were engaged in a game of "eight ball." They all looked at us briefly, and then went on with their games.

We walked back to the far end of the basement, where Mr. Greene put our suitcases down, and then unlocked the door to the storage room. Then he took our suitcases, and stored them away inside. The room was crowded with all kinds of stuff: furniture, boxes, trunks, and more suitcases.

Mr. Greene came back out, and locked the door, then looked at us.

"Now," he said. "I'll introduce you to some of our boys."

We went back to the rec area, and he cleared his throat loudly, but none of the kids paid any attention to him.

"Hey guys!" he said real loud. "I need to speak to you for a second!"

All activity, and talk came to a halt, and I started feeling very self-conscious, because you could tell they didn't want to be bothered. I was pretty sure they wouldn't be thrilled about meeting Billy and me either.

"Guys," he said. "I'd like you to meet our two newest boys. This is Tommy Janicek, and this is his brother Billy."

There was an awkward pause, and when none of them responded, I spoke rather meekly.

"Hi."

"There!" Mr. Greene said. "Now, why don't you guys go around, and introduce yourselves."

I fidgeted nervously, feeling their eyes on us. Their names, and faces became a blur, and were forgotten almost as soon as they told us. Afterwards, they all went back to their games, and Mr. Green said he'd see us later, and left.

Billy, and I walked over, and stood, and watched the ping pong game and then he turned to me.

"I think I'll go watch some tv," he said, and started walking towards the stairwell.

"Go ahead," I told him. "I'm gonna stay here for awhile."

He went on out the door, and I continued to watch the game in progress I was hoping one of them would offer to play me when they were finished. I liked playing ping pong. I'd played it at the church the Bryan's attended, and we used to go to a Youth Group there on Wednesday nights. I wasn't too bad a player.

When they were done with their game, I thought they might ask me if I wanted to join in, but they just ignored me, and started another one. After they did that, I decided to go upstairs, and watch some tv with Billy. I was tired of standing around, and being made to feel like I wasn't worthy of their attention.

As I turned around, and started towards the door, suddenly the ping pong ball whizzed past my head, and went out the door. It wound up bouncing around the stairwell, making a goofy, almost tinny, sound before finally shuddering to a stop.

"Hey, you!" a voice shouted. "Mick! ... or whatever yer name is! Bring me that ball!"

I stopped in my tracks, and anger began to to take over any of the anxious feelings I'd had about being in this place. I'd be willing to bet almost anything, that the ball had been hit at me on purpose and now I was supposed to fetch it like I was a dog or flunky.

"Hey!" he shouted again. "I said git me that ball! You deaf or sumpthen?"

I wanted to turn around, and tell him to go to hell, but I didn't.

Instead, I went out the door, got the ball, and walked back in, then threw it towards the ping pong table. I didn't even look at the two players. Then I turned around, and started to leave.

"Hey, what the fuck you think yer do'en asshole? Come back here!" this guy yelled.

His tone of voice made me stop, and I froze, then slowly turned to see which one of them was cussing me. My anger was being replaced by the anxiety again that I'd felt before. The rec room had gotten awful quiet, and I heard someone snicker. I felt my face flush with embarrassment, and a sliver of fear began to grow inside my gut as I walked back towards the table.

One of the kids who'd been playing came up to me. He was about my age and size, but he sounded older, and looked mean.

I couldn't remember his name; Sonny or Donny, something like that. There was a tough look, about him that unnerved me. His dark, brown hair was cropped close in a crew-cut, and his cold bluish-grey eyes, flickered over me, and when they fixed on mine, I cringed.

"I threw it back to ya," I said meekly.

He walked up, and put his face close to mine, and I swallowed nervously, and felt very weak, and alone.

"Look stupid," he sneered. "I asked ya to bring it to me, not throw it, stupid."

"Don't call me stupid," I said, trying to sound outraged.

He moved his head closer, so that we were nose to nose, and I could feel his hot breath on my cheeks. I tried to move away from him, but he stayed right on top of me.

"Why! Whut'cha gonna do about it, stupid?" he taunted.

I'd finally had enough, and summoned up all the courage I could muster, and pushed him away. He stumbled back, then came straight at me. I started to put my hands up to shove him again, when suddenly, his fist landed on my cheek, and a flash of lights went off in my head, and I landed on my ass. I put my hands out, to keep from going over backward, and hitting my noggin on the hard cement floor. Stunned, I sat there dazed for a moment, then I scrambled to my feet, and faced him. I wasn't hurt that bad, just angry. I'd been hit harder, and getting slapped or punched wasn't something new to me. I was almost used to it. But I was tired of people going out of their way to pick on me.

"You dirty bastard!" I screamed. "Leave me alone!"

His eyes narrowed, and he threw another punch, but I stepped back towards the door, and he missed. I began to turn away from him to make a run for the stairs, when suddenly, a pair of hands reached out, and grabbed me by the arm, and spun me around. Then I was raised up, and slammed against the wall by the door. I found myself staring into the face of one of the older boys. He resembled the kid who'd hit me, and he had the same cold, bluish-grey eyes. I thought, Oh no, another brother act, just like the Bryan boys."

"Watch out who yer calling names, you little fuck'en creep," he snarled, "or else yer gonna git hurt. Now get the fuck outta here!"

He threw me towards the door, and I staggered backwards, hitting the block wall, and looked around for some sign of help or support, but there was none.

Suddenly, Uncle Harry came to mind. He'd said if anyone bothered me, to come to him. I bolted for the door with jeers from some of the boys ringing in my ears, and I hurried up the stairs.

When I scurried through the tv room, Billy glanced over at me, and he could tell there was something wrong, but he didn't say anything. He was used to seeing me get into one scrape after another. If I wasn't falling, and hurting myself, then someone else was doing it for me. Trouble seemed to follow me around.

When I got to Uncle Harry's office, he was standing by the door talking to Mr. Greene, and they gave a start, when I burst in trembling, and a little out of breath.

"Uncle Harry," I whined. "One of those boys downstairs hit me."

"Who hit you?" he asked irritably.

"One of the boys playing ping pong," I sniffled. "I don't know his name."

"Sounds like Ronny or Timmy," Mr. Greene said. "They were playing when I came upstairs. You want me to handle it?"

"No, I'll deal with this myself," Uncle Harry told him.

He walked over, and opened a drawer in his desk, and pulled out a belt that looked like it was made out of braided plastic. One end was all gnarled, and twisted.

"Alright," he sighed. "You'll have to show me which boy hit you."

He looked very mean, and menacing now, and not like the grandfatherly figure who'd talked so kindly to me earlier, when my dad was here.

We left his office, and when we reached the tv room, the boys there looked concerned when they saw Uncle Harry with the belt. Billy just shook his head.

"Why'd he hit you?" Uncle Harry asked.

We were walking out of the door of the tv room, and when we turned towards the basement stairwell, I started to explain.

"I don't know. He …"

I stopped because the kid who'd punched me, met us at the top of the stairs that led into the basement. His friend was right behind him, and when they saw who was with me, they both halted, and looked concerned.

"That's him!" I said excitedly, pointing. "That's the guy, Uncle Harry!"

"Did you hit this boy?" Uncle Harry asked in a threatening manner.

"Yea, I'm sorry Uncle Harry," he said. "I didn't mean to."

Uncle Harry's eyes narrowed, and he raised the belt to strike, and the kid put his arms up in a feeble attempt to ward off the blow, but it didn't help. The belt made a nasty, whistling sound, as it cut through the air, but even worse was the sharp, slap the braided plastic made when it hit flesh. I winced, and now wished I hadn't said anything. The boy began to scream in pain as the beating went on, and I felt sorry for him. Especially when I saw the ugly, red welts appear on his arms.

Uncle Harry finally stopped, and he was breathing hard. The kid had backed up against the rear door, that led into the kitchen, next to the upper stairwell. He was crouched down, with his arms covering his head. Now that the assault was over, he slowly brought them down, and stood up. I expected him to be sobbing, but to my surprise, he wasn't.

There were tears in his eyes from the beating, but when he saw me staring at him, there was a look of anger that made me wish I hadn't said anything.

Just then, I saw the older guy who'd threatened me, coming up the stairs behind the other kid. He looked really angry, and I backed away from the stairwell, and pointed him out to Uncle Harry.

"And that guy threw me against the wall, and called me a fuckin creep, Uncle Harry!"

"Yeah, because he called Ronny a bastard," he retorted nastily.

"Yes, but he …"

I never finished speaking, because Uncle Harry slapped me across the chest with the belt. I yelped in pain, and surprise, and took a couple of steps backwards. I couldn't understand what I had done wrong.

"Enough!" Uncle Harry snapped. "I don't want to hear anymore out of you! Nobody likes a tattletale! … Now! … If I hear about anymore fighting amongst you kids, I am going to beat your asses raw! Have you all got that?"

He glared at each of us, and when we nodded our heads, he turned around, and left which scared me. Now I was alone with the two brothers, and their friend. I had no idea what they would do to me now that Uncle Harry wasn't there.

"You've had it, ya fuckin snitch!" the older guy said.

I was standing in front of the outside door, and I thought if they came at me, I'd run out-doors. I didn't have any idea where I'd run to, but I knew it wouldn't be to Uncle Harry. Maybe I could go to John. He'd be nice.

But they turned, and went back down the stairs, and I waited until their footsteps died before moving. I thought I'd go up to the dorm, so I could be as far away from them as possible. I scooted past the basement stairwell, and climbed the steps, and made my way to the Middle Dormitory.

Once there, I laid down on my bunk, and thought about what had just occurred. Jeezus, I hadn't even been here an hour, and already I'd managed to get in a fight, and make a couple of enemies, and get a half-assed beating. This place was starting out to be as bad as the Bryan's. Gawd, I hoped not.

A wave of hopelessness washed over me, and I wondered what other kinds of torture this joint had in store for me. Judging from what I'd seen so far, the future didn't look very bright, and my spirits were pretty low.

I was really wrapped up in my thoughts, and I jumped when a voice broke into the silence. I hadn't heard anyone come in.

"How're ya do'en?" someone asked.

I turned my head, and looked up, and saw a young kid about my age, standing just over my shoulder. He had an average, round friendly face, topped by a thatch of light, sandy brown hair, and pale, blue eyes which just about described me. He was grinning in a self-conscious sort of way, and I couldn't help but grin back at him.

"Okay," I lied, and sat up, and put my feet on the floor. The rubber cover crackled and I hoped he wouldn't notice.

"My name's Tommy," he said. "Whut's yers?"

"Hey! So's mine! My name is Tommy too!" I told him happily. "Whut's yer last name?"

"Madsen," he said, "Whut's yers?"

"Mine's Janicek," I told him, and we shook hands.

"Janicek?" he said. "Whut's that? Polish?"

"Nope Czech," I answered proudly.

He sat down on the bunk across from me, and we stared at each other for a moment, and shared a smile.

"How long have you lived here?" I asked him.

"Oh, I dunno," he said. "About a year, I guess. That's when my grandma died. My mom had me put in here cuz she couldn't always find someone to watch me while she worked."

"Oh." Boy that sounded familiar.

I couldn't imagine spending a year in this dump. Hopefully my dad wouldn't leave us in here that long, but I wasn't going to hold my breath over that.

"Man, that Uncle Harry sure is mean," I told him, and gingerly rubbed my chest. "He hit me with that weird looking belt of his. Whut happened to it anyway?"

He told me that a kid had stolen the belt out of his desk, and then taken it out to the Home's old concrete incinerator and threw it on top of a bunch of newspapers, and lit them on fire.

The only problem was, the old man saw him doing it, and he got it out of there, and saved most of the belt. It was still warm when he used it on this kid.

"Whut'd Uncle Harry hit'cha for?" he asked me curiously after he was done speaking.

I told him about those two guys ganging up on me, and how I went to the old man to let him know about it, since that's what he'd told me to

17

do. And then all of a sudden, I'm getting hit, and I hadn't done anything wrong to my way of thinking.

He started shaking his head halfway through my story, and when I reached the end, he was frowning.

"Whut's wrong?" I asked him uncertainly.

"Man, if ya want to stay healthy here," he said, "I wouldn't make it a habit outta runnen to Uncle Harry every time someone does sumpthen you don't like."

"Why?" I asked worriedly.

"The big guys'll take ya out back of the garage and give ya a 'Ratso, Fatso, and Japso'," he told me.

"A whut?" I didn't like the sound of that at all.

"I'll show ya," he said, and stood up. "Cum'on."

He started towards the door and I got up and followed him. We walked down the hallway, and just as we reached the stairway, a dark-haired boy appeared coming up the stairs towards us. We moved off to the side, as we started to pass him.

"Hey Joey," Tommy said.

"Hey," the kid answered.

This guy stopped, and stared at me curiously, so we halted, and faced him.

"This must be one of the new guys'" he said.

"Yea," Tommy replied. "His name's Tommy too."

"Oh yea?" he said, and made no effort to shake hands, or even act friendly.

He turned, and walked away, and I decided I didn't like him. There was an air about him, that told me he and I were not going to become best buddies.

Tommy, and I continued on down the stairwell, and I hoped we wouldn't meet those other guys, but the first landing was empty. We came to the door that led outside, and when we opened it, there was a short set of concrete steps, and we went down them. Then I asked him about the kid we'd just met. Something told me he wasn't someone you'd want to trust.

"His name's Joey Mendoza, and you gotta watch him," he told me.

"Why's that?"

"Well to start with, he's crazy. He's the one who stole Uncle Harry's belt, and threw it in the incinerator. And he'll steal anything that isn't nailed down, and besides which, he's a dirty fighter," he explained. "He'll kick ya right in the balls."

When I heard the part about stealing, my thoughts instantly went to my locker, and more importantly, to my medallion. The guy had been headed in the direction of the Middle Dorm, and I halted, and Tommy did too.

"Whut's the matter?" he asked.

"Does this Joey live in the Middle Dorm?" I questioned.

"Yeah." He answered.

"I'm just trying to remember it I locked my locker," I said nervously.

"Did ya?" he asked.

"Yea, I locked it." I answered.

"Well," he cautioned. "If you've got anything ya don't want stole, keep it locked."

"Yea, that's what John said," I told him.

"Who? Oh? Ya mean Greenie?" he laughed.

"Greenie?" I asked. "Is that whut ya call him?"

"That's whut everyone calls him. Ya know, like a great big, green goober?" he grinned.

"Yea," I answered. "Why do ya call him that? He seems pretty nice."

"Oh, you'll find out," he said with a knowing smile.

He took off before I could ask him anything else, and he headed in the direction of a large, brick garage. I hurried and caught up with him.

This part of the home was like a small, fenced in courtyard compared to the rest of the yard. I noticed the clothesline upon which I'd hang my sheets on in the mornings, and I looked away because I didn't like to be reminded of my nightly affliction.

I hoped my seemingly, new found friend wouldn't think less of me because of it. That'd really be a drag.

The alley that dissected the houses, and businesses on the block, cut into the Home's property, which like the building, wasn't laid out square. I noticed the old, fire blackened concrete incinerator that Tommy had told me about sitting alongside the chain-link fence, as the cement passageway made its way towards us.

The fence abruptly ended, and there was a large entryway, and the alley made a sharp, ninety degree turn in front of the gap, and then continued on until it reached the street behind the Home.

The wire enclosure in the meantime, started up again by the garage and like the alley, made its way back until it came to the sidewalk, and then turned, and resumed its journey around the rest of the yard.

Inside the garage, was a big, yellow bus, and a black Oldsmobile 88, which I assumed was Uncle Harry's car.

Once you got this far, you could begin to see more of the sparsely, tree lined playground.

There was a tetherball pole on the other side of the Home, and some kids were playing a game. A little further away, was a parallel bar, and that was it, as far as recreational equipment went. There wasn't even a swing set.

The rest of the big yard was just barren dirt.

After we walked around, and behind the garage, the home was completely out of sight. Tommy stopped, then pointed to a crude-looking face that had been painted on the reddish colored bricks with white paint. Underneath it was the word, "Ratso." There were two other faces in line with the first, each one spaced out about three or four feet apart. The other two read "Fatso" and "Japso". They'd been there for some time, and were weather-worn, and rather faded.

I gazed at them for a moment, and I was puzzled, then looked at Tommy.

"Whut do they mean?" I asked mystified.

He seemed to take great pleasure in my ignorance, which was kind of annoying.

"The first one's Hitler, then Mussolini, and then Tojo," he explained. "Ratso", "Fatso, and "Japso."

"Oh … yea."

World War II had ended in 1945, but was still fresh in the minds of a lot of people. I was born on June 23, 1943, right in the middle of the war for the United States. I was, of course, too young to remember it.

My dad served in the Navy in the South Pacific with Admiral "Bull" Halsey's 7th Fleet. The ship my dad served on, was the U.S.S. Crosby, a WWII destroyer escort … a "four-stacker." The Crosby was a sister ship to the U.S.S. Ward, the one that sank the Japanese sub, just before the attack on Pearl Harbor on December 7, 1941.

The day I was born, my father's ship was landing some troops on an enemy island, somewhere in the Solomon Islands. Dad didn't hear of my birth until August. The Crosby was involved in a lot of battles, and was credited with shooting down twenty four Jap planes. Dad was a Third Class Gunners Mate, and he and his gun crew were responsible for downing seven of the enemy aircraft. The ship, had also sunk two Jap submarines, and I never tired of hearing my father talk about his wartime experiences.

I was fascinated by the War. There was a mystique about it that really got my juices flowing. I read every book about World War II that I could get my hands on, and I loved to watch war movies, like John Wayne's "Sands of Iwo Jima." They made the War seem so noble, and heroic. The good guys against the bad guys. Ratso, Fatso, and Japso. I should've know that, and I felt kind of foolish.

"I thought I'd better warn ya," Tommy said. "If the big guys think yer a rat, they'll take ya out here, and work ya over, just like they would've Ratso, Fatso, and Japso."

"But they already know I'm one," I said fearfully. "I told on those two guys, and the oldest one said he'd get me."

"That was Ronny, and Larry Collins," he said. "Since yer new here, I wouldn't worry about it too much. Just don't do it again or else they'll make life miserable for ya."

That didn't help ease my fears any, but at least I knew better than to go to Uncle Harry whenever I had a problem with someone. From now on, I was just going to have to tough things out. I was beginning to hate this place more, and more.

We walked back to the main building, and went in the tv room. Billy was still there watching television, and I introduced him to Tommy. We talked a bit in between commercials, and then Billy got up, and left to go use the bathroom. Tommy said my brother seemed like a nice kid, but he sure was quiet.

"Yea, he's always been like that," I told him.

Sometimes I envied my little brother. Especially when I got myself into situations like this. He never ran off at the mouth like I did, and people seemed to like him better than me.

There were a couple of younger kids there watching also, and they seemed friendly enough, but I was at a point where I didn't care if anyone liked me or not. I tried to lose myself in the shows, but I kept thinking about those two brothers.

About that time, Mr. Greene came in, and sat down with us, next to Billy. He looked past him, and asked me how I was doing.

"Okay," I told him.

"Did you get that hassle with the Collin's boy worked out?" he asked me. I didn't know what to say, so I just nodded my head.

"Well, the next time you have a problem like that, feel free to come get me, and together we'll see what we can do about it," he said.

When Tommy heard him say that, he glanced over at me, and shook his head in disgust, I remembered what he'd said about the guys beating me up, if you snitched on them. I knew better now, but I appreciated the fact that Mr. Greene was willing to help me out, and that was comforting.

Ever since Mr. Greene had sat down, I noticed how Tommy had made a point of ignoring him. I remembered how he'd called him Greenie, and said "you'll find out." I wondered what he problem was. He didn't seem like a bad guy to me.

Mr. Greene watched a program with us, and then he left. When he was gone, I felt uneasy, because while he was there, I knew I wouldn't be bullied.

"Mr. Greene seems nice," I told Tommy. "How come you don't like him?"

Tommy just rolled his eyes, and laughed.

"Whut's so funny?" I asked irritably, and he leaned over towards me.

"Ol' Greenie's a queer!" he whispered.

The shock of hearing that made me sit back in my chair, and Billy looked over at us. I could tell he was concerned too.

I knew what the word meant. I'd overheard the Bryan boys talking about a kid, in school, who'd offered to give a blowjob to the older boy, and he said he'd punched this queer in the stomach, and then spit on him. I remembered how disgusting they made the whole thing sound.

So evidently, if someone was a homo, then it was okay to abuse them. Or make fun of them. Of course, I was so naive, putting Old Man Bryan in the same category as a queer, didn't even enter my mind. He was too big, and mean to be a faggot. But now, to hear that about the first decent adult I'd met here, was a real letdown.

"How do ya know that?" I asked, hoping he was wrong.

"Watch him. He's always coming in the bathroom when we're taking showers, and sneaken' peeks," he answered. "I think he's a peckerchecker."

"Yea, but that don't mean he's queer," I told him.

"Wait, there's more," he insisted.

"Okay."

"One of the big guys caught him jacking off in his room," he said knowingly.

"So?"

"Yea, well finally, he takes guys in his room for talks, and they're in there for a long time." He nodded then sat back with a smug, smile on his face. "I don't think they're playing tiddlywinks. Well, maybe Ol' Greenie is, but he ain't using tiddlywinks."

"Oh yea," I told him. "How do ya know whut he's do'en? Has he ever tried anything with you?"

"No, but you watch," he said. "He's slimy. Just like a big, green goober. You wait. You'll understand after you've been here awhile."

That kind of talk made me uncomfortable, and I tried to concentrate on the tv. Tommy could see I was kind of upset, and dropped the subject. Billy, as usual, never said a word, but I knew he'd picked up on everything that was spoken.

As I watched the tv set, my mind was racing with all the events of my short stay here. This place was proving to be worse than I thought. I was really going to have to watch myself from now on.

My lousy mood was heightened, when Ronny, and his friend, Timmy Miller came in, and I tensed up. They saw me, and I heard them say something about a "rat." There were some empty chairs behind us, and they sat down.

I tried to ignore them, but they kept making remarks, and kicking the legs of my chair. This went on for a while, until I finally turned around, and told them to stop it.

"Stop it, stop it," they mocked, then Ronny sneered.

"Whaddaya gonna do? Run to Uncle Harry, Ratface?" he taunted.

Tommy turned around, and tried to stick up for me.

"Hey, Ronny, he's new," he said. "He didn't know any better."

Ronny gave Tommy a mean look, and then stood up. I grew concerned because I thought he might hit Tommy, so I stood up also. Ronny then turned his attention on me, and he smiled, but there was no humor or warmth in his features, just cold, dislike.

"Stay out of it, Madsen," Ronny said, never taking his gaze off me. "Unless ya wanna knuckle sandwich."

"Look, I'm sorry," I told him sincerely. "I didn't know Uncle Harry was going to beat ya like that, or I wouldn't have said anything to him. Honest."

Suddenly, his eyes saw something, and all the toughness seemed to melt away, and then he was just a scared, little boy. I couldn't figure out what was causing this amazing change, and I turned around, and saw a figure coming towards us from the doorway of the dining room. A huge figure. It was Buck Bucholz, the other counselor.

Tommy had told Billy, and I about Buck, and how big and bad he was. After seeing him for the first time, I realized how inadequate Tommy's words were in describing him.

Buck stood 6'4", weighed 275 lbs., and was in charge of the big guys. He was ably qualified to handle that chore, judging from his size.

The thick, dark hair on his head was receding to the point of baldness, and the harsh lines in his face made him look older than his thirty years. He had piercing blue eyes that seemed to look right through you, and any stupid lies you might tell him. Buck didn't talk a whole lot, but when he did, you know you'd better listen or risk bodily harm.

But the thing that made him so feared was just the sheet, physical presence, he had about him. He looked very menacing, and when he fixed those eyes on somebody, it made them want to crawl in a hole, rather than face him, when he showed up. Everybody was on their best behavior, because they weren't keen on having him pick them out. Buck Bucholz was just one mean, intimidating, ass-kicking son-of-a-bitch.

He walked up to us, then put his hands on his hips, and glared at Ronny first, and then me with a wicked scowl.

"Is there a problem here guys?" he asked in a thin, raspy voice.

I was surprised by his voice, because I thought it would be deep, and booming.

"No," Ronny said meekly. "We were just talken, Buck."

"You wouldn't be lying to me, would you?" said Buck, and skewered Ronny with his eyes.

"No, no, honest, Buck," Ronny squirmed. "We're not argu'en or nuthen."

Buck then turned his gaze on me, and I looked down in fear. He was really scary looking.

"Is that true?" he asked me.

"Y ... yessir," I answered, and looked at his chest to avoid his eyes.

"Is your name Tommy?"

"Yessir." I gulped nervously.

"Uncle Harry told me you two had a little get together this afternoon, so I thought I'd better check to make sure you guys were getting along now," he said.

"Yessir." I really didn't know how to answer him. "Everything's ... fine sir."

He gave me a hard look, then he saw my little brother sitting there, and I glanced up, and Buck's features had seemed to soften a bit. Billy had that effect on people. Especially when they got a load of those eyes. Those big, sad eyes. The ones that were staring at Buck right at that moment, unblinking, and unafraid.

"You must be his brother, Billy?" Buck asked him.

"Yessir," he said.

"If you have any questions or problems, Billy, don't be afraid to come see me. "Alright?" he told him.

"Yessir," my brother answered.

"And I would really like to hear from you if these two clowns give you any shit!"

He jerked his thumb in the direction of Ronny and Timmy, who looked like they wanted to crawl under their chairs, and hide.

"Okay?" he told Billy.

"Yessir."

"Then he looked back at me, and I averted his eyes.

"I hope you aren't going to become a real pain in the ass," he said in a flat tone.

I was at a loss for words, and then he turned, and walked back out the doorway. When he did, Ronny and Timmy, made their way out the other door. I sat back down, and looked over at Tommy, who had a knowing smile on his lips. I'd just met him, and I liked him, but I had an overwhelming desire to just reach over, and slap him.

"Whut'd ya think of Buck?" Tommy asked.

"I don't care if I ever see him again," I told him truthfully.

"He sure liked Billy," he said, looking over at my brother.

"Yea, everybody likes Billy," I answered in a jealous manner.

Billy glanced over at me, and smiled faintly.

"Sorry," he said then turned his attention back to the tv.

"Well, at least he got rid of those jerks," I told Tommy.

"Buck was a marine like my dad during the War," Tommy said, changing the subject.

"Really? Does Buck talk about being in combat?" I asked hopefully.

"Naw," he replied. "He don't say nuthen. The only reason I know he was is cuz I told him once about my dad's service, and he said he'd been one too."

"How about yer dad?" I went on. "Does he tell ya about fighten any Japs?"

Tommy got real quiet, and a sad look took over his features.

"He was killed on Okinawa," Tommy said sadly.

"Oh jeez, I'm sorry Tommy," I told him.

"Aah," he said. "Don't worry about it."

That threw a damper on the conversation, and so we watched tv for a while, and there wasn't a lot of talk, and that was okay. As long as I stared at the screen, I could blank this place out for a while. I loved watching television.

I never got to see my first one until 1950, when I was seven. That was when my mom's parents, Grandpa, and Grandma Brewer, got theirs. I remember how exciting it had been.

After dad went to Korea, and we were living with the Bryans, sometimes Grandpa, and Grandma would pick us up on Friday nights, and we would spend the weekends at their house.

Our Uncle Melvin lived with them, and my greatest pleasure was watching Friday night wrestling with him, and Grandpa. We always rooted for "Gorgeous" George whenever he took on the villain he was having problems with at the time.

Grandpa, and Grandma loved us kids, and spoiled us rotten, and I hated going back to the Bryan's after those great weekends. I wished that Mom would've let us stay with them, but they lived in a small, two-bedroom house, with Uncle Melvin, and there just wasn't any room for two growing boys.

I don't know why she didn't let them babysit us while she worked, instead of leaving us with the Bryan's. I guess she had her reasons.

I always wondered though, what would've happened if I'd said something to mom about what Old Man Bryan was doing to me in the bathroom. I don't know how things would've turned out, but at least we wouldn't have had to stay with them.

But I never did talk about it. I was afraid. Besides which, I didn't think anyone would believe me anyway. Who'd take my word over a grown up's?

Now I had another problem to deal with. This place. But like I said, at least they had a tv, and I concentrated on that, and the day passed by rather quickly.

The afternoon sun was starting its journey into dusk, and as the light shining on the shades of the windows in the room darkened, so did my mood.

I began to feel depressed, and my head was filled with gloomy thoughts.

Shit! Just what I needed! One of my lousy spells was coming over me.

Several years ago, when I was about six or seven, I remember I was staring at a beautiful, rosy sunset, when suddenly, a dark wave of melancholy came over me. I was filled with a sense of bittersweet nostalgia, and I felt so lonely, I almost ached. It was scary, and I couldn't figure out what was going on. The feeling didn't last very long, and finally, to my relief, it went away.

After that, these assaults on my senses would happen once in a while, and when they did, I dreaded them because they made me so sad.

This was one of those times. As the dark, lonely emotions spread their heavy, black cloaks over my slumping shoulders, I wished I'd never consented to come here, and that dad could've found a better place for us to stay. This boys home sucked.

I tried to shake off the feelings, and I really focused my attention on the tv, and that helped some. Having Tommy on one side, and Billy on the other, did some good also. As least I wasn't all alone, and there were two people I could share my misery with.

Finally, the emotions subsided, and I was able to concentrate on the shows we were watching, and I was fairly fine afterwards, all things considered.

This being a Sunday, most of the boys were away on visits with their respective families. The Home employed a cook who had living quarters right behind the kitchen. I learned she was a sweet, dark-haired lady in her mid-forties named Miss Sarah. On Sundays, good meals were scarce with Miss Sarah gone. We were fed bologna sandwiches and soda pop by Uncle Harry, and his wife. It was time for supper and we headed for the kitchen.

Aunt Alice seemed nice enough. She was slender, wore glasses, and had dark hair that was streaked with grey. We walked through the kitchen, and were given two sandwiches, then chose our sodas from a stack of wooden pop bottle crates. We weren't allowed to go in the dining room, but were free to eat wherever else we wanted.

Billy, Tommy, and I went to the first stairway and walked up to the landing between floors, and sat down to eat. I was hungry, and was the first one done. After taking a big swig of my pop, I then proceeded to let out a loud belch, which echoed back down the stairwell. I heard someone walking by, and he hollered up at us.

"Hey! Who's the pig up there?"

I turned red with embarrassment, and Tommy put his hand over his mouth and his eyes were all crinkled up in laughter. Billy even smiled.

"I'm sorry!" I yelled.

"You got that right!" the guy replied, and walked away.

After he left, Tommy let one go, which rivaled mine, and all three of us laughed. Suddenly, Uncle Harry walked out of the kitchen doorway, and shouted up the staircase.

"Alright! That's enough! Who's doing that?"

We all choked on our laughter, and Tommy spoke up.

"I'm sorry, Uncle Harry!" he said.

"Who is that?" he asked irritably.

"It's Tommy. I'm with the other Tommy, and his brother!" he answered.

"Well knock it off up there!" he ordered and went back in the kitchen.

When we were done, we went back down the stairs. After putting our pop bottles in a crate just inside the kitchen door, we decided to go up to the Middle Dorm.

We sat on a couple of bunks, and told dirty jokes.

"Knock, knock" Tommy came up with one.

"Who's there?" Billy and I both chimed.

"Argo," he told us.

"Argo who?" we both answered.

"Argo fuck yerself." he joked.

We broke up in laughter, and I was so glad that I'd met Tommy. He had shown me the ropes around this dump, and I was grateful. Tommy was really making this place more pleasant for me. At least with him around, I knew there'd be a few laughs to help me get through all the bullshit. It was a blessing that his mom had to work on this particular Sunday.

We thought we'd go back downstairs, and watch some more tv. As we got to the stairwell, a boy in his early teens, came up the stairs towards us. He was homely, tall, and lanky, with long, stringy hair. There was a prominent Adam's apple bulging from his throat, and a lot of pimples spotted his pasty, white face, and surrounded his big nose, beady, blue eyes, and a large mouth. Overall, not a very, pleasant, looking sight.

"Hi, Elmer," Tommy said.

"Hey," the guy said as he passed us.

After he left, I looked over at Tommy, and grinned, as we descended the stairs.

"Who was that?" I asked. "Gawd, he's ugly."

"Shh ... he might hear ya," Tommy cautioned. "Believe me, you don't wanna piss him off."

"Why?" I asked unsurely.

"That's Elmer Lehr," Tommy said. "He's kinda crazy. I'll tell ya whut, he may be ugly but he's strong. I mean real strong!"

"Is he?"

"You oughta see some of the things he does," Tommy told me.

I didn't think he looked that muscular, but he was wearing a long sleeve shirt. I was going to ask him some more questions, but we'd reached the first floor landing, and I started to hurry on by the basement staircase.

"Let's go down here, and we'll talk." Tommy said, pointing at it, and I stopped, and put my hand on his arm.

"Wait!" I told him. "What if Ronny's down there?"

"Na!" he said. "Nobody's down there. They lock the door every day at six."

"Oh" I felt relieved, and Billy, and I followed him down the stairway to the basement landing. We sat on the steps, and then I asked him about Elmer.

"He can do thirty pull ups on the bar outside," he told us. "Nobody can beat him at pull ups."

"Thirty?" I could barely pull myself up once.

"Yea! And you should see him in the trees," Tommy said. "He's a regular Tarzan."

"Whadda ya mean?" Billy asked him before I could.

"He can swing from one limb to another, just like a monkey." Tommy replied.

"Oh, bullshit!" I told him. "I'd like to see that."

"No bullys," he said. "Just wait, you will … oh, yea, and you'll really git a kick outta Elmer when we're at camp."

"Why's that?" I asked, becoming intrigued.

"On Sunday nights, we have bonfires, and roast marshmallows, and all kinds of stuff, but the neatest thing happens when Elmer sneaks off, up in the trees with a flashlight. Then he puts it under his chin, and turns it on."

He paused for dramatic effect, and Billy and I never said a word. Tommy had our complete attention.

He said seeing Elmer's white face, outlined against the black background, was creepy to say the least. Then he'd turn off the light, and a bunch of the guys would set out to try, and find him. The woods were very dark, and spooky, and Elmer would wait until everyone was close, then he'd jump out, and grab someone, and then bite him.

"Bite?" I repeated.

"Hard, too," he answered, "Like I said, he's crazy."

The camp sounded like great fun. He said just about everybody built their own forts. Then he told us about a neat, log fort, that a guy had built years ago, and was still standing. Nobody could build one like this kid's. As Tommy talked, I got more excited about going there.

"Oh man," I told him. "I wish summer would hurry up, and get here."

We talked a while longer, and then decided to go watch some tv. When we walked in, Ronny, and Timmy were there but so was Greenie, and they left me alone, except for some dirty looks.

A lot of kids were coming back from their visits, and the tv room was filling up with boys of all sizes, shapes, and hair colors. Tommy introduced me to some of the guys he liked.

There was Jeff Russek, who was nine, blue-eyed, and blond haired, along with his five year old brother, Jason. And red-headed Benny Martinez, who was eight. Then there was Vern.

Vernon Goldman was Jewish, eleven, with black hair, and eyes, an olive complexion, and retarded. The guys liked to tease him, but he always took it in stride, and smiled sweetly. In fact, he seemed to enjoy the attention. I found out he was a bedwetter too. I wondered what these guys would think when they saw me carrying my wet sheets out to the clothesline. I hoped they'd still like me.

We were sent to bed at 8 clock. Some of the kids grumbled, but not me. I was worn out from all the stress, and worry and I was ready for some rest.

When we reached the dorm, I undressed, then headed for the bathroom which was down the hall. It was a big, square room that had two toilets facing each other, with a urinal between them on one side, and over across from them, was a large shower stall with three shower heads.

In the middle, as you entered, were three sinks, with a big, long mirror above them.

A couple of older boys were standing by the sinks talking when I came in. one of them was Ronny's brother Larry. I'd never seen the other guy before, but he looked mean. He had dark, curly-hair, and his well-muscled body was straining against his tight t-shirt.

When they saw me, I tensed up, and hesitated. But my full bladder urged me on, so I went hurriedly over to the urinal. Just before I could get a hold of myself to pee, I heard someone behind me, and suddenly my head was jerked back.

The guy who'd been with Larry, had me by the hair, and I was staring up into his nostrils. My bladder let go out of fear and a stream of urine stained my underwear, running down my bare legs.

"I hear yer a fuck'en rat!" he said roughly.

"No!" I gasped.

"You call'en Larry a liar?" he asked.

"No! No!" I cried. "I mean I won't do it again, honest."

"You better not jack off, if ya know whut's good for ya," he said threateningly.

He let go of my hair, and I almost fell over backwards. I scurried back to the dorm, changed underwear, then sat around and talked to Billy, and Tommy, and Jeff, until it was time for lights out. After that, we listened to the programs on the old radio, that each dorm was provided with. That helped to soothe me some.

Gradually, everyone went to sleep, but I still tossed and turned, thinking about the events of the day. I'd been so glad to get away from the Bryan's, and now, this. The Home was worse than I thought, and was going to take some getting used too. The biggest difference so far, between the Bryan's, and here, was that as long as I minded my own business, hopefully, I could get lost in the crowd. And try to stay out of the way of Uncle Harry, and the counselors, especially Buck. I was really going to have to watch my step. But at least some of the guys here were nice, and thank God I'd met Tommy. Finally, I drifted off to sleep.

Of course, when I awoke my bed was wet. Vern, me, and another kid named Bobby Johnson, had to strip our beds, then make the embarrassing trip to the clothesline out back.

When Ronny saw me carrying my sheets, he called me a name which I came to detest—a hated name which burned its way down deep into my soul. For the rest of my life, the sound of that word would affect me like a cold, hard slap across my senses.

"Hey, Pissass!"

Part
3

The next few days found me busy enrolling in school, and settling into the routine of the Home, and becoming good friends with Tommy, Jeff, and Benny. Billy seemed to be adjusting to our new way of life too.

I tried to avoid Ronny, and Timmy as much as possible, but we were in the same classes in school, and they tormented me whenever they had the chance. I continued to take their abuse without saying or doing anything, because I figured sooner or later they'd lose interest.

One of the ways I got away from them was to go to the library, and curl up with a good book, and get lost for awhile.

And then there was the radio, which had been my refuge growing up. Especially when we lived with the Bryans. A lot of the stations were filled with kids shows on Saturdays which was my favorite day of the week. In the morning, that's where I could be found, wound up in a fetal position on the rug, lost in a dreamy, swirling world of fantasy. The voices, and music coming from the speaker created for me in my mind's eye, a wonderland, where nobody got hurt, and people were gentle, and kind. Looking back now, I really miss that time.

Television seemed to make it even better. I sat enthralled that first Saturday, watching "Fury," "Mighty Mouse," and the like. While they could never replace the wondrous images I carried in my head from the radio programs, the tv helped me forget about the realities of life in that stinking hole for a while. I could get lost in the flickering pictures, and stories.

In the afternoons, we younger boys would go to the Saturday matinee at the Bijou. The older guys went to the Majestic Theatre on Friday nights.

On Sunday, Dad came to pick us up for our visit. He asked us how we liked the Home so far, and I lied, and said "okay." Billy went along with me, and agreed. What I really wanted to do was tell him it was a load of crap, but I didn't. Why? I don't know. Maybe it was because I didn't want him to feel bad about putting us in such a shitty place.

He'd made a change that he thought would make us happy because he'd sensed that we didn't like staying with the Bryans. And now, it was too late to tell him that we weren't any better off at the Home.

But I didn't want to talk about that place anyway. It was nice to just get away for awhile.

We went to Dad's favorite bar, where his girlfriend, Roberta, worked. My father ordered dinner for Billy, and I, and afterwards, he took us to a movie theatre, and dropped us off.

We sat in the dark, eating popcorn, and candy, getting caught up in the story being told on the screen. I loved the movies. The bright, square screen flashing it's images in my mind's eye, wrapped me up in a cocoon of fantasy, protecting me from any harm that might be out there in the real world.

I never gave much thought to the fact that my dad took us to the theatre, instead of spending more time with us.

After the movie was over, Billy, and I would wait outside. When dad came to pick us up, we'd go back to the bar, and drink pop while he sat, and swapped lies, jokes, and beers with his friends. Then he'd take us back to the Home.

I don't ever remember being upset or questioning this routine. His parents were both gone, but Dad had a brother, and two sisters, and we used to go to their houses for Sunday dinners once in a while. But most of the time it was the bar, eat, movie, then back to the Home. That's just the way it was for Billy and I.

I don't think we realized how different our life was, compared to other families, and I guess we thought everyone had problems like us. Being at the Home didn't help change that viewpoint either, since just about everyone there had a situation similar to ours.

It was during my third week at the Home, while playing out in the yard, that I was first told the story that caught my fancy, and so filled my head with wonder, and enchantment.

A bunch of us were pretending to be at war, and after getting clonked in the head with a dirt clod, I crawled into one of the many foxholes that littered the yard, to recover from my wound. Since this was January, the clod was a little frozen, and it had stung me pretty good. I didn't know which clod have thrown it, but I wanted to find out so I could return the favor.

I think I should explain that our foxholes were actually just small depressions in the ground, since we weren't allowed to dig holes. But we made them as deep as we could.

About that time, Tommy jumped into my hole, and a dirt clod followed him in. Tommy reached over, grabbed the clod, and heaved it back in the direction it came from. Then he popped his head up, and pretended to let off a burst of a submachine-gun fire. He was firing at a kid in another hole, named Stan Martell, who was eight.

"Brrt-brrrrt-brrt! Yer dead, Stan!" Tommy hollered. "I gotcha!"

"Bullshit!" Stan screamed. "I nailed yer ass with that grenade!"

"Bullys! It didn't go off until I threw it back!" Tommy yelled.

"Ah, bullshit!" Stan repeated.

"No stinking bullies", Tommy said. "Yer dead!"

He lowered his head, and grinned at me. I just frowned, and rubbed the side of my head.

"Whutt'sa matter?" He asked.

"Ah, some jerk nailed me with a dirt clod," I whined. "Is it bleeden?"

He leaned over, and inspected the side of my head, then laughed.

"Na," he said. "It's skinned a little, that's all."

"It was probably that lousy Stan," I told him.

He started to say something, when suddenly, a dirt clod hit him right on top of the noggin. I turned my head, and put my arms up, to keep from getting hit with flying pieces of dirt. Then, when I looked to see if Tommy was okay, he was cussing, and running over to the hole where Stan was, who then stood up, and started hauling ass as fast as he could, towards the safety of the Home. I watched as first Stan, then, Tommy disappeared around the side of the building. Jeff, and Benny, and my brother came over to my hole to find out what happened.

"Oh, Stan hit him with a dirt clod," I explained.

"Really?" Benny said. "That Tinken Stan's always do'en that kind of shit."

"Yea, I know," I told him, rubbing my head.

Suddenly, Tommy appeared, and walked back in our direction and when he got close, I asked him if he'd caught Stan.

"Naw," he said. "Greenie showed up. I'll git him later. Hey Tommy! Is my head bleeden?"

He lowered it, and I examined his skull. Other than a pink mark, there was no blood that I could see.

"Naa," I said, then remembered something my dad had pulled on me one time. "Wait!"

"Whut?" Tommy exclaimed, alarmed.

"There's a hole," I told him.

"Where? Where?" He said, searching around frantically with his fingers. "I can't feel nuthen."

"Oh. Nevermind. It's just yer ear," I joked. "For a second there, I could see clear through to the other side."

He gave me a funny look, then he scowled as the others laughed.

"Oh, fuck you," he said.

"Yea, well, yer lucky that wasn't a rock," I told him.

"Or a real grenade," Benny added.

"Yea, really," I said. "Wouldn't it be neat to have a grenade from the War?"

"My dad has a German Luger he took off a dead kraut," Jeff bragged.

"Wow!" I exclaimed. "You should ask him if he'd bring it here so we could see it."

"Aw, I doubt it," he said. "He keeps it locked up, and he won't let us touch it."

"I know where we could get some machine guns from the War," Tommy told me.

"Where?" I asked him skeptically.

He told us that when they were at the camp last summer, a boy had told him that during a snowstorm in WWII, a B-17 Bomber had crashed on a mountain near there. It was named Mt. Baldwin, and was climbed every year by the guys from the camp.

Legend had it that the only survivor had been the tail-gunner. It was said that despite numerous injuries, including a broken leg, he'd managed to crawl down from there, and been rescued.

During the first couple of years following the crash, the guys tried to figure out where it was, but they couldn't find it. Finally, though one summer, some of the boys had been fortunate enough to find the crash site, and they had brought back some souvenirs.

But since that time, no one else had been able to find it again, and the location of the wreckage remained hidden.

The more Tommy talked about it, the more excited I got. Gawd, this was really something special. I asked him if he'd gone up there last year, but he said he'd been too young to go.

"Wouldn't it be cool if we did find it, and there was a machine gun?" I was thrilled at the prospect.

"Yea," Billy said excitedly. "We could take it to school for 'Show and Tell.' That would really be neat."

Tommy gave Billy a disgusted look.

"Na. That's kid stuff," he sneered. "I'd use it on cruds like Joey Mendoza. He'd shit his pants."

We all laughed at that. Nobody liked Joey.

So that's how my dream about finding the plane began. It quickly grew into an obsession, and I became preoccupied with the very thought that I might be able to locate the crash site once I made the hike up to the Mountain.

Billy seemed to feel the same way, and that first night before lights out, we discussed our chances of doing that. It was nice to be able to share something with my brother that we both agreed upon, which didn't happen a lot.

We both could hardly wait for summer to arrive so that we could begin to search for the wreckage of the ill-fated bomber.

The excitement that I felt about it began to wear off after awhile, but the thought was never far from the level of my consciousness, ready to spring into action once I heard someone mention the plane. Or whenever I saw the photograph of the camp in Uncle Harry's office. Then I would bring the dream out into the light, and I would fantasize for a time, before storing it back in my mind, like some treasured object. One morning, not long, after that, I awoke just as my bladder was about to burst, and I got up from my dry bed, and hurried into the bathroom to relieve myself.

Vern was taking a shower when I rushed in, and he smiled. After I was done peeing, I turned around, and he held out a washcloth towards me. He'd gotten used to me getting up, and taking a shower with him whenever we each had an "accident."

"Not today, Vernon," I announced proudly.

He almost looked disappointed, but continued to smile. I went back to bed, and dozed until it was time to get up. Seven year old Bobby Johnson, the other bedwetter, was stripping the sheets off of his bed, and I felt pretty good about not having to do that this morning.

After I was up and dressed, I headed for the bathroom to brush my teeth. Vern, who slept in the bunk next to mine, was walking with his sheets ahead of me. As we got to the doorway, Ronny and Timmy were walking back from the bathroom. When they saw Vernon with his wet sheets, they pretended like they were afraid, and jumped back.

"Look out! Look out!" Ronny said in a high falsetto voice. "Pissing the bed might be contagious!"

Vern had paused, as did I, and now he laughed, then made his way down the hallway. In the meantime, I'd been debating whether to go back to my bunk, rather than face my two, main tormentors. I decided to keep going, and as I passed them, they gave me dirty looks.

"Hey, Pissass!" Ronny taunted.

Again, the shocking slap across my ego. Again, the zing of anger, and resentment at the hopelessness of my situation. To me, there was nothing more humiliating, and degrading, than to wake up in the morning, lying in a puddle of piss, feeling as helpless as a baby. I felt ashamed, and to have people make rude remarks, only made me feel worse. Any sense of self-worth was low. People acted like I did it on purpose, which couldn't be further from the truth. In those days, I would have given anything if I could quit wetting the bed. Knowing I had no control over this particular body function was very frustrating.

So I did my best to ignore people like Ronny, who didn't care or understand how much I hated being a bedwetter. I detested what I did, but there wasn't anything I could do about it. And when people called me names, it really hurt.

But it was special whenever I awoke to a dry bed. For a while, I could feel like a normal person, instead of some kind of freak … a Pissass!

That evening was our night for showers, and I was beginning to understand what Tommy had told me about Ol' Greenie. Whenever we took showers, he'd come in, and look like he was checking out all the naked flesh.

This particular night, Greenie came in while I was drying off, and told me when I was done, he wanted to see me in his room. When he left I looked over at Tommy, who was putting on his underwear, but he just shrugged his shoulders.

I finished toweling off, then slipped on some clean shorts, and nervously went to Greenie's room. He was standing over a phonograph player, putting on a record. He looked up, and smiled at me. I felt self-conscious, and didn't know what to do with my hands, so I just folded my arms.

"Come in, Tommy," he said invitingly. "Please shut the door."

He then told me to make myself comfortable, and sit on the bed. When I did, the springs let out a eerie "screech," and the sound seemed to echo loudly in the room. I felt clammy, and cold. He pulled the chair from behind his desk, and turned it towards the bed. Then he sat down, and smiled at me again.

"How'd you like to stop wetting the bed?" he said.

I couldn't believe my ears! Yea!

"I'd give my right arm," I told him excitedly.

"Well, I might be able to help you," he replied.

"How?" I asked, all ears.

"I'm going to use hypnotism," he said, matter of factly.

"Oh," I said hesitantly, because I wasn't really sure what he meant, and a seed of doubt began to break through.

"Now, I need you to lie down and completely relax," he told me gently.

I did as he said, and laid perfectly still, although I was far from relaxed. Then he told me to clear my head, and think pleasant thoughts. He was talking in a soothing monotone, and as he continued to speak slowly, I did, indeed begin to calm down. After that, he turned on the record player, and a man's voice came on. He basically said the same thing Greenie did, and I wondered how long it was going to take, before I was hypnotized.

Then Greenie turned off the record, and told me he was going to count to ten, and when he reached it, I would be under a trance. I waited, but

THOMAS BECK

when he was done counting, I was still aware of my surroundings, and didn't feel any different than when I came in.

I didn't want to blow this opportunity to stop my bed wetting, so when he asked me if I was still awake, I didn't say anything. Then he asked if I could hear his voice.

"Yess," I said sleepily, not exactly sure how a person in a trance should sound.

Greenie said he was going to massage me, and that would help me to strengthen my bladder control. Soon after he began, I realized all this hypnosis stuff was just a sham. All he wanted to do was fondle me. I lay there for what seemed like an eternity, too embarrassed to protest.

When he was through, Greenie said he was going to count back from ten, and when he reached one, he would snap his fingers, and I'd wake up. I went along with the farce, and "woke up." Then he asked if I remembered anything.

"No," I answered, having a hard time looking at him.

"Well, there's no guarantee," he said. "But hopefully, this will help."

"That'd be great," I replied, trying to sound sincere. "Thanks."

"You're welcome."

When I returned to the dorm, everyone was talking, laughing, and running around. Billy asked me what Greenie wanted, and I told him a half-truth.

"Aw, he said he could hypnotize me, and that would help me stop wetting the bed."

"Really?" He seemed impressed. "Whut'd it feel like?"

"Whut?" I said guiltily.

"Ya know, to be hypnotized?" he asked.

"Oh. I don't know." I was uncomfortable talking about it. "It must not've worked 'cuz I didn't feel nuthen."

"Oh." Billy looked disappointed.

About that time I saw Tommy, and Jeff headed over in my direction, and I braced myself for another round of questions. I really didn't want to talk about my visit with Greenie anymore, and just at that moment, he walked through the doorway, and flicked the light switch to get everyone's attention.

"Okay guys," he said authoritatively. "Let's hit the sack. Let's go!"

Reluctantly, guys headed for their bunks, including Tommy, and Jeff, and I was glad Greenie had showed up. He waited until everyone had gotten in bed, before switching off the light, and told us goodnight. After he left, guys started talking, and laughing, but I didn't feel like doing either.

Ronny turned on the radio, but even that didn't seem to help my state of mind, and I couldn't relax.

Eventually, the dorm settled down, and everybody seemed to be asleep, except me. I was restless, and stared up at Billy's mattress above me. My mind was racing with all kinds of thoughts and images.

I didn't know what to do about my encounter with Greenie and wondered if this was going to lead up to him screwing me in the ass like Old Man Bryan. Jeez, I hoped not.

I was getting to where I hated adults. They were supposed to help us kids, but all they ever wanted to do was fuck, fondle, or hurt us, and I felt helpless around them.

Then I thought about Mom, and began to feel sorry for myself. Nobody seemed to care that I'd lost my mother. Or that I missed her terribly, and needed her to sooth this ache deep inside of me. The ache that had been there, ever since Billy, and I had been told she was dead. At first, I hadn't believed Old Man Bryan when he said that. It just wasn't possible. When I asked him how, he said she died in her sleep from natural causes. Whatever the hell natural causes meant.

Gawd, she had been the most beautiful mom I'd ever seen. Her dark, brown hair had always seemed to frame her head perfectly, even when she first got up in the mornings. And her beautiful, dark eyes. Those deep, haunting eyes. How could someone so beautiful be dead? I didn't understand why God let her die, and then let terrible things happen to Billy, and I.

When I remembered how sweet our lives had seemed, before dad went off to the Korean War, I began to weep silently. So much had changed since then, and now we were stuck in this stinking place. Life was unfair.

It was late before I was able to sleep. In the morning, I woke up to a wet bed, and for the rest of the day I felt pretty rotten. I never told anyone about what Greenie did, not even Billy, although I think he, and Tommy suspected. Thank the Lord, that was the only time Greenie ever did that to me, but at the time, I had no way of knowing if he'd do it again. And so the thought of another session with him was always lurking there, just below the level of my consciousness. Like Tommy had said, he was just a great big, slimy, green goober.

A couple of weeks after that, I got into trouble over Greenie. There was a song going around that one of the older boys had made up about him. The melody was "Whistle While you Work," the popular song from "Snow White and the Seven Dwarfs," Tommy, and Jeff, and I, thought we'd serenade Greenie, whether he wanted us to or not.

Although it was February, we were having a mild winter. This particular day was nice, and sunny, and Greenie's window was open. Jeff had checked to make sure he was in his room, and then he joined us outside.

"He's setten at his desk readen," he said.

We gathered below his window, which was right above the kitchen, and we were standing by the outside door.

"We'll start at the count of three," he whispered. "Ready? One … two … three!"

Then, we began to sing.

"Whistle while you work."

Greenie is a jerk.

Greenie went and bit my wienie,

"Now it doesn't work!"

We broke out in hysterical laughter, and hearing a commotion from up above, we took off running wildly. Just as we rounded the corner of the building, a voice came roaring out of the window, that struck us between the shoulder blades with a searing bolt of fear.

Buck! Oh, shit! Evidently, he'd stopped by Greenie's room, and now he'd heard our song too.

As I ran, I looked around in panic, but there was no place to hide. We hadn't counted on getting caught. Now we were really sunk!

I couldn't see any use in continuing to run, so I came to a halt. Tommy must've had the same thought as me, because he quit running too, but Jeff, who was ahead of us, kept on going. He disappeared around the other side of the building.

Tommy slumped against the brick wall, and hung his head in despair. I just stood there miserably, and waited. I had my back turned towards the

42

approaching terror, and it didn't take long to appear. I heard Buck come running around the corner of the building, and then slow down when he saw Tommy, and I standing there. As he walked up behind me, a shiver of dread went through me, and I squinted my eyes, and braced myself.

Buck slapped me with his heavy hand on the back of my head, and my brain seemed to explode with bright light, and burning pain, and I fell to my hands, and knees. Then he walked up to Tommy, and grabbed him by the arm, and slapped him also Tommy would have fallen, if not for Buck's strong grip. Then, he came back, and roughly grabbed me by my arm, and hauled me to my feet.

"You clowns think you're funny?" he asked us.

"No, Buck," I said. "It was just a joke."

"Let's go ask John if he thought it was a big joke," he said.

With both of us on each arm, we walked around to the side entrance. We saw Greenie standing in front of the door, and he looked a little pissed. When we walked up to him, he gave us each a dirty look, then spoke to Buck.

"Did you see the other guys, Buck?" he asked.

"No," Buck said. "These were the only two I got a look at."

He still had a hold of our arms, and now he shook both of us.

"Who else was with you?" he asked.

"I bet Jeff or Benny were part of it," Greenie said nastily. "They're all thick as thieves."

If Buck hadn't been there, I would have laughed. Thick as thieves. That was rich.

"No, it was just me and Tommy," I told them.

Buck let go of my arm, and slapped me across the back of the head again, and stars danced around my eyes. I was still recovering from the first slap, and the second one hurt even worse, although he didn't hit me quite as hard. Then he grabbed my arm again, hard.

"Don't lie," he threatened. "I don't like liars."

"No. Please don't hit me again, Buck," I pleaded. "There's nobody else, honest."

Something in my voice made him relent a little, and he let go of my arm, as well as Tommy's.

"Okay, then" he said. "You two want to take all the punishment, it's no skin off our noses."

"That's right, Buck," Greenie answered. "Now, get you're sorry asses upstairs."

As we trudged into the home, I looked at Tommy, and his face was filled with fear, and dread, and mirrored the way I was feeling. We both knew what kind of punishment was coming.

During the summer at Camp, Aunt Alice taught arts, and crafts. The most popular, was making plastic lanyards out of braids of different colors, the kind referees wear to hold their whistles. They are very tightly braided, and when one of them meets flesh, the pain is indescribable.

Whenever we were being punished for something like smarting off, the counselors would use them on us. They'd make you hold out your hands, palms up, and then hit them with the lanyard. If you pulled your hand away, the person swinging would usually hit themselves on the leg. That wasn't a very good idea, because they'd hit you across the arms, and back too.

I'd heard Joey Mendoza was good at doing that, but then he was crazy. I'd seen a couple of guys get beat that way the week before, and it wasn't very pleasant to watch.

Now my turn was coming, and I wished I'd never let Tommy, and Jeff talk me into pulling this stupid stunt. I'd gone along with them, because at the time it had sounded like fun, and I hadn't thought about the consequences, as usual.

Buck, and Greenie took us to the shower room, and made us wait until they came back with the lanyards. While we waited, Tommy and I never said a word, and we suffered in silence.

They were back shortly, and had us stand side-by-side. Buck was across from Tommy, and I was stuck with Greenie. They made us hold our hands out and a shiver of dread went down my spine. Greenie looked over at Buck.

"How many?" he asked, meaning swats.

"I think ten on each hand, should make them sing a different tune," Buck said sarcastically.

Greenie narrowed his eyes at me, and I wondered if he knew I was aware of what he did the night he tried to hypnotize me. I guess it didn't matter now.

In the meantime, some guys had gathered out in the hallway, and Ronny and his friend Timmy were there, but I just ignored them.

The first blow hit my left hand, and it felt like a fierce, powerful shock of electricity hitting me, and the pain shot all the way up my arm, to my brain. Before I could even think about how much it hurt, the same thing happened to my right hand. After the third or fourth whack, my hands got numb, but that didn't seem to lessen the pain. If anything, it seemed to intensify. The feeling was like a thousand, sharp needles striking my flesh with each sharp, jolting, slap of the lanyard. My fingers, and palms felt like they were on fire, and some of the blows hit my wrists and forearms, which just made the beating that much more unbearable.

I prided myself on being able to take a whipping, but I'd never experienced anything like this before. I started screaming in excruciating pain, and begged Greenie not to hit me anymore, and finally, mercifully, the punishment ended.

When Buck, and Greenie left, Tommy, and I were both in tears. My hands throbbed, and burned fiercely, so I went to one of the sinks, and I thought I'd run some cold water over them when I turned on the faucet, Tommy came over, and turned it off.

"Whatta ya doen?" I asked tearfully.

"Man, you don't wanna do that," he blubbered, and wiped some tears with the back of his hand.

"Why?"

"It just makes it hurt worse," he said, and sniffed.

"Whut can ya do to help?" I asked hopefully.

"Nuthen" he said sadly. "Not a stinken thing. Ya just gotta wait till it quits."

Tommy folded his arms, and put his hands under his armpits, then he bent over, and let his arms dangle down. I imitated his moves, but it didn't help. Like he'd said, there wasn't a whole lot you could do, but wait. We compared wounds, and inspected the ugly, red welts, on our forearms. But by far, our hands were the worst. They were swollen and our fingers looked like fat, pink sausages. Finally, the pain began to subside, and we went out to the yard. When we met up with Jeff, we proudly showed off our battle scars. He tried to touch the welts but we shied away from him with dirty looks. They were still pretty tender and sore.

"Yer lucky, Russek," Tommy told him. "You know Buck was up there, and he tried to get us to rat on who else was in on it, but we wouldn't say nuthen."

"Thanks, guys," Jeff said gratefully.

"Sure," we answered.

If Buck had slapped me one more time, I'm not so sure I could've kept my mouth shut, and instead of praising me, Jeff would have been cussing. But at least I didn't rat on him, and that made me feel good. We all laughed when we talked about how Greenie must've looked when he heard the words to our song.

Eventually, the pain went completely away, and by that night, you could hardly tell that Tommy, and I had been beaten. The welts were hardly noticeable.

A couple of days later, I got into a fight with a kid because of Vernon. We were playing in the yard one afternoon, when this guy stuck his foot out, and tripped Vern who fell awkwardly. He rolled over in the dirt, and sat up, and began crying. This guy's name was Kenny Kongaleski, and he laughed cruelly when Vernon fell.

I ran over to where Kenny was standing and I was angry. Vernon was harmless and I didn't like to see him get bullied.

Not that I was any angel when it came to that kind of thing. I'd pushed Vernon around a couple times when he'd gotten on my nerves, but this was different. I just didn't like Kenny. He was about a year and a half older, but he wasn't much bigger than me. Whenever he was around our little clique of guys, he always seemed to have a smirk on his face, like he was laughing at us.

"Hey!" I yelled. "Why don't you pick on someone a little tougher than Vernon?"

He just laughed at me and I grew angrier.

"Whut the hell you laughen at?" I told him.

"You, Pissass!" he chuckled, and shoved me.

I reached out and shoved him back, and he quit smiling, then came at me swinging. I tried to fight back, but it didn't do any good and he hit me with three or four hard punches and with each one, bright lights went off in my head. I fell to my hands and knees, and I curled up in a ball, so Kenny got down on top of me, and grabbed my hair with one hand, and let me have it with the other before he finally quit.

"Fucken Pissass!" he snarled. "Don't ever touch me with those stinken piss-hands again! Ya hear me?"

I nodded my head, and he stood up and walked away.

I was crying big tears because his punches hurt, and I'd looked like a real pansy in front of my friends, and everyone else. It was very frustrating, especially in a place like the Home, where fighting was almost a requirement. Those who wouldn't or couldn't fight were considered to be pussies, and were treated with contempt, and scorn.

Tommy came over after Kenny left, and helped me up. I brushed off the dirt, and kept my eyes averted because I was ashamed.

"Thanks, Tommy," I mumbled.

"That was nice of ya to stick up for Vernon," Tommy said.

"Yea, for all the good it did," I retorted.

We helped Vernon to his feet and he'd skinned up his knee pretty good, so we went with him to get a band-aid from Greenie. Getting skinned up at the Home was a common, occurence, just like it was getting punched out. A few guys cried, and whined a lot, but they were looked down on. I tried not to do that.

One incident, however, was unusually painful, and was something I'd never learn to take in stride, just like the lanyards.

This one day, I was outside playing, and I ripped my jeans in the back. I was really embarrassed, because I didn't have any underwear on, so I went up to the Middle Dorm to change. I took off my tennis shoes, and pants, then opened my locker, and got out another pair of jeans. As I did, I suddenly remembered they were wrapped around the box which held my medallion, and it fell to the floor, and came open. The medal, and chain clattered on the linoleum, and I bent down, and put it back in the box. When I straightened up, Joey Mendoza was standing off to one side, watching curiously.

I was startled, because I hadn't heard him come in. When I first walked in the dorm, there was no one around, but Joey was sneaky, so that wasn't surprising. I tried to avoid him at all times, but in a place like the Home, that was hard to do. He'd called me Pissass a couple of times, but I'd just ignore him, even though he'd made me mad. Joey wasn't very big, but according to Tommy, he was fast, and liked to kick people in the balls. That was enough to convince me that I was going to do my best to stay completely out of his way. But now, here he was.

"Whut's that?" he asked, and I felt a little panicky.

"Nuthen," I lied. "It's nuthen."

"Let me see," he ordered, and walked right up to me.

"No!" I exclaimed, and hid the box behind my bare bottom.

"Come on," he said impatiently. "I ain't gonna steal it."

He tried to reach behind my back, and I got desperate, and shoved him with my free hand. I was a couple of inches taller than Joey, and outweighed him, so when I pushed him, he staggered back a few feet. His dark eyes narrowed in anger, and I felt a sinking feeling of fear in my bowels.

"Tu pinche cabrone!" (Loosely translated: "You fucking bastard!") he snarled.

He came at me in a flash, and before I could react, his foot caught me right in the genitals.

I screamed in agony, and let the box go, and grabbed myself, then sank to the floor, with my cheek meeting the linoleum. I'd never experienced pain as bad as this, not even the lanyards.

It felt like the wind had been knocked out of me, and there was a burning, sharp, ache, that went all the way from my testicles, to my throat. The deep, throbbing pain was almost unbearable, and I writhed back and forth on the floor. My screams turned into moans, and I was nauseated, and felt like I could throw up. I opened my eyes in time to see Joey bend down, and grab my medallion, which had fallen from the box again. I could only watch helplessly through the pain, and the tears.

Then suddenly, he dropped the medallion, and I could hear scuffling, and punches being thrown. I managed to sit up, and I was surprised to see Ronny Collins beating on Joey, who was backed up against the locker next to mine, doing his best to avoid punches.

Joey tried to kick him like he had me, but Ronny turned sideways, then quick as that, he was back on the attack. He landed two or three more hard punches, one of which bloodied Joey's nose.

After Ronny landed a couple more, Joey started pleading for him to stop. When he did, Joey took off in a hurry.

Then, Ronny, and Tim came over to where I was sitting, still trying to recuperate, and when they stood over me, I expected a smart remark. But, to my surprise, they didn't make one.

I looked up at them, then groaned, and got to my feet, and sniffed.

"You okay?" Ronny asked.

"Yea," I replied, trying to sound like I was.

"If yer gonna mess around with guys like Joey," he advised, "you better learn to protect yerself, or else yer gonna wind up wearing yer balls around yer neck like a bow-tie."

Before I could say anything else, they turned, and walked away. They went over to their lockers, and got something, then left.

I picked up my box, and put the medal, and the chain inside, and started to put it in my locker. Then, I had a thought, and instead, stuck it in the pocket of the pants I was going to wear. I didn't want to take any chances of losing it now.

Then I inspected my groin area. Although I was sore, everything still seemed to be there.

I was putting on my jeans, when Greenie came in, and saw me.

"Did somebody just hit Joey?" he asked. "He's in the bathroom washing blood off his face, and I noticed there's a trail of it leading right back in here. Do you know what happened?"

"I dunno," I told him innocently. "I'm just changing my pants."

He looked annoyed, and then left without saying anything else. I heard him go back to the bathroom, and I zipped up my jeans, then slipped on my tennies, and headed back outside.

I found Tommy, and Benny, and I told them about Ronny sticking up for me against Joey. I mentioned how I didn't think he liked me, and Tommy laughed rudely.

"Believe me, it's not because he likes you," he said. "He just don't have any use for Joey. Ronny can't stand him."

"How come?" I asked curiously.

Tommy told me that when Ronny first came to the Home, he was about eight, and he, and Joey got into it. Of course, Joey kicked him in the nuts. They were out in the yard when this happened.

When Larry saw that, he went ballistic, and he dragged Joey behind the garage. Then while he refereed, Larry helped Ronny put a Ratso, Fatso, and Japso on him.

So, since that time, whenever he saw Joey kick someone, he'd do a number on him, whether he liked the other guy or not. Ronny just hated Joey more then he did anyone else.

I was disappointed to hear that, but it was reassuring to know that as long as Ronny was around, I wouldn't have to worry about Joey kicking me. I was glad Ronny came in when he did, or else I'd have lost my medallion. And I was even more relieved that I'd decided to keep the box in my pocket, instead of my locker because someone broke into it later on. Nothing was taken, and of course Joey was the main suspect, but there wasn't much that could be done. Greenie said they would fix the locker door, because the hasp had been pried loose, lock and all. They didn't get around to it until a month later. I'm glad I didn't have anything worth taking in there.

That Sunday when dad came to pick us up, I gave him the medallion to save for me. I felt better then.

The weather continued to be mild that early spring, and I knew it wouldn't be long before school ended and we'd be headed for the Camp. Then we would check out the Mountain, and hopefully learn where the plane was. I could hardly wait.

Something happened though, about that time, that bothered me immensely.

One morning, Vernon, and I were up early, showering together.

Since coming to the Home, I had begun to take my sheets in the shower with me and rinse them off. Then I'd take them out to the clothesline and that way, they didn't stink when I put them back on the bed. Vernon got to where he'd do that too.

I was kidding around with him this certain day when suddenly he said something odd.

"Whut'd you say?" I asked.

"Art come in to see me last night," he repeated.

"Art? Who's Art?"

"He's nice," Vernon said with a smile.

"Who's Art?" I demanded.

"Sometimes he sucks my pee-pee," he went on.

"Whut?" I was alarmed.

"Art's a nice guy," Vernon said.

"Vernon, there is nobody named Art in the Home," I told him patiently.

"Art's a nice guy," he said again.

I gave up, and later that morning, at breakfast, I told Tommy about my conversation with Vernon. He gave me a funny look, and I asked him if he knew anything.

That was one thing I liked about him. If you had a question, especially if it had to do with the Home or Camp, all you had to do was ask Tommy, and he usually knew the answer. And if he didn't, he'd make something up.

So when I asked him about Vernon, he looked around to see if anyone was listening, then he leaned close.

"One of the 'Night Crawlers' must've showed up," he said.

"Whut? Whut the hell're you talken about?" I said.

"The homos," he explained. "Ya know? Queers?"

"Yea. I know whut queers are," I answered. "But whut've night crawlers got to do with it?"

Jeff had been listenting, and now he put his two cents worth in.

"That's whut Tommy likes to call them," he laughed. "Because he sez they crawl out from under rocks at night."

"Oh," I said.

Then I pointed at the head table where Uncle Harry, and the counselors sat.

"Don't they know about these guys coming in here at night?" I asked curiously.

Tommy looked at Jeff, and they laughed.

"Na," Tommy grinned. "Shit, if Greenie knew, he'd prob'ly jump in, and join 'em."

"Yea, really." I had to agree.

That explained a lot, but now I had something else to worry about. Queers. And somehow, they were getting into the Home late at night.

When I told my brother later, Billy responded like he normally did.

"Oh yea?"

I couldn't tell if he was concerned or not, but I was. There were people sneaking into the Home at night, and nobody seemed to be upset, except me. My silence about what Greenie did, and my failure to tell someone, was my own fault. But this was a little different, because they were strangers, which made it even worse. I don't know why none of the kids had ever said anything or complained to Uncle Harry about these guys.

When I thought about how they were getting in, there was an easy explanation. Guys used to sneak out of the Home after the outside doors were locked, to either smoke, see a girlfriend, vandalize, car prowl, whatever. The easiest way to get out, was to go unlock one of the windows, and screens, and you had it made. They were suppose to be checked every night by the counselors, but with guys slipping out all the time, windows remained unlocked, and that's how these people were getting in. You never knew when they would show up. Like something slimy, crawling out from under rocks at night, to prey on young kids. I hoped they wouldn't bother me.

As the weather got nicer, I began to spend more time outside, although I still liked to rest on the sofa, or one of the soft chairs, in the library, and read. But the sounds of laughter, and shouts, from the yard, would beckon to me like an ancient Siren's Song, and I would put my book away, and go outside.

There was always some kind of game going on, whether it be softball or football or something else. That was one of the few things I liked about the Home. We never lacked having enough players for a game.

My favorite was tag. Our version of the old, children's game, consisted of one kid being chosen as the "tagger." The rest of us would line up along the fence, in the yard, and try to reach the other side without getting caught. The distance covered, was one city block, so you needed to be quick, and in good shape if you expected to last in this game.

The tagger would stand out in front of us and holler:

"Ready!..Set!..Go!"

We'd take off running and this guys job was to tag as many of us as he could.

There were usually around twenty of us, and it always turned into a wild, screaming melee. The dust would swirl around our legs, as we darted, dashed, and dodged, finally crashing into the fence on the other side, laughing, and out of breath.

You were "safe" then. We were elated at having not been caught, but that good feeling only lasted for a short while, because then you had to line up, and do it all over again. Only this time, there were usually one or two more guys looking to catch up and plant a "tag" on you. It could get rough out there, and sometimes it was more like shove than tag with guys getting skinned up and sometimes fights broke out.

Soon after we'd done this three or four times, only the fastest guys were left, one of whom was usually Ronny Collins. He was only eleven, but could outrun everyone, even the big guys. Ronny was always one of the last guys to be caught.

At times like that, I forgot about how much I hated being there. I didn't want the game to end, and it felt like I could run forever, in the soft, spring air.

Then Buck or Greenie would holler at us to come in. When they did, the magical spell was broken. Everyone would reluctantly head for the side door, full of the devil, laughing and joking, not ready to settle down.

We always stopped to get a drink in the washroom, but the bed wetters were only allowed one drink of water at night, and that was it. To a thirsty boy, this was pure torture. The knowledge that I couldn't have a second or third drink, made me even thirstier. The craving for water became an obsession, and I got pretty good at sneaking drinks.

After we were sent upstairs for the night, and lights out, there were usually a couple of threats by Greenie, or a smack with the lanyard, before everyone would settle down enough to stay in our bunks. Then we'd listen to mystery programs on the radio, like "Mr. and Mrs. North."

I loved lying in bed at night, listening to those shows. They were comforting, and you didn't have to look at a screen, to know what was going on. I'd close my eyes, and drift off into a dream world, where brave, strong people lived, and they were smart, and always caught the bad guy. They did the right thing, and they could be counted on when times got tough. I wished I could meet someone like that.

That was my favorite time of the night. Listening to the calm, peaceful voices of reason, and understanding. When the world didn't seem so scary and, full or worry, fear, and disappointment.

I'd always been afraid of the dark but being in a dormitory full of kids, made me feel secure. And then there was the light from the shower room, that was left on all night, so that we could use the toilet. The light that helped to keep the monsters, that hid in the deep, black shadows at bay.

One evening, just before the sunset, Tommy and I were lying in one of our foxholes, talking. This one was situated along the back-fence line, behind the garage.

Suddenly, we saw a couple of big guys go around to the rear of it to have a smoke, which was against the rules. We could tell who they were, and one of them was Larry Collins. The other guy was Danny Henderson. He was the one who grabbed me by the hair the first night I was here and made me piss my pants.

They lit up their smokes, and their faces flashed briefly against the dark background of the garage. We watched as their cigarettes made orange arcs of light as they took a puff, then dropped their arms back down to their sides.

"That Danny's sure mean," I said, and told Tommy about my run in with him.

"Shh, they'll hear ya," he muttered nervously.

"Whut?" I said. "We're not doen nuthen wrong."

"Will ya shuddup!" he hissed, then ducked his head. "Shit! They heard us!"

I looked over, and saw one of them heading in our direction. From the way Tommy was acting, I began to worry. The guy walking towards us was Larry, and he strolled up, and leaned over to see in the dusky light. Tommy had his head down.

"Is that you, Pissass?" Larry asked.

"Yea." Gawd, I hated that name.

"Who's that with ya, Tommy?"

Tommy lifted his head.

"Hey, Larry," he said.

"Unless you guys want yer asses kicked," he threatened, "You better not say anything about us smoken."

"Naw, we wont say nuthen Larry," Tommy promised.

"Me either," I added.

"Okay, but remember whut I said," he warned, then turned, and walked back to the garage.

We breathed a little easier, then decided we'd go in, and watch some television. When we got up to go, we gave the garage a wide berth. As we walked up to the side door, Buck came out. We stepped aside as he went by, and he didn't even look at us. His full attention seemed to be on the garage, and judging from the expression on his face, someone was in trouble. Namely, Larry and Danny. Evidently, somebody had told Buck about their smoking, and now he was going out to catch them.

I don't know what possessed me, but suddenly I hollered:

"Hey Buck! Ya going for a ride?"

Buck stopped, and looked back at me. There was a moment of stunned silence, and I thought, "Jeez, whut've I done?" Then he motioned for me to come to him. I looked at Tommy, but he just shook his head sadly, and walked away, then went in the side door. I slowly walked up to Buck, shaking in fear. When I was within reach, he slapped me hard across the face.

A bright, flash of light, tinged with yellows, oranges, and reds, exploded behind my eyes. The crack of the blow deafened me for a moment, and it felt like a firecracker had gone off in my head. I stumbled backwards, and almost fell. I brought my hand up to my cheek which was stinging, and I cowered. The slap had really hurt, and the whole side of my face tingled, like it was on fire. My ears were ringing, and my eyes filled with tears from the pain. I hoped he wasn't going to hit me again.

"You stay right here until I get back," he ordered coldly.

He hurried around the corner of the back of the garage. Larry and Danny must've been watching from the other side, because suddenly they appeared, running towards the side entrance. They ran past me, and had just made the steps leading to the door when Buck came roaring around the opposite side of the garage.

He hollered at them to stop, but they went on in. I was still standing in the same spot, felling lonely, and dejected. Me, and my big mouth. Buck walked up, and jerked me by my arm.

Suddenly, Uncle Harry shouted from a window in his living quarters, which jutted out from the main building. He could see the garage from there.

"What's the trouble Buck?"

"Oh, I found a couple of kids were smoking behind the garage, but 'Loudmouth' here hollered before I could catch them," Buck explained.

"Who's that?"

"It's Tommy Janicek," Buck said. "Danny Henderson was one of the smokers and Larry Collins was the other."

Uncle Harry gave a snort of disgust, and told us to meet him in his office. Buck took me inside. When we passed through the tv room, Tommy looked at me like I was a condemned prisoner being led to the gallows, and to tell the truth, that's how I felt.

When we got to Uncle Harry's office, he was sitting at his desk. He had that wicked-looking belt, and was tapping it lightly on the arm of his chair. Buck told me to sit down on the bench, then he looked over at Uncle Harry.

"I'll be back with Larry and Danny as soon as I find them," he said, and left.

I was downcast, and slumped on the bench, staring at my feet.

"Sit up straight!" Uncle Harry snapped.

I did as he said, and sat rigidly until Buck returned with the two guilty parties. They looked sullen and angry. Uncle Harry got up, and walked over to Larry.

"Let me smell your breath," he ordered.

When Larry breathed on him, Uncle Harry made a face. Then he walked up to Danny, and had him do the same. Then he stepped back.

"Were you kids smoking?" he asked, and you could tell he already knew the answer.

"No," Larry muttered. Danny shook his head.

Uncle Harry reached over, and slapped Larry with his free hand.

"Don't lie to me, dammit!" he roared. "I can smell it on your breath."

Then Uncle Harry started whacking him with his belt, and Larry put up his hands in an attempt to protect himself. The Old Man hit him three or four times, then stopped, and turned his attention on Danny.

"And I suppose you weren't smoking, either?" he said sarcastically.

Danny didn't answer, and just looked down at the floor, and Buck smacked him on the back of the head with his open hand.

"He's talking to you, gawdammit!" he said.

"Okay, okay," Danny said dismally. "Yea, we were smoken."

Uncle Harry then proceeded to hit him with the belt, but Danny didn't even move, although I'm sure it must've hurt. While Uncle Harry beat him, I got the feeling that if Buck hadn't been there, Danny could've taken the belt away from the Old Man, and used it on him if he wanted to. Uncle Harry was big, but compared to Danny's well-muscled body, he looked old and flabby.

When Uncle Harry was done, he told them he'd better not catch them smoking again, and then he sent them off. I knew my turn was coming and I was filled with dread.

"I'll take care of Janicek," he told Buck, who walked out of the office.

Then Uncle Harry had me stand up.

"Just what were you trying to prove with your stupid stunt?" he asked harshly.

"I dunno," I answered honestly.

"What do you mean, you don't know?"

When I didn't say anything, he began to hit me with the belt. I yelped in pain, as the braided plastic bit into my skin, I was crying and begging for mercy, and he finally stopped.

"Don't ever let me catch you pulling another stunt like that," he warned. "Now get out of my sight!"

I hurried out to the dining room, and sat in a chair, and checked my injuries. There were welts all over my body, and they burned intensely. I sniffed back a tear, and waited for the pain to go away.

Tommy walked in from the tv room, and sat down next to me.

"How ya doen?" he asked.

"Okay," I mumbled, and tried to wipe the tears from my eyes.

"Man, yer crazy," he said, with a little bit of awe in his voice. "You'd never catch me doen sumpthen like that. Speshly when Buck's around."

"Believe me, I won't ever do it again," I told him.

I was gingerly rubbing my fingers on some of the sorest spots. They hurt like hell, but by bedtime, they'd quit burning, and there was hardly a mark on me.

The next day at school, Tommy, Jeff, Billy, and I were out in the yard skimming lids. We used to get in the incinerator, and look for the tops from the big, commercial cans of fruits and vegetables that went into our meals.

There was an old fashioned can opener in the kitchen, which you turned with a big handle, and after it was used on a can, there was about a quarter of an inch of sharp metal left around the edge of the lid, which was razor sharp.

We'd bend part of it down, and grasp it between thumb and index finger, and let them fly. When thrown properly, they'd almost hover in the air.

I was really a moron when it came to skimming lids. They usually wound up bouncing along the ground. Billy, now, could make them hover, and so could Jeff. Tommy was in my class.

I noticed Danny Henderson watching us, and he motioned to me. I walked over to him hesitantly, and wasn't sure what to expect. He sensed my nervousness, and grinned.

"Hey, Tommy," he said. "I just wanted ya to know I appreciate whut ya tried to do last night."

"Aw, that's okay," I replied shyly.

I was flattered that one of the toughest guys in the Home, was paying me a compliment, and I looked down at the ground, and scuffed the dirt with my shoe.

"Hey, that took guts, kid," he said, then surprised me with his next words. "I gotta favor to ask ya."

I looked up at him curiously. A favor? What in God's blue heaven could I possibly do for Danny?

"Whut?" I asked, perplexed.

He saw my brother and friends watching, and he told me to come with him. He took off walking, and I followed.

We wound up going behind the garage, then to the corner of the back fence. He looked around, then put his hands together in a cradle position.

"Come on," he said. "I'll give ya a boost over the fence."

I was so caught up in the excitement of the moment, I didn't even hesitate or question his order, and after placing my foot in his hands, he easily lifted me to the top of the fence. I grabbed on and let myself down to the other side.

Danny effortlessly climbed over, and landed besides me. He glanced around to make sure nobody saw us, because we weren't supposed to leave the grounds, and we would get a chewing out, and a beating if we got caught. But the only people watching were Tommy, Jeff and Billy.

"Let's go before someone sees us," Danny said.

We took off hurriedly, and my heart was pounding with fear, and excitement. Once we were out of sight of the yard, we slowed our pace.

The neighborhood around the Home was made up of a lot of houses with trees lining the streets, and yards. Most of the homes had large verandas with neatly trimmed lawns, and flower gardens. They were solidly built, and had a comfortable, serene quality about them that was appealing to me. I envied the people who lived in those houses. I wished I could live in one, and have a regular family life like other people. As we walked down the street, I was curious about what Danny wanted.

"Where're we goen?" I finally asked.

"To the store," he answered. "I want ya to steal a lock for me. The one I got is broke."

My heart seemed to leap up in my throat, and I was instantly filled with fear. I stopped dead in my tracks, and Danny turned to see what was holding me up.

"Whut's the problem?" he asked.

"You … want me … to steal a lock?" I stammered.

He walked back to me, and tried to be persuasive.

"Hey, come on," he said. "There's nuthen to it. Look, they'll be watching me, cuz I'll create a scene, and when they're not looken, you can slip it in yer pocket, and nobody'll be the wiser."

He stepped closer to me, and then glanced around quickly, I grew tense because I wasn't sure what was coming next, but nothing could've prepared me for his next move. Danny put his hand on my crotch, and began to rub me. The shock of this unexpected assault on my body almost made me jump. His eyes were half closed, and his breathing had quickened.

"Ya do this fer me, and I'll make it good to ya. You know?" he said.

About that time, a man walked out of his house, and the screen door slammed shut behind him. That brought Danny out of his trance, and we started walking again. When we reached the corner, he stopped.

"Look," he said. "Are ya gonna do this fer me or not? I thought ya had balls."

"I … I wanna help ya … but … I've never done nuthen like this." I told him sincerely.

"It'll be a breeze. You watch, afterwards you'll laugh cuz it was so easy," he smiled convincingly.

I thought about it, and decided that no matter what happened, I was going to go through with it. I wanted the big guys to think I was cool.

"Okay … if you say so," I told him.

As I walked the rest of the way, I tried to steel myself for what was coming. When we got to the department store, he sent me in ahead of him. Nervously, I took off. I wandered through the store until I was able to find the hardware section, and the locks in particular.

I looked around for Danny, and spotted him about thirty feet away. He looked like he was trying to find something, and he glanced over at me, and winked, then continued with his act.

Suddenly Danny reached out, and pulled some stuff off a rack, and then he cursed, and acted like he was trying to keep things from falling, but a couple of items hit the floor. The commotion caused some customers to look over at him, and I saw a clerk head in his direction.

I decided that now was as good a moment as any, and I grabbed a lock, and with my heart pounding wildly, stuck it in my pocket. Danny had told me that as soon as I had one, to get out of there as quickly as I could, and he'd meet me a block away. I took off, nervously making my way to the door that led outside. Once I got that far, I began to let out a sigh of relief, and I slowed down as I walked through it.

Just as I reached the sidewalk, a man grabbed me by the shoulder, and I just about jumped out of my skin in alarm as he turned me around.

"Okay," he said. "Hand over the lock."

"Whut?" I answered innocently. "Whut lock?"

"The one in your pocket," he told me, matter of factly.

My shoulders slumped, and I began to shake with fear. Jeez, I'd really screwed up this time. I reached into my pocket, and handed the lock to him. My hand was shaking, and I began to cry.

"I'm sorry, Mister," I whined. "Honest, I didn't mean to take it, please don't arrest me."

The man didn't say anything, and instead took my arm, and led me back into the store. As we walked by shoppers, they all seemed to be staring at us. I didn't see Danny anywhere.

He took me to the managers office, and when we walked in, I was told to sit down. Then the manager, and the guy who caught me, went out in the hallway to talk. I was left alone in a state of abject depression.

Why had I listened to Danny? I was minding my own business until he came along. Jeez, I could be out in the yard right now, sailing lids with Tommy, Billy, and Jeff, instead of sitting here in this crummy office, facing a scary future in jail. Shit!

The manager, and the other man came back. I was slumped down in the chair, hanging my head. I heard the manager sit down behind his desk, and shuffle some papers. Then he spoke in a very businesslike manner:

"What is your name?"

I looked up, and saw he had a pen and paper in front of him. I told him and he wrote it down.

That must be for the police, I thought. Then they'll probably take me to jail. I shivered with apprehension.

"Where do you live?"

I told him the address of the Home, and he gave me kind of a funny look, but continued to write. When he asked me for the phone number, I really fell apart.

"I'm sorry," I sobbed. "I won't ever do it again, I promise. Just don't call, please."

He seemed to soften a bit, and then he asked me how old I was.

"Ten," I sniffed.

"Have you ever done anything like this before?" he asked.

"No," I answered truthfully.

"What made you do this?"

I hesitated. I wasn't about to tell him Danny had talked me into it. But I had to tell him something. Suddenly I had an idea.

"The place where I live … has a lot of guys who steal, and … and one of them broke the lock … for my locker." Yea. That sounded good.

"Why didn't you just ask someone for the money to buy you a new lock, instead of trying to steal one?" he questioned.

"My mom is dead, and my dad don't make much money, which is why I'm in that place," I told him truthfully.

I played that statement for all it was worth, and put on a sad face. It seemed to work because he crumpled up the sheet of paper, and then threw it in the waste paper basket by his desk. Then he looked at me sternly.

"You're not the first boy from the Home that I've had to deal with, regarding the stealing of merchandise from the store. I usually just turn

them over to the authorities, and let them deal with these individuals …
but in your case, I'm going to let you go on the condition that you promise
me you'll never steal anything from this store again."

I couldn't believe it! They were going to let me go! I almost shouted
with joy.

I let out a big sigh of relief, and shook from all the pent up emotion.

"I promise," I said. Shit! I'd have promised anything.

"Okay Tommy, you can go now," he said, and then smiled.

"Thank you Mister," I told him.

When I stood up, my legs felt weak. After I walked out of the office,
I could hardly believe my luck. I hurried to the exit door before they
changed their minds. It was only after I reached the sidewalk, that I felt
relatively safe.

As I walked back to the Home, I looked around for Danny, but there
was no sign of him. I didn't really care, though, because I was so happy
to be free.

When I got back to the Home, it was just about suppertime. I snuck
back in through the entrance by the garage, without getting caught. I
looked for Tommy, Billy, and Jeff, and found them watching tv.

"Whut happened between you, and Danny?" Tommy asked.

I looked around to make sure no one else was listening, before I
answered.

"You wouldn't believe it," I told him in a low voice. "Danny asked me
to steal a lock for him at Monty's, and when I did, they caught me, but
then they turned around, and let me go."

"Oh bully's," he said skeptically, and gestured with his hand.

"No bullshit, man," I replied.

I guess I should explain here about Tommy, and his saying "bully's."
I'd never heard of the Texas Longhorn's football team or their "hook 'em
horns" sign. I don't know if they were doing that during games at that time,
but we were doing it in our neck of the woods. For us, it meant bullshit.

Whenever someone thought you were lying, they'd flash you the sign,
and say, "bullys." Tommy used to like doing that.

"Why'd they let you go?" he asked.

"I just told them I was poor, and put on a sad face, and that was it,"
I told him.

"Whut about Danny?" he asked.

"He wasn't around when I got caught." I answered.

At supper, later on, I saw Danny, but he didn't even look in my direction.

Afterwards, Tommy, Benny, Billy, and Jeff, and I were headed outside when Danny called my name. I stopped, then turned around, and walked back to him. We were standing by the side door.

"Whut happened?" he asked. "I saw that guy grab ya. You didn't say nuthen about me, didja?"

"Naw," I said.

"Well, good," he answered. "I'm on probation, and I could get my ass in a sling."

I told him what happened, and he grinned.

"Yer okay, Tommy," he said. "We'll try another store."

"I ... I dunno." I sure didn't want to go through another hassle like that again.

His face took on a hard, mean look.

"Whut? Don't tell me yer gitten chicken?"

"No ... I just ... dunno."

I felt trapped, and didn't know how to get out of it. At the same time though, I didn't want to pass up a chance to prove myself.

Suddenly, Danny sensed something, and looked back over his shoulder. His eyes widened in fear, and I looked past him, and saw Buck standing in the doorway of the tv room, watching us. I'd never been so glad to see him.

"What's going on?" he asked.

Danny tried to look innocent.

"Nuthen Buck," he told him. "We're just talken, ain't that right, Tommy?"

"Yea, we're just talken, Buck," I parroted.

"See ya later, Tommy," Danny said, and walked over to the far stairwell, and went up the stairs in a hurry.

Buck watched him leave, then fixed me with that merciless stare. I tried to act like there was nothing out of the ordinary.

"Was he bothering you?" he asked again, and I avoided his eyes.

"No."

He let out a disgusted sigh, and slowly shook his head.

"You know, Tommy," he said. "I don't know why you stuck up for him and Collins that night, but if you keep messing around with guys like them, you're headed for trouble and you're going to wind up just like them—losers."

"Yea?" I answered, not sure what to say.

"Yea, now beat it," he said, disgustedly.

I left, and went outside to play. I was sure glad Buck showed up when he did, but there was still the problem of what to do about Danny. After my close call, I didn't want to try my luck someplace else. When I got to playing tag, I forgot about it.

But after we were called in, I started worrying again, and when we went upstairs to shower, I thought about what Buck had said. He'd made it sound as if I'd turn out to be like Danny. Me? I looked down at my puny body, and tried, to imagine being fifteen or sixteen with muscles like Danny, but I couldn't even picture myself as being that old, I felt like I was never going to grow up, and be a big guy.

We were taking showers, and Tommy, and Billy were sharing the showerhead with me. Tommy was soaping himself by my side, and he noticed me gazing downward, and he grinned.

"Whutsa matter?" he asked. "You act like ya got a boner or sumpthen."

I snapped out of my daydream, and a remark came to mind that I'd heard one of the Big Guys say. I thought it was pretty clever.

"Shit, mine's bigger soft than that pimple of yers is hard!" I told him.

We laughed, and engaged in some horseplay, and I soon forgot all about what Buck had said.

Danny looked me up the next day, and when I balked at going with him to steal a lock, he pushed me in the face. I fell down, and he called me chicken, then walked away. Although I was relieved at not having to go through that again, I still wanted him to think I was cool. But not if I had to steal something to prove it. And I never told anyone about Danny groping me, because I didn't want him to find out I'd said anything. He'd kick my ass, and I didn't think anyone would believe me anyway.

One night not long after that, I woke up with a strong urge to urinate. I was ready to throw back the covers, when suddenly, I heard whispering voices. I looked around, and finally saw a figure bending over five year old Jason Russek's bed. At first, I thought it was Greenie, but then I slowly realized that what I was looking at was a Night Crawler. I was filled with disgust, but also fear at the thought of a stranger coming into the dorm while we slept. There was a creepiness about it, and I realized how vulnerable we were to this type of person. I felt helpless about doing anything, and just covered back up, and waited for him to leave. I hoped I could hold my bladder.

Finally, he left. I got up, then noticed Vernon wasn't in his bed. But that wasn't unusual, because no matter what time you got up, you could usually find him in the bathroom. I don't know what the hell he did in there, but that's where he'd be. I wondered how he still found the time to wet the bed.

I was kind of concerned because of the Night Crawler, but when I walked in, I was relieved to see him. I went over to the urinal, and Vern walked up to me. He was smiling.

"Art came to see me tonight," he said.

"Did he?" I told him disgustedly.

"Yes," he said. "Art's a nice guy."

"Yea, sure he is."

I finished peeing, then headed back to bed. I was concerned about this Art guy, and I vowed that in the morning I was going to tell Uncle Harry about him, but I didn't. Why? I don't know. I never said a word. It was just another thing that we had to put up with while living there.

During that time, I found out how strong Elmer Lehr was. He'd work out on the parallel bar, and now that he was wearing t-shirts, you could see the muscles ripple along his arms, and chest.

The best part though, was when he got up in one of the trees that ran along the fence line in the yard, and like Tommy had said, swing from the branches like Tarzan, or an ape anyway.

He had broken his leg last year falling from a tree, and Uncle Harry had told him to stay out of then. But of course he didn't.

One day, he was performing for us, and Buck just happened to see him. He walked out in the yard, and started towards the tree.

In the meantime, Elmer was doing his thing, and just as he was about to grab a branch between swings, Buck yelled, and that threw him off.

He missed, and then fell from the tree, and landed on his back with a thud. The dust flew up around him, and he laid still for a moment. Then he began to roll from side to side.

Buck ran up to him, and bent over, and grabbed hold of his belt, and then began to lift him up, and down until Elmer was breathing normal again. Then Buck helped him to his feet.

"Elmer," he said. "If you don't stay out of the dammed trees, you're going to wind up killing yourself. Quit clowning around before you really get hurt. You got that?"

"Yessir," Elmer told him.

Buck turned around, and started walking back towards the Home. As he passed by me, and Tommy, I swear there was a hint of a smile on his face.

Maybe it was because he got as big a kick out of Elmer as we did.

The days began to go swiftly by, and it wasn't long before school let out. Now, at last, we'd be going to the Camp, and I was really looking forward to seeing the place I'd heard so much about. This was going to be exciting.

Part

4

There was a special quality about making the move to the mountains. The change from being at the Home and going to Camp, seemed to put everyone in a good mood. Even Uncle Harry seemed more cheerful than usual. I know I couldn't remember when I'd been so worked up about packing up, and moving. At last, I was getting my wish, and soon I'd be about to see the legendary Mountain.

There was almost a carnival atmosphere surrounding us, as we got everything arranged, and we headed out on the road. We had a regular convoy, what with Uncle Harry's Old's 88, Buck's Chevy, and the bus that Greenie drove. Tommy, and I were in the back of the bus and we were in high spirits. On the way, we sang songs, and waved at the people in other cars.

We finally ascended the mountains and the sights that popped up with every curve in the highway looked wonderful to me.

I'd been on this road before, with Mom and Dad when I was younger, but I didn't remember it being quite this beautiful. The panoramic view of the trees, rocks, and mountains held our interest, and we were far from being bored. The air was clean, and fresh, smelling of pine trees and wild flowers.

The drive took quite a while, and I wanted them to hurry up, and get there. But the passing scenery gave us plenty of things to see, and talk about, and the time went by rather quickly.

Finally, we came to the stretch of highway that led up to the Camp, and Tommy said it wouldn't be long. As we drew closer, I became more anxious, and excited. We rounded a curve, and Tommy pointed out the window.

"We're getting close," he said. "Look, there's Old Baldy, and Twin Peaks."

Finally, I was able to gaze upon the storied Mountain that had fired my imagination, and filled me with so much anticipation.

When I got my first look at Mt. Baldwin, I was kind of disappointed. I'd pictured it in my mind as being like Mt. Everest, a craggy castle of granite, whose battlements were covered with sheets of ice and snow. A forbidding, fortress, shooting up through the clouds, that inspired awe. But it wasn't like that at all.

The Mountain was pretty frumpy looking by comparison. Most mountains usually come to a point. It's expected of them, to my way of thinking. But instead, Mt. Baldwin was round, hence the nickname: "Old Baldy." It was almost like some great giant had dragged his foot, stepping over the Mountain and had knocked the peak down. There were a few flecks of snow on it's sandy-colored face and overall, Mt. Baldwin was not very impressive looking.

Now, the set of peaks next to it, looked like real mountains, or at least, how I thought they should look.

They weren't as high as the Mountain, and had formed up into twin cones of reddish-yellow rocks on the one side of Old Baldy. The peaks appeared to be separate from their larger, fat sister. (I began to refer to them in feminine terms right away, don't ask me why).

There were some big, tree covered hills, across from the twins, and between them, they created a framework of rocks, and forest with Mt. Baldwin in the middle.

Whenever I heard the word "mountain," the ones like twin peaks came to mind.

But despite its appearance, there was a special quality about Mt. Baldwin that made it different from all the other mountains I'd ever seen.

Somewhere on the Mountain was the wreckage of a WWII Bomber, and I was bound, and determined to find it. I looked up at her long after most of the guys had shifted their attention elsewhere.

"Where's the plane?" I asked the Mountain. "I'm going to find it."

We went around another curve, and there was a tree lined bluff up ahead that overlooked the highway. Tommy pointed it out to me.

"That's where the Camp is," he said. "We're almost there."

I looked at where he was pointing, and really got worked up as we neared the end of our journey. I could hardly wait to see the Camp, and all the things Tommy had told me about.

After we reached the bluff, it began to slope downwards as we went along until finally, it was level with the highway, and we reached the entrance. It was across the highway from us, and we pulled off to the side of the road, and stopped. There was a gate that appeared to be locked, along with a sign that had the name of the Camp on it.

Uncle Harry got out, crossed the highway, and unlocked the gate, and opened it. Then he went back to his car, and we pulled away, and followed him through the entrance. The road began to slope upwards, and the bus groaned as Greenie shifted gears.

The outgrowth of trees, and bushes were so close on the one side, you could almost reach out and touch them. The thick, green walls of foliage almost looked like the jungles I'd seen in war movies. I turned to Tommy.

"It looks like a jungle," I told him.

"That's what it's called," he said. "The Jungle."

I was impressed. I'd have to check it out.

When we got to the top of the incline, the trees and bushes thinned away, which created an open space with only a solitary tree here, and there. The ground continued to rise up on one side, and we came to a place where the road split. The one we passed by had been carved out of the side of the hill behind the campsite.

Tommy said it was called "The Old Sawmill Road," and it snaked it's way back about eight or nine miles. He said there was an old lumberjack camp at the end of it. I was really intrigued.

There was a small rise ahead, and when we reached the top, and started down the other side, I got my first glimpse of the Camp.

It was arranged military style, with each building lined up next to each other in a row. There was even a flagpole. The large, open area in front of everything extended clear out to the edge of the bluff. The forest began behind the buildings and that's where we stopped. The first building was the little guys bunkhouse, and I figured that's where I'd stay, then the chow hall, with living quarters for the cook, the big guys bunkhouse, and then a small, guest cabin. Across from it was the shower house, which contained a wash room, laundry facilities, and showers. All the buildings were painted a faded, light green color.

The ground started to slope upwards behind the buildings, and that's where the Old Man's summer home sat. It had a big, wooden veranda, and a large picture window that gave him a great view of everything.

We jumped out of the vehicles chattering excitedly, and the counselors organized everyone to help unload our belongings.

Because the little bunkhouse could only hold so many kids, I found out I was going to be in the big bunkhouse, along with Tommy who was ten now. I really liked that. I'd be with the big guys, and it was nice to know that I wasn't considered young enough to stay in the other bunkhouse. (Billy was).

But the pecking order of the Home was even more clearly defined at the Camp. There were some do's and don'ts. The biggest don't concerned the two wooden outhouses that were provided for our use. They were close to the edge of the bluff, where there was a barbed wire fence that ran the entire length of the camp property.

They were called "Joanerholes," and each one had two holes. One was for the big guys, and we younger kids had to use the other. If the big guys found a little guy in the big Joaner, they would kick his ass, and then stick his head down one of the holes and try and make him puke.

I didn't know what the cut-off point between big and little was, but I knew that I wasn't going anywhere close to the Big Joaner.

But I wished I didn't have to use one. I couldn't stand them.

I remembered when I was about four, we lived next door to Grandma and Grandpa Brewer's house in an old, tar-paper shack that had no indoor toilet. We had to go to an outhouse that sat nearby.

It got awful cold in there during the winter. I hated to use it, and I remembered the horrible smell that came from the hole. I didn't like to sit on it because I just knew that a spider or something was going to grab me by the ass, and pull me down inside.

And now I was going to have to get used to it all over again. But then it occurred to me that if I wanted to, I could always use the woods to pee or take a shit.

The adults had a Joanerhole that was close to Uncle Harry's house.

My dad had bought Billy, and I a couple of small trunks for our stuff, and when I carried mine inside the bunkhouse, I was reminded of the barracks that I'd seen in Army pictures. Everything was wood, including our bunkbeds. They weren't your ordinary bunkbeds though. They had been built so that there were two beds nailed together, top and bottom, and each one had high wooden sides.

I was hesitant about taking a bed for myself, and I watched as other guys came in with their trunks, and then pick out bunks for themselves.

About that time, Tommy walked in, carrying his trunk.

"You picked out a bed yet?" he asked.

"No, I was waiten on you," I lied.

"Well, let's take these," he said, indicating the bunks I was standing by.

I set my trunk down, and then I noticed there weren't any mattresses on the top bunks, just the bottom ones.

"How come there ain't any mattresses up here?" I asked him, quizzically.

"Oh, they give us sleeping bags, and then we go out, and pick some boughs, and put them in here to sleep on," he explained. "I used to help Johnny do that last year."

Tommy had been in the little bunkhouse last summer, which just had regular bunkbeds. Johnny had been an older friend of his who had since left.

"Hey!" I told him. "That sounds like fun! Let's go git some to put in our beds!"

"Aw," he explained gently. "If ya wet the bed, they won't let you sleep up here. You have to sleep on the bottom."

"Oh." Again, I cursed the fact that I was a bedwetter.

There were boards laid across the rafters above the bunks, and I helped Tommy hoist his trunk up to them so he could store it there.

Ronny, and Timmy had taken some top bunks nearby, and when they saw me helping Tommy, they made some disparaging remarks.

"Peeuu!" Ronny said. "You smell whut I smell?"

"Yea!" Timmy wrinkled his nose. "A pissass."

"Hey, Buck!" Ronny yelled. "Does Pissass hafta sleep in here? You should make him sleep outside with the skunks!"

Some of the guys laughed, and I was embarrassed. Gawd, I wished they would let up on me.

The counselors slept in the bunkhouses with us, and now Buck looked up from where he was storing his belongings by his bed which was next to the front door.

"Nevermind all the shit!" he ordered. "You guys on the top bunks better worry about getting your bunks filled, unless you want to sleep on bare boards tonight. But first you better get over to the chow hall, and get a couple of sandwiches, because that's all there is until supper!"

Some of the guys, including Ronny, and his friend, headed for the doors, where Buck had laid down some stacks of gunny sacks, and they grabbed a couple, and left.

Tommy asked me if I would help him, and I told him he didn't even have to ask. Then we picked out two sacks, and went to the chow hall where they were handing out sandwiches, and pop.

When we walked in, the first thing to catch my eye was a huge American flag that hung from the ceiling to the floor on one wall. It was the biggest one I'd ever seen.

We got our sandwiches, and pop, then sat down at one of the tables to eat. Tommy, and I were facing the flag, and I mentioned how big it was.

"Count the stars on it," he said.

"Why?" I knew how many stars were on a flag.

"Just count 'em," he insisted.

I did, but I could only come up with forty-six. I gave him a puzzled look.

"There's only forty-six," I told him. "They left two out."

He started laughing, and I couldn't figure out what was so funny.

"Whut?" I asked.

"You dumb shit, it's only got forty-six 'cause that's all the states there were when it was made. That's how old it is," he explained.

"Oh," I said, feeling kind of stupid.

Off in the corner, of the same wall as the flag, I noticed there was a bookcase, and a couch. The first chance I got, I was going to check it out.

When we were finished eating, Tommy and I got the gunny sacks, and set out to gather some boughs. Billy, Benny, and Jeff came out of the chow hall behind us, and we asked them if they'd like to come with us, but they said they were going to go explore.

Vernon was standing nearby, and he asked if he could come along.

"Sure Vern," Tommy said. "Let's go."

We walked back to the rise, and went down the way we'd come in. Tommy led us close to the Jungle, but just before we got there, he left the road, and started walking down a path off to the side towards some trees, and we followed him. I began to hear the sound of rushing water, and the trail started to slope sideways down towards a pond that was encircled by some bushes, and trees.

Once we reached the bottom of the path, I got my first, good view, and it was really pretty. The pond had been created by a small dam that some beavers had built. The pine trees, and aspens around the edges, shrouded it in shades of light, and dark, and there was a peaceful, soothing quality about the setting. Especially with the shafts of sunlight that flowed down through the branches of the various trees.

A small, mountain brook fed the body of water at one end, and then the water went on to filter through the dam on into the Jungle. This accounted for the thick growth of greenery on the other side. Then the water continued to flow through it until it reached a big culvert that was under the highway.

"This is called 'The Old Mill Pond,'" Tommy informed us.

The trickling sound of the water, and beauty of the setting kept me spellbound, until Vernon ruined the moment by throwing a rock in the pond.

"Hey! Don't do that!" I told him irritably, then turned to Tommy, and pointed at some trees. "Let's go get us some branches."

"The ones around here aren't the right kind," he said. "I'll show you where we need to go."

Tommy took off, and when he reached the dam, he began to walk gingerly across the dam because there were gaps in it into which your foot could easily slip. I followed, and did my best to avoid the holes along the way.

Once safely across, I turned around to see if Vern was following, and he was slowly making his way over to us, and he had his arms raised up from his sides like he was some kind of tightrope walker.

"C'mon Vernon!" Tommy hollered at him impatiently. "We ain't got all day!"

"Ahh, let him be Tommy," I said. "If he tries to go any faster, he'll prob'ly fall in."

Finally, he reached us, and then I took in our surroundings.

The pond, and Jungle were near the end of a wide, long ravine that took off in the direction of the "Old Sawmill Road." There was a long, winding footpath that started out from where we were standing, and it meandered along beside the bottom of the steep slope that rose up higher, the further back you walked. The tinkling stream wove itself close to the path in places, and then it would take off into the trees and bushes that lined the trail on the other side.

There was a mystical, magic look about it, and I asked Tommy about where it went to. It was quite beautiful and charming.

"This is called 'Indian Trail'," he told me. "It goes back about a mile, and the big guys have a fort up there at the end."

"After we're through picking boughs, I'd like to see where it goes," I said.

He told me we could only go so far, because if the big guys caught us messing around up there, they'd kick our asses.

"Oh," I replied.

Shit! Again with the big guys. They sure could make life lousy.

Tommy led us off in the opposite direction towards the highway. The ground was pretty level, and the trees began to spread-out, and we walked though a green, grassy meadow. Up ahead, I could see some trees that lined the asphalt road, and we began to walk along beside it towards them.

That's where Tommy said we needed to go to find the evergreens that he was looking for. He said they had the best boughs for sleeping on.

Before we got there though, he stopped, and cursed, and I asked him what was wrong.

"Ahh, those other guys beat us to them," he said disgustedly, and pointed.

He was gesturing at the trees we were headed for, and I could see some guys up in the branches, and I recognized Ronny, and Tim amongst them. I thought we didn't need to get any closer.

"Now whut?" I asked him.

"Ahh, those ain't the only good ones," he answered. "There's some more back this way. We're just gonna have to walk a little further."

We turned around, and retracted our steps, but instead of going back to the pond, we just kept walking in a straight line up to where the foothills started. As we climbed upward, we kept an eye out for the trees we needed to find.

But, when we reached the place that he'd told us about, there were some older boys there already.

"Hey! Git the fuck outta here, you little pricks!" we were told.

Man, I hated big guys!

Tommy wound up taking us to a spot further back, and we hoped we wouldn't run into anybody else. I was getting tired of the bullshit.

But, when we arrived there, it was deserted, and we walked up to the trees, and began to gather boughs. The needles were soft, and pliable, and I understood why Tommy preferred them.

At first, Vern, and I were breaking off every branch in sight, but Tommy told us to pick the smaller ones. If they were too big, it was like sleeping on rolling pins. We got the right idea, and it wasn't long before we'd filled the two sacks.

Our hands were sticky with sap, and we started rubbing them on our jeans, but Tommy stopped us.

"The best way to git it off is put some dirt in yer hands, and rub real hard," he said.

We did as were told, and most of the sap came off, but it left black splotches on our palms.

Then Tommy, and I put the bags over our shoulders, and we took off. The sack wasn't heavy at all.

After we'd gone a short ways, Tommy asked me if I'd like to go down the cliff that ran alongside Indian Trail, and I said yea.

We walked over to the top of the hillside, above the path, and made our way down the steep slope. The dirt beneath our feet was kind of loose, and I tried to be careful so as to not slip. There were some trees and bushes, but they were sparse.

Like I said, the sack wasn't very heavy, but it seemed to have a mind of its own, and it rolled over my shoulder, and wound up on my chest. I tried to throw it back over, but all that did was cause me to lose my balance. The sack slipped out of my hand, and I tripped over it, and began to plummet down the slope.

I dislodge some rocks, and Tommy, who was below me, did his best to get out of the way, as I whizzed past him.

I was trying to slow down, but I wasn't having much success. When I got to the bottom, the ground seemed to rise up at me, and I flew across Indian Trail and fell right into some bushes. They cushioned my fall but bit the shit out of me at the same time. I'd just missed hitting a tree.

I land there for a moment before moving. I'd kicked up some dust, and I spit. Then I untangled myself, and stood up. I noticed that I'd scratched my arms on the branches of the bush, and they itched, and had started to bleed. I licked my fingers and rubbed them on my wounds. I did this a couple of times and I could taste the blood and I spit out some red balls of saliva. I was a mess, and I tried to brush the dust off of my clothes.

Tommy had reached the bottom, and laughed at me.

"Oh, fuck you," I told him, and picked up my sack, and together, we put back some boughs that had spilled out. Then we waited for Vern, and when he reached us, we took off.

As we walked along, I admired the scenery around us. It was really beautiful, especially with the little stream that flowed besides the trail, weaving in and out of the trees, and bushes.

We came to the Old Mill Pond, and I got across it with no problems despite the sack. Then after waiting for Vern, we made our way back to the Camp.

When Tommy, and Vern, and I went in the bunkhouse, we climbed up, and emptied our sacks in his bunk. We spread the boughs out evenly, and then Tommy unrolled the sleeping bag provided, and after placing it over them, he laid down on his back, and sighed.

"How does it feel?" I asked him enviously.

"Great."

"Can I try it?" I asked.

"Sure," he said, and we traded places.

I laid back, and it was so very soft, and springy. It really felt comfortable, and again, I cursed the fact that I wet the bed.

"Wow, this is really nice," I told him.

"Yea, it is," he said.

"Don't they git purty dry after awhile?" I asked him, meaning the boughs.

"Yea, we haf'ta taken 'em out every week, and start over," he explained.

"Oh," I said, then changed the subject. "Let's take a hike. I wanna see some of the other places around here."

"Sure."

I asked Vernon if he wanted to come along with us, but he said he was going to stay, so Tommy and I took off.

We walked towards the shower house, and once past it, the trees began and the ground sloped down sharply into a large gorge. Tommy said it was called the "The Gully." Some guys were on the far side standing above the rutted ravine, and they were swinging from a long, heavy rope that had a round piece of wood attached to it. It was tied to a huge, pine tree on the side of the gully, and when they got to going, they must've swung above it by a good twenty feet. I had to tilt my head all the way back to see where the rope ended, but there were too many branches in the way. Whoever had climbed up there must have been very brave or foolish. I asked Tommy if it was Elmer's handiwork, but he said some other guy had done it years ago.

"If ya take the rope, and swing hard enough, you can touch the trees on the other side," he told me.

"Have you done it?" I asked him.

"Na," he said. "I ain't that brave. You wanna try it?"

"Not right now," I replied. "Maybe later."

Tommy grinned, but I ignored him.

"Where to now?" I asked him, and he told me to follow.

We went down to the bottom and started up the other side. We continued up the steep slope, and we didn't go very far before losing sight of the camp, behind the trees. The afternoon sun had begun to drift behind some gray storm clouds and the wind picked up, and smelled fresh and clean. Our surroundings became muted and gray, as our footsteps crackled on the carpet of dead pine needles, and aspen leaves.

It began to mist as we climbed past lichen-covered rocks and occasional felled trees, that had become soft and old. I stopped to kick one of the latter and the wood felt spongy as the bark split and the log began to roll down the hill. The guts of the tree spilled out in a reddish-orange mass that slowly fell apart and tumbled lazily down the slope.

We finally reached the top where there was a large outcropping of rock, and from there, you could look out over the camp and surrounding area.

Despite the rain clouds that had driven off the sun and were trying their best to spit some moisture, the view was still beautiful.

"It sure is purty up here." I told Tommy.

"Yea, this is called 'Crow's nest,'" he said.

We must have been at least a hundred feet above the camp, and I could see the river that ran beside the highway as it snaked its way along the valley floor. There was a place where the flow of water curved sharply and Tommy told me that it was called "Big Bend." That was where we went swimming.

As I looked around, I could see several summer homes and ranches scattered across the valley between the foothills and ravines. The levels of green color varied as you swept your eyes around and I liked the contrast of the dark, emerald trees and the lighter pea-colored meadows. Overlooking all of this was the Mountain and the two smaller peaks. Mount Baldwin clearly dominated the surrounding terrain.

"Look at the Mountain and Twin Peaks," Tommy told me. "Then tell me whut they remind ya ot."

"Whutta ya mean?" I was puzzled.

"Whut do the peaks look like?" he asked.

Suddenly, it dawned on me.

"Tits!" I exclaimed.

"Yea," Tommy said. "if ya really look at it, you can see a woman layen there."

I looked again, and indeed, if you used your imagination, you could make out a reclining female form. More importantly though, this particular lady held a secret.

Somewhere up there on her massive form, was a place that filled me with a longing, just like a lover who desires to conquer the object of his affections.

Just looking at her now, filled me with impatience, and excitement. I hoped there was enough of the plane left so that we could crawl around inside. That'd really be neat. Or as Tommy liked to put it, "neato keeno." From what he'd said about the tail gunner, it sounded like there was.

"Man, I can hardly wait until we climb it this year," I told him.

"Well, you better put on a couple of years between now and then if ya expect to go on that hike," he said.

"Why?" I asked, with a sinking feeling.

I felt my spirits crumble as he told me that only the older boys got to go on the trek up to the Mountain. It wasn't climbed until August, and saved for the last hike of the summer. It practically took all day to go up it, and down. The young guys went to a park some miles down the highway.

When I heard that, I was really disappointed. I'd been waiting for six months to make the climb, and now I was going to have to wait even longer. Dammit! Just my luck.

We took off, and Tommy showed me some of the other sights. I loved the beautiful landscape, and there were lots of places I could go if I wanted to get away from everyone. All I had to do was walk into the forest.

Tommy, and I finally returned to the camp, and met up with Billy, and the guys. We goofed around, and played until suppertime.

Later on, as the sun was going down, one of my melancholy moods came over me. I was in the bunkhouse, and I had to pee, so I got up, and went out the door. I started towards the joanerholes, but then I stopped.

The sky had darkened, and everything that had been peaceful, and charming in the light of day, had taken on a somber quality. The minions of the Black Spirit, of the night were spreading their wings over everything in sight, and were making the surrounding terrain take on an ominous, sinister look. Their color was everywhere, and I felt all alone, and depressed.

As the waves of emotion washed over me, I looked up at the Mountain and the Twins and hoped that the positive feelings that they held over me would help rid me of these thoughts. But they were awash in pink colors from the sunset, and their flanks were beginning to become shrouded in gray tones. They looked cold, desolate, and like me, isolated, and all that did was make me feel worse.

Everywhere I looked, there was emptiness, and gloom. Inside the bunkhouse, I could hear the loud sounds of raucous talk, and laughter, and music from the radio, but I felt far away, and totally down. I just stood there, and waited for the mood to pass. I hoped it wouldn't be long.

About that time, Tommy came out onto the small porch of the big bunkhouse, and saw me standing off by myself.

"Hey Tommy!" he said. "What'cha doen?"

"Nuthen," I lied.

"I gotta go use the joaner," he told me. "Ya wanna come along and help me pee?"

"Fuck no!" I said. "But I'll hold yer little hand on the way down there if you want."

He came down off the porch, and walked up to me with a smile, and then held out his hand, which I slapped away. Now that he was here, I began to perk up.

We walked down to the joaners, which were surrounded by some bushes, and trees. Darkness really had a firm grip on the landscape, and there was a murky atmosphere around, that made me nervous, even though I was with Tommy.

I've stated that I'm afraid of the dark. But this was far more worse than the dark in the city. There was so much of it here, and there were tons of places for the monstrous things of the night to hide in.

As long as I was around lights, and people, I was okay, and whatever it was that was out there, lurking in the darkness, could just stay there, and leave me the hell alone. But take that away, and I was screwed.

When we reached the joaners, a guy came out of the big joaner, and I must have jumped a foot off the ground when the spring door slammed shut behind him.

Tommy laughed, and I felt kind of foolish.

When he went in to use the little joaner, I hesitated to follow him. Now that we were here, I didn't want to go inside even though I was with my friend. It was pitch black in there. So, instead I peed in the bushes by the side of the outhouse, and when Tommy came out, he grinned.

"I wasn't gonna ask you to hold it, if that's why ya didn't come in," he joked.

"Oh, fuck you," I retorted. "I just don't like the smell." That was true anyway.

"Smell? Whut smell? I didn't smell nuthen," he laughed.

"That's cuz it's rotted yer brain," I told him.

Now that we were done, I couldn't get away from the joanerholes soon enough. The lights of the big bunkhouse beckoned, and I knew once I got there, I'd be okay.

I didn't know what I was going to do later on if I had to piss. We weren't supposed to pee around the bunkhouses, but I sure wasn't going down to the joaners.

When we returned to the bunkhouse, I was feeling better, and my mood had gone away. I got caught up in the horseplay, and joking around, and when it came time to go to bed, I felt pretty good.

I thought I wouldn't have any problem falling asleep, but after awhile, I found myself wide awake while those around me seemed to be sleeping soundly. But that was okay, because that way no one would bother me.

Especially the night crawlers. I wouldn't have to worry about them here, and that was comforting.

The change from the city to the mountains was going to take some getting used to. For one thing, there were the different smells, such as the scent of wood combined with the odor of the evergreen boughs.

Another thing was the peace and quiet. I was accustomed to the noise of the bustling town, especially the traffic going by the Home at night.

Now, there was only the sound of the wind as it lightly passed by, sighing through the trees behind the bunkhouse, and then playfully singing along the shingles on the roof. I liked the calming effect it had on me.

Suddenly, off in the distance, I could hear a truck laboring up the highway. The deep, roaring sound of its engine was spreading itself along the valley floor towards the camp, and then echoing off the foothills, and ravines.

I could make out the roar, then a pause as the driver shifted gears, then a roar, then a pause, then roar, and so on. By the time he got to our vicinity, the sound of his engine had reached a loud crescendo. This kept up for what seemed like a long time. Gradually, the engine noise gently faded into the night until all that I could hear was the sound of the soft, whispering wind.

There was a comforting quality about it, and I finally drifted off to sleep. In the morning, I woke up to a wet bed, and after dressing, I took my sheets out to a line by the shower house, which I'd been told to use. I wanted to take a shower, but we couldn't use them like we had at the Home, so instead, I went to the wash room, and cleaned up as best I could.

The bright, morning sun cheered me, and I forgot all about my fear of the darkness from the night before. I took a breath of the cool, mountain air, and thought about how great it was to be alive.

Then I headed for the chow hall where I met up with Tommy. As we are breakfast, I looked at the slate board next to the doorway of the kitchen that was used to post daily activities. That day, only "free time" was written on it.

After eating, Tommy, Jeff, Benny, Billy, and I, took off to see what we could get into. We decided to go up the Old Sawmill Road. We walked along, and skipped over the ruts that had been gouged into the road from countless years of melting snow. The landscape was bright green, and it was a pretty day for a walk. I was enjoying the moment.

Tommy found a big rock off to the side of the road, and began to push on it. We stopped and watched him, and he looked up at us.

"Hey guys!" he said. "Help me with this."

We all went over, and then took turns pushing, and tugging, until it broke free, and began to tumble down the hillside next to the road. As the boulder picked up speed, it smashed right through young aspens, and pines, and the noise echoed throughout the hollow. It finally rumbled to a stop, and afterwards, the air was filled with the sharp odor of Sulphur of the boulder hitting other rocks.

There was something really satisfying about getting it to roll down the slope. The deep, crunching sounds that the boulder made, seemed to fill a primeval thirst within us that could only be quenched by destroying something.

We hunted for more of them, but they were scarce as a result of guys doing the same thing in years past. We did find one on the side of a hill, and Jeff was pulling on it when the rock broke free, and he just about followed it down.

We continued on our search, and then Tommy turned to me.

"Hey Tommy," he said. "Remember that fort I told ya about?"

"Yea."

"It's up here a ways," he said. "Wanna see it?"

"You bet," I told him.

"You mean the 'Fort?'" Benny said. "It's really cool."

"Whutta you guys talken about?" Jeff asked curiously.

"A really, neat for T," I told him. "Tommy sez we're gitten close. I'd like to see it."

"I think I oughta tell you if the big guys catch us messing around up there, they'll kick our asses," he said.

"Oh, to hell with them," I told him bravely. "Let's do it."

"Yea," Jeff said.

We continued for awhile, and then Tommy started looking around.

"Are we close?" I asked.

"Yea. There's a path around here somewhere," he said, then pointed. "Look! That's it!"

I did, and there off to the side of the road, was a faint trail that cut-through the wild grass, angled down to some trees. We followed Tommy single-file, and no one of us spoke as we made our way from the bright sunlight into the cool, blue-green-shadows of the forest. We walked downward along the side of the hill until we came to a small glade at the bottom of it.

There was a place where a small spring had gathered into a pool before moving on. A rugged, moss covered table of rock over looked the water, and it created a charming, mirrored setting.

The fort sat at the far end, and the ground started to slope upwards right behind it. The trees on all sides enclosed the glade into a tranquil, dark world of beauty. I was overcome by how charming, and peaceful it was there. It was like a large, green cathedral in the forest.

When we got closer, I could tell the fort was made out of aspen logs, and looked like a cabin you'd see in a western movie. After we walked up, and checked it out, I put my hand on one corner, and pushed, but there was no give. The guy who'd built it knew what he was doing. There were notches in the logs, and it all fit together snugly. It was really something. The fort stood over five feet high, and there was a doorway on one side. We all went in, and there was room enough for everyone.

"Whutta ya think?" Tommy asked me.

"This is sharp," I told him. "I wish we could build one like this." I knew we couldn't.

We stayed there a while, talked about how great the fort was, and the way it was built, and we made plans to try and build one like it. But, as I said, this was a little out of our league. Then Tommy said we should take off before any big guys showed up. As much as that annoyed me, I knew he was right.

When we left, I couldn't get over how great the fort was, and what a beautiful place this guy had chosen to build it on. I could understand why the big guys were hogging it all to themselves.

We took off up the trail with Tommy in the lead. I hung back because I was reluctant to leave. This place really soothed me, and I just loved it.

I was bringing up the rear behind Benny, when suddenly, I saw Tommy, then left start back with looks of panic on their faces.

"Big guys! Big guys!" Tommy whispered loudly. "Hide! Find a place to hide!"

Everyone got off the trail, and hid behind trees, and bushes. Tommy, and I wound up behind a gooseberry bush, and we laid on our stomachs. All of my brave talk about the big guys, and how I was tired of them telling us what to do, had flown south, and been replaced by fear.

We watched as they walked past us talking, and laughing. Danny Henderson, and Larry Collins were among them. There were six of them, and I hoped they wouldn't see us. Finally, they were out of sight.

We scooted out of there as quickly, and as quietly as we could, and it was only after we got to the road, and started walking back down, that we spoke.

"Man, that was a close call," Jeff said. "I'm glad we heard them talken. We would've walked right into 'em" I just about shit my pants."

"I thought that's whut I smelled." Tommy said. "you must've shit your pants, Tommy."

"Yea, well, I'm not so sure it wasn't you," I told him.

"Oh no. Close though," he said. "Ya wanna check my shorts? Put yer hand in there?"

"Fuck no," I told him. "Git away from me."

We got back to the camp, and went over to the gully where some guys were swinging on the rope. I thought about trying it, but decided to just watch. So did the others.

Then it was lunch time, and afterwards Tommy and I went down to the little joaner.

Once you walked in, and the door shut, there wasn't a lot of light, except for what was being let in from a couple of square holes near the roof, one on each side.

I was peeing when I noticed something that someone had written on the wall beside me and I leaned over to read it in the half-light.

"There was a young man from Nantucket,

Who lured a young mare with a bucket,

He got in past his balls,

Was kicked over some stalls,

So that now when he sees a horse, he sez, fuck'et."

I laughed, and Tommy asked me what was so funny.

"Oh, I was just read'en this joke," I said.

"You think that's funny, you should see some of the stuff in the big joaner," he told me.

"Really?" I said. "Let's go over there."

"Yea well, we gotta make sure there ain't any big guys around," he cautioned.

We left the joaner, and looked to see if we were alone. As far as we could tell, the only ones nearby, were some little guys playing cars by their bunkhouse.

We walked over, and opened the door, then stepped inside. We'd just come from the other joaner, but my nose wasn't prepared for that first blast of foul odor that came out of the two holes. After a few months, it didn't seem quite so bad, but I would never get used to that smell.

Tommy was holding the door open, and I forgot about it as I began to read the graffiti on the walls. I chuckled at them.

There were sayings like: "The Ruptured Chinaman by One Hung Low," and "Cream of the Russian Youth by Ivan Yakinoff," or "Anyone Can Piss on the Floor," Become a legend and Shit on the Ceiling."

Then there were some rude verses.

"The moon was out, and the sky was blue,

And down the street, the shitwagon flew.

It hit a bump, a scream was heard,

And a man was killed by a flying turd."

And there was a long, obscene one, but I won't repeat it here.

I envied anyone clever enough to think things up. It was beyond my imagination to make up verses that rhymed or were funny.

When I was done reading, we hurried out of there before one of the big guys saw us. Man, I wished I could be like them.

I admired guys such as Danny Henderson, who looked tough, and were insolent towards adults. I wanted to grow up, and be like Marlon Brando in the movie "the Wild One," where he, and his motorcycle gang go into a town, and intimidate the people there. They didn't take crap from anyone.

I yearned to be like that, but I was such a coward. I didn't think that would ever happen. Maybe when I got bigger, and older, that would change. I hoped so.

The next day, we took our first hike of the summer. It was a long ass trek to a place called Trounce Park. The little guys, like Jason, got to ride with Uncle Harry, and Aunt Alice in the bus. The rest of us hiked with the counselors. At first we were full of pep, and enthusiasm. But after the first few miles or so, the younger kids like me began to fall back, and we were strung out over a long stretch of the highway. Buck was up front with the older guys, while Greenie was helping to bring up the rear.

The road seemed to go on forever. Our only amusement came whenever a truck went by. We'd begin to pump our arms up, and down to try, and get them to blow their air horns. When they did, we'd wave, and cheer. If they didn't, we'd give them the finger, and sometimes they'd flip us off in return.

Most of us didn't have canteens, so we got pretty thirsty. When we complained, Greenie told us to put a pebble in our mouth, and suck on it, and said that might help. Another way was to grab some of the timothy grass that grew alongside the road, and then chew on the sweet stalks. Neither one helped much, and I just wanted a long, cold drink of water.

As we continued along, some of us began to get blisters. Uncle Harry showed up in the bus, and took the worst ones with him back to the park. The rest of us continued on. I started to develop a blister, but I wanted to finish the hike on my own.

Finally, we arrived at the park, and I felt pretty good, despite my burning heel. I hadn't needed anyone's help to get there.

We ate a lunch of sandwiches, and cold pop. My soda really tasted good, and helped to quench some of my thirst, but then I went over to a nearby stream, and drank to my heart's content. That ended that problem.

We played, and explored for quite a while, and then it was time to head out. The little guys, and the casualties from the hike drove back to the camp in bus. The rest of us started walking, and waited for Uncle Harry to drop them off, then return to pick us up. Hiking wasn't exactly my favorite thing to do. It was too much work.

Sunday's, just like at the Home, were for visits. The mornings began with church services in the chow hall conducted by Uncle Harry. The catholics amongst us went to the camp about a mile down the road where mass was held in a small chapel.

The service at the Camp consisted of Uncle Harry reading from the Bible, and Aunt Alice leading hymns on the piano.

After church was over, some of us would head out to the barbed wire fence at the edge of the bluff, and watch for our relatives.

That first Sunday, Tommy, Jeff, Benny, Billy, and I sat together looking at the weekend traffic, talking, and singing hymns. Jeff was the first one to spot a familiar car, and he, and Jason took off with their dad. Then it was Tommy's turn, and then Benny.

After they'd left, I grew impatient. I wished Dad would hurry up and get here. I hoped he hadn't changed his mind about coming up to see us. He had promised us that he would. I turned to Billy.

"I wonder if he's go'en to show up?" I asked.

"He'll be here," he said confidently.

I wasn't convinced and there was a long silence as we watched the passing cars. Then I spoke again.

"I don't think he's goin to come," I said, dejectedly.

"Sure he is," he told me, then pointed. "Look! There he is now!"

I did and sure enough, I saw dad's 47 Plymouth coming around the curve in the highway. We went over by the road, and waited for him to show up.

When his car pulled in, we ran up to it. I reached in, and hugged him, and I saw that Bert was with him. She must've had the day off.

"Hi Dad!" I told him excitedly. "I didn't think you were ever going to get here."

"We'd have been here sooner, but Bert had to go check out the bushes on the side of the road a couple of times," he chuckled.

"Oh you," she said, and slapped him on the arm.

I understood what he was talking about, but I had a hard time picturing a woman taking a leak or a dump like guys did.

"Aren't you boys going to say hi?" she told us.

"Hi Bert," I said, and Billy did too.

Roberta was a pretty brunette, who always had the pleasant smell of a musky cologne surrounding her. She was nice to Billy, and I, and I liked her, but when she was with Dad, I always felt left out of their conversations.

"Well guys," dad said. "Let's go check this place out."

We went for a short tour of the camp, then drove off to take in some of the other sights. After awhile, we found a spot for a picnic, and unpacked the lunch Bert had made. There was fried chicken, potato salad, and a dessert of cherry pie. It was delicious. We made a fire, and toasted marshmallows. Dad had brought a couple of gloves and a ball, and we played catch.

Those Sundays my father drove up to see us were special. I felt closer to him than I ever did in the city.

I really enjoyed myself, and then too soon it was time to return to the camp. I hated to go back, especially on a day like today, when I was feeling the closeness of family.

As we drove up the hill, I felt sad. It was back to the insults, and indifference I had to put up with there.

As we watched dad's car drive off, my heart felt heavy. I moped around for awhile until Tommy showed up.

"Yer gonna come with me to git some wood for the bonfire, aren't cha?" he asked.

"Oh. Yea." I'd forgotten about that, and I quit moping. This was going to be fun.

Billy came with us. We went up the Old Sawmill Road, and some guys passed us dragging small, dead trees down to the bonfire area which was in the open space between the joanerholes, bunkhouses, and chow hall.

We continued on until we found a good spot off the road. Someone else had already been there. There were aspens that had been in a competition with some bigger trees, and they had lost out. They were brittle, and most of them weren't very tall. There was a fair-sized one on the ground, and I hoisted it to my shoulder. It was kind of heavy.

In the meantime, Tommy, and Billy had selected some smaller ones.

"That poles too big," Tommy told me. "Why don't cha grab a couple like these?"

"I got it," I said.

"Okay," he replied with a smile.

We took off and right away I knew I'd made a mistake, because every time I went over a bump, the tree dug into my shoulder. I felt like dropping it, and getting a smaller one, but I wasn't about to admit Tommy was right.

As we walked along, it seemed like I was hitting every rut in the road. We followed the crisscross patterns of the other logs that had been brought down before us, and by the time we reached the camp, my shoulder was bruised and scratched. We laid our poles down with all the other ones, and then headed back for more.

This time I had no problem picking out a couple of smaller ones, and Tommy grinned at me.

"Now yer getten the right idea," he said, but I ignored him.

It was much easier coming down the second time. When we got back, Buck and a couple of big guys were arranging the poles for a foundation. They began with three medium sized ones, and then they tied them together at the top, with some rope. Then they raised them up, and spread out the bottom of each one, and the poles stood upright on their own. The bonfire pit was below them, and it had been filled with papers, cardboard boxes, and what not.

Then they began placing poles around the wooden triangle, and when they were done we had us a large, wooden teepee. I could hardly wait to see it burn.

Then we filed into the chow hall for our supper of sandwiches, and pop. After that, we goofed around until it grew dark. Then Tommy, Billy, and I, along with our friends, went and sat on the crude, wooden benches that had been built in a semi-circle around the bonfire area, and talked, and joked.

As the sky blackened, the stars appeared, and we pointed out constellations like the Little and Big Dippers. The neatest thing though, was when we saw a shooting star.

They would slash across the blackboard of the sky, leaving a thin, bright, white line, that in the blink of an eye, was just as quickly erased. Then we would crane our necks looking for another one.

Doing this made me a little uncomfortable, because it reminded me of an incident that happened when I was about four or five.

I was playing out in the yard of the tar-paper shack, and I remember laying down on the grass, and staring up at the sky. Mom and Grandma both, had told me there was a God up there who looked down on, and watched over us. I was trying to get a glimpse of Him, but all I could see was a vast, expanse of clear, blue skies.

Suddenly, I realized that if I could fly, and took off into space, I would just keep going into the pitch-black reaches of the cosmos forever, and ever, and never reach the end of it.

That thought so frightened me, I got up, and went into the house, and played with my toys to try, and forget about what I'd just experienced. I never did that again.

The Sunday night bonfires never began until Uncle Harry, and Aunt Alice showed up. When they finally did, they had some lawn chairs that were set up. Miss Sarah was with them, and I noticed that she'd brought her accordion case.

Everyone had to take turns working in the kitchen, and while some of the guys complained, I enjoyed it. Besides being able to eat leftovers. I just liked being around Miss Sarah. She was one of those gentle souls who accepted people just as they were. Miss Sarah always had a smile for us even when we were being ornery.

She wore her dark hair, in a bun, and had round, black-rimmed glasses that framed her sweet, pretty face.

When we had finished our chores in the kitchen, Miss Sarah would get out her accordion, and serenade us with tunes. She always tried to play any request we made. Miss Sarah was the nicest person I'd ever met.

Seeing her now, I know it wouldn't be long before we'd have a sing-along with her.

I liked to sing, although some of the guys didn't seem to care for my voice.

As soon as the Old Man, and the women were settled, Greenie helped one of the little guys light the fire. After they got it going, we watched eagerly as the flames began to lick the outside of the stack with reddish-yellow tongues of fire. The top of it started to smoke, and then throw out brightly lit sparks, that made it appear to be a huge Fourth of July firework.

Soon, it was engulfed in flames, and the cool, night air was filled with the sweet, smoky scent of the burning wood, and it tickled our nostrils. Those of us who'd ventured too close moved backwards as the heat intensified.

We watched spellbound as the flames continued to shoot upwards into the night sky. It was fascinating.

"I bet there's some people who think it's a forest fire," I said to Tommy.

He told me that they'd had such a big bonfire last year, the fire department from Redrock, which was about six miles from us, had showed up because somebody had thought that very thing.

Now, it wasn't very long before some people in a car showed up to see what was going on. Buck went over to talk to them, and they watched for awhile, then left.

After they had gone, I thought it was kind of neat to know that the fire could be seen for miles, and I was part of the event.

The pillar of wood was beginning to lean as the fire continued to eat away at it. Suddenly, it fell with a great crash, sending orange embers, and yellow sparks flying up into the air as we cheered.

Uncle Harry had brought some bags of marshmallows, and now everyone lined up to receive a couple to eat or roast.

Most of us had gotten sticks, and now Tommy, and I looked for a good place for us to melt ours. After mine was done, I blew on it, and started to take a bite, but it fell off, and landed on the ground.

"Shit!" I said disgustedly.

Tommy laughed, and I gave him a dirty look.

"It's still good," he said. "Pick it up, and eat it."

"I don't want it now," I told him.

"Hey," he said. "I'll eat it."

"Go ahead."

He bent down, and picked up the marshmallow, and brushed off some of the dirt, then stuck it in his mouth.

"Jeezus," I told him. "How can you stand to eat that thing?"

"Hey, a little dirt ain't gonna hurt," he said.

Tommy made a big production out of eating it, but I just ignored him, and instead just concentrated on roasting my other one. This time, I was able to get it to my mouth, without falling, and it tasted good.

Tommy in the meantime, was busy with his second one, and while he was doing that, I noticed he was spitting out pieces of dirt once in awhile. What a moron.

I heard Miss Sarah start up her accordion, so we walked over to where she was sitting with Uncle Harry and Aunt Alice. We sang songs for awhile, but it wasn't long before the Old Man, Aunt Alice, and Miss Sarah retired for the evening.

After they'd gone, we stood around in groups, staring at the fire, and feeding more wood to it while we talked.

Suddenly, one of the guys hollered, and pointed at the trees on the hillside behind the camp.

"Hey! Look over there!"

We looked in the direction he was pointing, but saw only darkness.

"Whut'd ya see?" someone asked.

"I saw a vampire's face!" he said.

"It's Elmer," Tommy told me.

I felt a thrill go through me as we looked for some sight of him. Suddenly, we saw a face glowing eerily back in the trees, and we shouted excitedly. Then it vanished.

"Hey, let's go find him," someone said.

"Yea," most of the guys agreed.

We set out with some older kids in the lead. There must have been sixteen or seventeen of us and, we were talking, and laughing in anticipation of what lay ahead of us. Buck noticed.

"You kids be careful out there in the dark!" he said.

"We will!" we chorused.

I'd forgotten all about my fear of the darkness because I was caught up in the excitement of the moment, and the search for the pretend monster. And there were a lot of guys around.

We reached the trees behind the camp, and we walked up the dark hillside. The moon was out, which lent an ominous, shadowy threat to every tree, and bush.

We put on a big show of bravery, but we were grouped together for protection. As we continued along, I thought about how crazy Elmer had to be to go out in the scary woods by himself. It was very spooky.

Judging from where we'd last seen his face, Elmer was drawing us further and further away from the camp. I was expecting an attack at any moment, and I was filled with excitement at the thought of the coming event.

Suddenly, we saw his face up ahead, and he ran at us growling horribly, and the flash of light was bobbing across his features, making him appear even more frightening than he already was.

We scattered trying to get away, and as for myself, I just about ran over the top of Billy who was behind me. I plunged through the forest running as fast as I could, trying to avoid the trees, and bushes.

Suddenly, I hit my foot on a rock or something, and I went asshole over appetite, and I landed on my butt. I sat there stunned for a moment, and I could hear guys running, and hollering nearby.

My toes were aching, and I rubbed them through my tennis shoe. Despite the pain, I was laughing at the situation. This was a blast.

Then, the realization came over me that I was all alone. The sounds of everyone running off had grown faint, and I began to get scared. I felt a great need to get away from there, and go back to the safety of the bonfire.

I scrambled to my feet, and headed back towards the camp. As I hurried along, I kept looking back over my shoulder to see if anything was behind me.

Pretty soon, I could see the fire through the branches of the trees, and the fear inside of me, began to subside, and I slowed my pace. I felt a sense of relief at getting away from the dreaded, dark woods.

Suddenly, Elmer jumped me from behind and growled. The shock of that almost made me piss my pants. We fell to the ground, and then he bit me on my lower back, and I screamed in pain. Then, as quickly as that, he was gone.

I laid there for a moment, and I could feel the numbing pain where he'd bitten me, and I tried to rub it. Then I got to my feet, and headed towards the bonfire again.

When I got there, Tommy and the other guys asked me what had happened. They heard my scream, and I lifted up my t-shirt to show them.

"That crazy son-of-a-bitch bit me," I told them.

"Wow!" Tommy said and whistled. "He really nailed ya."

"Yea, he did," I asked.

We talked about going out to look for him again, which I wasn't too keen on but then we saw Buck, and a couple of big guys carrying buckets of water towards the bonfire.

For all intents, and purposes, the evening's festivities were over.

We stood, and watched them throw the water on the reddish-orange embers which hissed, and bubbled in protest. Great clouds of steam, and smoke rose up in to the still, night air. Then Buck looked over at us.

"Why don't some of you kids help Pete, and Chuck carry some water?" he said "It's getting late."

Tommy, and I volunteered, and Buck got us some buckets, and we went to the water pump that was between Uncle Harry's place, and the big bunkhouse. We filled our buckets, then carried them to the bonfire, and after another couple of trips, the fire was out.

We put the buckets away, and then headed for the bunkhouse. After going to bed, I thought about what a fun day it had been, what with the picnic with dad, and Bert, the bonfire, and our search. I realy enjoyed being here as opposed to the Home.

The next day, Tommy, and I decided to build a fort. We picked us a spot a long way behind Crow's Nest in a thick stand of Aspens and Pines so that it would be difficult for someone to find, and then wreck it.

Our efforts to come up with one like the fort were futile, and the best we could do was to build a wooden teepee. It wasn't much to look at, and it leaked when it rained, but we liked it.

We did come up with a really neat idea for a place to hide our comic books, and model cars that we took up there.

Tommy, and I had seen a prison movie where the inmates had dug a hole for illegal contraband, and then covered it with a rock to keep it hidden, and nobody was the wiser.

We set about making a hole, and put a small, cardboard box in it, then we placed our toys, and comic books inside. After finding a flat rock, we put it on the hole, and spread some dirt, and pine needles over the top.

When we were done, you couldn't tell where our stash was. We were really proud of it. I really liked our little private domain, and I spent a lot of time there.

The week of my eleventh birthday, I got into a jam with the big guys. It all started because I was so gullible, and naïve, and I got involved with Dewey Ledbetter.

He was a big, slow talking, sixteen year old who looked mean, but seemed friendly enough. Dewey had a great sense of humor, and he liked to make up words to songs.

One day, after lunch, Tommy, and I were headed for our fort, when suddenly, I had the urge to go take a dump, and I told him I'd see him later, and took off for the joaners.

When I was done, I stepped out, and saw Dewey sitting in the doorway of the other joaner. He was holding the door open with his leg, and was smoking. I waved at him, and he waved back. I decided to go over, and engage him in conversation.

He had his head slightly lowered, as he watched me approach, and I was reminded of the way James Dean posed in the movie magazines.

Dewey had brown hair that he combed straight back, but the front of it fell down carelessly over his forehead. His eyes were slit like he was having trouble seeing, and were the same color as his hair.

Like I said, he looked mean, but unlike most of the big guys, he would talk to us, younger guys, and tell us jokes. I liked him. He seemed to like me.

"Hi," I told him.

"Hey," he said. "Whutcha up to kid?"

"Nuthen Dewey," I told him, eyeing his cigarette, and he offered it to me.

"Wanna drag?" he asked.

"Me?" I answered stupidly.

"No, that tree over there," he said sarcastically. "Of course you."

When he saw me hesitate, he grinned knowingly.

"Ain't you ever smoked, kid?" he asked.

"Yea." I'd never even tried.

"Bullshit," he said. "Here, I'll show ya."

Dewey put the cigarette to his lips, and took a drag, making the tip glow, then pulled it away. Then he opened his mouth, and inhaled. The smoke disappeared, then came out in a slow stream. After that, Dewey looked at me, smiled, and held the butt out in my direction.

"Now you try it," he said.

Nervously, I took the cigarette from him, and then raised it to my lips. The sharp acrid smell of the smoke, tickled my nose. I took a puff, and inhaled, and when the smoke got to my lungs, I began to choke and gag. It was horrible, and I coughed a couple of times then spit.

He took the cigarette from me, and laughed.

"Hey," he said. "Ya got the right idea. Just don't choke."

"How do ya keep from coughing?" I asked him.

"Practice, Ace, practice," he told me.

"Hey Dewey," I said, changing the subject. "Sing me a song."

"Well, I got a new one I've been working on," he replied. "Wanna hear it?"

"Yea!"

He started singing, and I started laughing.

What he'd done is take the melody of one of my favorite hymns, "The Old Rugged Cross," and made up his own lyrics.

"On a hill far away,"
Stood an Old Chevrolet,
Her insides all tattered and torn,
She ain't got no third gear,
But give me a year,
And I'll have her back running to form."

"So I'll marry the Old Widow Ross,
She's got bread but her looks make me frown,
But I'll cling to the Old Widow Ross,
Till me, and the Chevy leave town."

"That's a good one Dewey," I told him when he was done.

He got up, then started walking towards the big bunkhouse, and I followed. I began to tell him a joke I'd heard, but when I was about half-way through it, he stopped me.

"Hey kid," he said. "That joke's about as stale as yesterday's piss. And besides which, it's too long. Don'tcha know any new ones?"

"No," I answered, feeling foolish, and he noticed.

"Hey, I didn't mean to hurt yer feelings," he said. "You just need to learn how to tell a joke. Keep it short, and sweet. Like this: Whut does a rooster, and Marilyn Monroe have in common?" he asked me.

"I dunno," I said.

"A rooster crows, 'cockle-doodle-doo,' and Marilyn Monroe sez, 'any cock'll do," he joked.

I laughed, and then told him I wished the other guys would treat me like he did.

"Whut guys?" he asked.

We'd reach the steps of the big bunkhouse, and I stopped, and pointed inside where some big guys were sitting on a couple of bottom bunks talking.

"Those guys," I told him. "Like Danny Henderson. They pick on me."

"Hey, ya just gotta show them yer cool, and not a rat," he said. "Then they'll treatcha better."

I told him about the incident with Larry, and Danny, and my getting caught stealing the lock, but they still didn't treat me any differently.

"Hey," he said. "You've just been going about it all wrong."

"I can't think of anything else," I told him, stumped.

Dewey said he knew a way, and he told me to unbutton my shirt. Puzzled, I did as he said. He took the two ends, and tied them together over my stomach. Then he knelt down, and began rolling my pant's legs. I looked down at him curiously.

"Whut're you doen?" I asked him.

"We're gonna make ya up like a girl," he said.

"Whut? Whut for?" I questioned. I had a feeling something wasn't right.

"Look kid," he sighed. "You want my fucken help or not?"

"Sure," I answered. "I just don't know how this is gonna help me."

"When ya walk in there like this," he explained. "They'll laugh, and think whut a character you are. It can't miss."

I wasn't too sure about that, but if Dewey said it was cool, then I guess I was going to have to trust him.

"Well, okay if ya say so," I told him hesitantly.

He finished rolling my pant legs up past my knees, then went over, and got the small rug in front of the doorway, and placed it on my head. I had to hold it with one hand so it wouldn't fall off. Then Dewey stepped back to check me out.

"How do I look?" I asked him.

"Great," he said. "Now, one more thing."

He wet his fingers, and then reached out, and twisted one side of my shirt, then did the same thing with the other. I looked down, and saw that the material was sticking our like two big nipples.

"That's perfect," he said. "Now, go in the bunkhouse, and shake yer hips like a chick with a hot ass. Then say, 'Hi boys. Looken for a good time?' They'll love it. Now go get 'em Tiger."

I was nervous as I went up the stars, and then inside. As I approached them, I decided to give it my all, and began to shake my hips.

They didn't notice me at first, but when I got close, a couple of them did. I pranced up, and stopped, then repeated what Dewey had told me to tell them.

Danny Henderson was the closest to me, and he stood up, and slapped the rug off my head. Then threw me to the floor. Then he knelt down on my stomach with one knee, and grabbed my hair, and slapped me across the face, which stung.

"You little fucken faggot," he snarled. "Hey Larry! Git me a dirty sock, and we'll stuff it down this creeps throat!"

"No, no!" I cried. "Wait a minute! Let me explain!"

He kneed me in the stomach, which knocked the wind out of me, and I struggled, trying to catch my breath.

"Hey you guys," Danny said. "Hold this son-of-a-bitch still for me."

A couple of them jumped in, and then Larry came back with a sock that he handed to Danny. He tried to stick it in my mouth, but I kept turning my head, and frustrated, he grabbed my hair again, and yanked real hard, and I opened my mouth to yell, and he stuck the sock in.

The rancid taste of it was terrible, and I gagged, and felt like I was suffocating. Danny had his hand over my mouth; and snot came out of my nose, which got on him, and he cursed, then wiped it off on my shirt.

I managed to spit out the sock, and then I heard someone say something about the Gully, and they picked me up, and carried me outside. I was sobbing, and pleading with them to let me go, and they told me to shut up, and one of them put his hand over my mouth.

They took me out to the Gully, and placed me in the old, rusty wagon that us kids played in. Then they wheeled me over to the steepest part, and in horror, I realized what they were going to do.

"Let's see how fast you can go, ya fucken queer," Danny said.

I couldn't believe this was happening to me, and I looked around for some kind of help. Where was Uncle Harry, and the counselors when you needed them?

Then I saw Dewey standing off to one side, and I thought maybe he could tell them why I'd pulled this stunt, but he was grinning, and I knew I was doomed.

They gave me a push, and I screamed as I began to plummet down the slope, my heart in my throat. I was hanging on for dear life to the handle of the wagon as it shuddered, and bounced. Suddenly, I hit a large rock, and was thrown out head first, screaming in terror. I rolled head over heels down the ravine, and landed in some bushes near the bottom.

I could hear them laughing, as I lay there sobbing. When I sat up, one of them hollered, and asked me how I liked the ride. Then they left.

I looked myself over, and aside from some scratches, I appeared to be okay physically. My shirt had come undone, and after buttoning it back up, I rolled down my pant legs.

I stood up, and cleared the bushes, then noticed some guys who'd been swinging on the rope. They were staring at me curiously, but I ignored them, and went down and then up the other side of the Gully towards the Crow's Nest.

When I got there, I sat on the rocks, and felt sorry for myself. Why were people picking on me? I just wanted them to like me. I never bothered anyone. And yet I was always getting my ass kicked. It wasn't right. I thought Dewey had liked me. I know I'd really liked him.

Then a flash of anger came over me. That fucken Dewey! Why did I listen to that asshole anyway? He was a big guy, and didn't give a shit about me! That fucken bastard!

I looked down at the camp, and stood up, and raged.

"I hope ya all die, ya sons-of-bitches!" I yelled.

The skies had been clouded over all day, and now in the midst of my anger I began to hear loud, rumbling sounds from above, and brief, white flashes, were going off around me. Since I was standing out in the open, I felt naked, and exposed. If a bolt of lightening came down, it would probably hit me.

But then I thought "ahh, who cares?" Nobody would give a shit anyway.

A wave of self-pity came over me, and I thought about how they would find me dead, huddled pathetically on top of the rocks. The big guys would be standing around after they brought my body down, and they'd probably feel bad about being so mean to me.

As I pictured it in my mind's eye, my eyes began to swim with tears.

Suddenly, there was a bright light, and a great crack of thunder split the sky, and I jumped in fear. Any thoughts of staying there to die, quickly disappeared. My only concern was to get the hell out of there.

I took off towards me, and Tommy's fort, hoping it wouldn't really start raining before I could reach our safe haven. But all it did was spit, and spat, and by the time I got there, it had completely stopped.

Tommy was sitting inside our fort reading a comic book, and I joined him.

"Where you been?" he asked. "I thought you was just gonna take a shit."

I told him about what Dewey had talked me into, and then how the big guys had kicked my ass. I was hoping he'd be sympathetic, but he wasn't.

"Jeezus," he said. "That was a stupid stunt."

"Oh, fuck you," I said, and then I told him how they put me in the wagon and pushed me down the Gully.

"Oh bullys," he scoffed.

"Hey, no bullshit man," I said, and showed him my arms. "Where the fuck ya think I got these scratches?"

Now that it was over, I was beginning to feel kind of proud of my experience. I felt like a daredevil who's come back from the brink of disaster, and harm.

We began telling each other lies about our near brushes with death, and I forgot all about my troubles with the big guys.

Tommy had a way of picking up my spirits when I was down, and he made the good times even better. Even though I was a little older than him, he had more sense than I did. He was more cautious than me, and that usually kept him out of hot water.

I was always blundering along, never seeming to use my head for anything more than a hat rack, and a punching bag. I was so glad that he was my friend.

That Sunday, Billy, and I celebrated our birthdays together just as we always did. His birthdate was one week after mine on the thirtieth. Our aunt, and uncle, and cousins were there with dad, and Bert, and one of my other aunts, Mary, who was unmarried.

We got the usual presents of clothes, and toys. But the best ones came from Bert. She got both of us silver chains that slipped over our heads. They glittered in the sun, and I fell in love with mine right away, and I gave her a big hug.

"Oh, thank you Bert," I told her.

"You're welcome Thomas," she said, then asked about the scratches on me.

"Oh, I fell playing," I lied.

"Well, you need to be more careful," she said.

Dad was listening, and now he reached out, and grabbed me around the neck, and gave me a knuckle rub across the top of my head, which burned.

"He's a Janicek," he joked. "He can take it."

He let me go, and I struck him in the stomach. He laughed, and we engaged in a mock fight. That is, if you could call it fighting on my part, since I wasn't any good at it. But I always enjoyed rough-housing with him, even though he tended to over do it, because he was so strong.

My aunt, and uncle had three kids. There was Gloria, Shirley, and Dougie, the youngest one, who was Billy's age. We were talking, and Dougie told me how much he envied us living in the mountains all summer, and I said, "me too."

Then I told him about the plane crash on the mountain, and he really perked up.

"Man!" he said. "That's cool. When you find it, bring me back something."

"I will," I promised. I didn't mention the fact that I was too young to go yet.

We spent a nice day with our relatives, and when we got back to the camp, it was later than our usual arrival. The wooden teepee was up in the bonfire area, and our friends were in the chow hall eating. I showed off my chain to them, but Billy didn't. When asked, he just said he'd gotten one too.

I loved my present, and wore it all the time, except when I took a shower. That's because I didn't want to dull any of its brightness. I'd take it off when I was ready, and I'd lock the chain in my trunk so nobody would steal it.

One day when it was time for our showers, I got to talking to Tommy, and I forgot to put my chain away. When I got to the shower house, I realized my mistake, and looked around to make sure no one was watching, and I slipped my chain from around my neck, and put it in the pocket of my jeans. It was awful crowded in there, and I couldn't tell if anyone saw me or not. Then I shed my duds, and shoes, and put them on one of the wooden benches that lined each side of the room, and then laid my towel on top. After that, I lined up, and waited until a showerhead was available.

When I was through showering, I went back, and got my towel, and dried off. Then I reached for my jeans, and put them on, along with my t-shirt, and then tennis shoes. After that, I stuck my hand in my pocket, but to my shock, and dismay, my chain wasn't there. Frantically I searched everywhere, under the bench, in my other pocket, but no luck. It was gone.

I felt so frustrated I wanted to cry. How stupid could I have been? I should have known better.

Then I thought about which crud had stolen my chain. Of course, Joey came to mind, but he wasn't the only one there who liked to steal. There were others who would take anything of yours if it wasn't nailed down.

I remembered that Joey had been in there at the same time as me, but I didn't think he saw me hide my chain. He'd been showering when I did. But someone had.

When I told Tommy about what happened, he asked me what the hell I was thinking about by taking it in there. I was just asking for it, and that had happened.

"I dunno," I said miserably. "I forgot about it till I was in here. But I'll bet it was that fucken Joey who took it."

"Probly," he replied. "But there ain't much you can do about it. You gotta prove it."

"That son-of-a-bitch!" I cursed.

I knew I was screwed. It wouldn't do any good to tell Uncle Harry, or the counselors. Like Tommy said, I needed proof.

I really missed my chain, and after that, I kept an eye out to see if anyone was wearing it. I don't know what I'd do it I did, depending on who it was. But, I needed to find my chain. I'd worry about what to do after I was sure I knew who took it.

After about a week, we were headed down to Big Bend to swim. We walked to the river in our swim trunks, and on this day, I saw something that really made me angry.

Joey Mendoza was walking up ahead with a friend of his, and there around his neck was a chain that looked exactly like the one that had been stolen from me.

Tommy was beside me, and I nudged him.

"Whut?" he asked.

"That fucken Joeys got my chain!" I told him, and pointed.

"Yea, it sure looks like it," he admitted. "But how're ya gonna git it back? If ya try to take it from him, he's just gonna kick ya in the balls. And ya can't snitch on him."

"I know it!" I fumed. "That son-of-a-bitch! He doesn't even care it I see him wearing it!"

The rest of the way to the river, I continued to stew about the situation everytime I looked over at Joey wearing my chain. There was no doubt in my mind that it was mine.

I finally couldn't stand it, and I decided to confront him. I didn't know what I was going to say, but I just had to do something. I wasn't going to stand around, and not do anything.

I steeled myself, and then waded over to where he was sitting on a big rock, talking to his buddy, Donnie Abernathy, who was a new guy. Donnie was twelve, chunky, dark-haired, and acted like he was tough. He'd gotten awful chummy with Joey since his arrival.

There were looks of contempt on their faces as they watched me come up out of the water in front of them, and stop. I was dripping water, and was unsure about what I was going to say. I felt very nervous, and unsure of myself.

"Whutta you want?" Joey sneered, although I was certain he knew.

"Somebody stole my birthday chain," I started out uncertainly. "And … uh … it looks just like the one you got."

"Whut? Oh fuck you!" he snarled. "My mom gave me this. Git the fuck away from me!"

"Yea Pissass," Donnie added. "Git the fuck outta here before ya git'cher ass kicked."

I turned around miserably, and went back in the water.

The rest of the day, I mulled over the loss of my chain to Joey, and what to do about it. There had to be something, and that night, I laid awake, and thought of ways to get even with him. At first I couldn't think of anything, then suddenly, the seed of an idea came to me.

It was rumored that Joey had a stash of stolen items, both here, and at the Home.

I wondered if he, and Donnie had a fort somewhere, and if they did, maybe I could get my hands on his stuff, and then smash, and throw it off a cliff. Then I'd wreck their stinking fort. It wouldn't get my chain back, but at least I'd feel some measure of revenge.

The more I thought about my idea, the better I liked it. But there was only one thing wrong with my plan. How the hell was I going to find the hideout if they had one?

The only way to do that was to try, and follow them. But that could be painful if I got caught. But I needed to do something, and I decided to hell with it. I was going to give it ago.

With that thought in mind, I went to sleep.

The next day I told Tommy about my plan, and I asked him if he'd like to help me, but he wasn't real keen on the idea. I guess I couldn't really blame him.

"Whut if they catch us?" he said.

"We just have to be careful so they don't," I told him.

"I dunno about this," he said.

"Cum on Tommy, I pleaded. "I'd do it for you."

"I donno," he repeated.

"Please Tommy," I cajoled. "Be a buddy."

"Well, okay," he said reluctantly.

And so we began our mission. We tried to spy on them without being too conspicuous, and at first, we didn't have any luck, because we were being too cautious.

But finally, a couple of days later after lunch, they took off up the Old Sawmill Road, and we followed them at a safe distance. They never did look back, and Tommy, and I had decided that if they did see us, we would take off into the trees beside the road, and hopefully they wouldn't come after us.

As we walked along off to the side, I hoped we weren't on a wild goose chase, and that they were just goofing off, and going on a sight seeing trip up to the fort.

But sure enough, when they got to the place where the trail began that led down in to the beautiful glade, they left the road, and began to make their way towards the trees, and the fort.

"Shit!" I cursed under my breath, then looked over at Tommy. "We followed 'em for nuthen. They're just goen to the fort."

"Wait," he told me. "Let's just make sure."

Anxiously, Tommy, and I followed, trying to keep them in sight without getting too close. For a moment, we lost them, and then Tommy held out his arm like he was leading an armed patrol, and we stopped. Then he pointed.

"Look," he whispered, "there they are."

I did, and could see them on the small hill behind the fort. They were making their way up in to the thick growth of bushes, and trees on the other side of the glade. Then they gradually disappeared from view. It was going to be a lot more difficult tracking them now, than it had been on the road. But I was right. It looked like they might have a fort here about.

We hurried across the glade, and up the slope, then began to make our way through the woods. As we went along, I became even more nervous than I already was. I was beginning to doubt whether this was such a good idea after all. If we ran in to them before we could hide, we'd get our asses kicked. The ground had leveled out ahead of us for quite a ways, but the bushes, and trees remained thick. I was about to tell Tommy to forget it, when suddenly, he held out his arm like he had before, and again we stopped then he gestured ahead, off to the side of us.

I looked, and could just make out Donnie through the branches of a tree. He had his back to us, and was peeing in a bush. We quietly back tracked, and got behind a bush of our own.

When Donnie was finished, he walked over to a fort much like ours, and entered. I could hear Joey's voice, and I looked over at Tommy, and smiled.

"All right," I said in a low voice. "We did it! We've found their hideaway!"

"Shh," he whispered. "They might hear ya."

Tommy, and I crept slowly away, and when we got to the fort, we decided to go up on the hillside nearest the road, and wait for them to leave.

While we waited, we played "Initials." This was where you gave the other person the initials of a well known celebrity, and then have them try to guess who it was.

After we tired of that, we talked, and aided our time. I couldn't wait to wreck their fort, and maybe trash some of their stuff. Hopefully they'd never find out Tommy, and I were responsible.

I didn't think they were ever going to leave, but finally they appeared. We waited for a good minute or two after they left, before we got up, and made our way back into the forest towards their fort. It took us awhile to find it, and I realized how lucky we'd been in our search. When we finally got there, I looked inside, and saw a big cardboard box with some plastic wrapped around it, and I brought it out in the light.

I took off the cover, and then opened the flaps. Inside the box was filled with all kinds of things, and I whistled. There were toy cars, comic books, cap pistols, you name it.

"Wow!" I exclaimed. "That Joey's some fucken thief! Look at this shit!"

"I know it," Tommy said, then reached in, and pulled out a compass. "Hey! This is mine! That fucken jerk! I lost it last summer! I figured it was Joey who took it!"

"Jeez!" I replied. "I wonder why he didn't hide this stuff like we did?"

"I dunno," he said. "Joey probly figured nobody would go past the fort. And it's purty well hidden."

"Yea, yer probly right," I answered. "We were lucky to find this place." Then, I told him I wished I knew what was Joey's stuff, but it didn't really matter because I was going to tear up what I could, and then throw what was left off a mountainside. But first, we needed to wreck their fort. As I started in, Tommy stopped me.

"Wait a minute," he said. "I got an idea."

"Whut?"

He reached in the box, and pulled out a red, and black lanyard that had been neatly and tightly braided. I was envious, because I wasn't any good at braiding.

"Guess who's lanyard this is?" he asked. "I saw him braid one almost exactly like this. I'll bet'cha it's his."

"I dunno. Who's?" I said curiously.

"Ronny's," he told me. "And if it is his, whatta ya think he'd do if he knew Joey had it?"

"He'd break his fucken arm," I said gleefully.

"If not more," he told me. "Hey! Let's take it to him, and see whut he does."

"Yea."

I liked the idea, and I hoped the lanyard was Ronny's if it was, I knew he'd jump Joey, and maybe he could get my chain back. That would be sweet revenge.

We decided to leave things as they were, and I returned the box, and put the lanyard in my pocket. Then we headed back to the camp.

When we got there, we searched for Ronny, and found him down in the Gully swinging on the rope. We sat down, and watched. I noticed Joey, and Donnie were there too, waiting for a turn. I wondered what they would think if they knew what Tommy, and I had done, and were planning on doing. We were both nervous.

Eventually, Ronny, along with Timmy, came up the slope by us, and I felt like showing him the lanyard now, but with Joey, and Donnie being so close, I decided to wait.

Instead, I kept an eye on them to see where they were going. He, and Timmy were walking in the direction of the joaners, and Tommy, and I followed.

They went in the big joaner, and we waited. I was anxious about what we were going to do, and how this was going to play out. I hoped it wasn't going to backfire on us.

When they came out, we hesitated, then walked up to them. They gave us dirty looks.

"Whutta you want?" Ronny sneered.

"I... uh ... I got sumpthen I think is yers," I said, and took out the lanyard, then showed it to him. He reached out, and snatched it from my hand, and I flinched.

"Hey!" he snarled. "That's my fucken lanyard! Whut're you doen with it?"

"I got it from Joey's stash," I told him hurriedly. I didn't want him to hit me.

I explained how Joey stole my chain, and the plan I came up with to get even. And how Tommy, and I followed him, and Donnie to their fort, and found the box of stuff.

As I talked, Ronny looked like he was having a hard time believing Tommy, and I were smart enough to figure this out on our own. When I'd finished speaking, he told me I'd better not be lying.

"I'm not," I protested. "Cum'on I'll show ya."

We walked up to the Old Sawmill Road, and started off. On the way, Ronny talked about what he was going to do to Joey if what I was telling him was true. I assured him I was.

As we walked along, I was worried about what kind of revenge Joey would take out on us, for what we'd done. Maybe we should've just wrecked the fort, and the stash, and called it good. But it was too late for that now. Oh well, at least I'd be able to see Joey get his ass kicked and hopefully, I could get my chain back. That'd be great.

When we got to the fort, we went up the small hill, and then finally to Joey, and Donnie's fort, and we showed them the stash. They took the box, then wrecked the fort.

After we started back down to the camp, I asked Ronny if he'd get my chain for me, and he said he would. That made me feel a lot better about the situation. He told us about a plan he had. When we got back, Ronny told us not to say anything to anyone. Then he, and Tim left with the box.

Tommy, and I went up to our fort, and tried to calm each other's fears. We'd set the wheels in motion, and now it was out of our hands, and we were going to have to live with it. It was exciting, but nerve-wracking at the same time.

That night at supper, I was scared about what was going to happen when Buck left to go play cards with the Old Man, and Aunt Alice. He, and Greenie did that a couple of nights every week.

When he was gone, I was to give Joey, and Donnie a message so that they would go down to the joaners, where Ronny would confront them.

After supper, I anxiously waited for Buck to leave. When he finally did, I walked over to where Joey, and Donnie were playing cards on a bottom bunk. They didn't notice me at first.

"Hey Joey," I said meekly.

He looked up irritably.

"Whut the fuck do you want?"

"Ronny wants to know if he can bum a cigarette from ya," I told him. "He's outta smokes. He's down at the joaners."

Joey seemed to be flattered by the request even though, he, and Ronny were enemies. He didn't even notice how tense, and apprehensive I was.

"He does huh?" he looked over at Donnie. "Ya wanna take a smoke break?"

"Yea, might as well," Donnie said.

They stood up, and then walked out of the door of the bunkhouse. After they left, I looked over at Tommy, who was lying on his bunk reading a comic book, and I went up to him.

"Wanna come down to the joaners with me?" I asked him.

"Nah, go ahead," he said, and wouldn't even look at me.

I couldn't blame him for not wanting to get anymore involved than he already was. But I had a bigger stake in this than him, and plus I just wanted to see Ronny kick the shit out of Joey, and hopefully Donnie too.

I left, and walked on down to the joaners. When I got there, Ronny and Timmy, along with some of the big guys, including Larry, were grouped around Joey, and Donnie. When I walked up, I heard Larry talking to Joey. The box was on the ground between them.

"So yer say'en all this shits yers?" Gary said.

"Yea," Joey muttered, looking down at his feet.

"Bullshit!" Larry said. "Yer a fucken liar."

Joey mumbled something, and Larry reached out, and grabbed him by the hair.

"Speak up, asshole," Larry said. "We can't hear ya."

"I dunno," Joey answered miserably.

Then Ronny walked up, and shoved his lanyard in Joey's face.

"And I suppose ya don't know nuthen about this either, jack-off?" he snarled.

When Joey didn't say anything, Ronny threw the lanyard to the ground; then punched him in the mouth. Joey staggered back, and Ronny followed, raining blows on his head. Suddenly Joey stumbled over a root from a nearby tree, and fell. Ronny landed on top, and continued to whale on him, while his enemy covered up as best he could.

About that time, Larry walked over, and reached down, and grabbed Ronny's arm in mid swing.

"Wait Ronny," he said. "I need'ja to referee a fight."

Then looked over at me.

"Hey Tommy!" I heard'ja got a beef with Donnie!" he said. "And ya wanna fight him!"

"Whut?" I was taken off guard.

"Yea," he said, then winked at his brother. "And Ronny's gonna be the referee."

"Oh yea." Ronny grinned, and got up, and walked over to Joey's friend, who looked scared. Then he motioned to me, and hesitantly, I went over to them. Ronny had us face each other, and he got between Donnie, and me. I hadn't expected to become this involved, and I was all shook up.

"Okay you two," Ronny said. "I wanna clean fight. I don't want to see any rough stuff, like this."

With that, he brought his arm up, and elbowed Donnie in the mouth, whose head snapped back and he acted dazed for a moment. There was a little blood in one corner of his lip, and he dabbed at it with the back of his hand. He seemed angry at first, but when he saw the mean looks on some of the faces of the older guys watching, his expression returned to one of fear. Ronny went on with his little game.

"And I don't wanna see any low blows like this either," he said, and punched Donnie in the stomach, who doubled up in pain.

When he did, one of the big guys named Chuck Gilmore, stepped in, and grabbed his head, then brought his knee up in Donnie's face, who staggered back, and fell, and began to cry. Blood was flowing from his nose, and he begged them to stop.

In the meantime, Joey had gotten to his feet, and now Larry hit him, and knocked him back to the ground.

"Watch it Ronny!" Larry said. "This asshole was try'en to jump ya from behind."

Ronny came over, and knelt down on Joey, and started hitting him again. Joey had his hands over his face, and was pleading for mercy, and finally, Ronny stopped, then grabbed him by the hair. Joey's face was all bloody.

"You gonna quit stealen shit?" Ronny told him.

"Yea," Joey gasped. "I promise."

"In case yer wond'ren who found yer stash," Ronny informed him, "it was the two Tommy's. But if you or yer buddy so much as pop a pimple on them I'm gonna come look ya up. You got that?"

"Yea."

Ronny let go of his hair, and then took my chain off Joey, and held it out to me. I walked over to him.

"Here's yer chain Tommy," he said.

"Thanks," I told him gratefully, and slipped it on.

Now that it was over, I felt kind of sorry for Joey and Donnie. It was nice to have my chain back, but it didn't seem that important compared to what had happened to them. They looked pretty pathetic now that the tough guy veneer had been wiped from their faces.

We walked away from them, and went to the big bunkhouse. Larry had the box, and when we walked in, he put it on a bottom bunk, and then told everyone that if they were missing something, they needed to come check it out, or else just help yourself.

When everyone was done, I noticed most of the toy cars were left, and Tommy, and I took them. I thought we'd share some of them with our friends, although we kept the best ones for ourselves.

Then one of the big guys took the box, and what was left in it, down to the big joaner, and threw it down one of the shitholds.

I told Tommy all the gory details about what had happened, and when I got to the part where Ronny had told Joey that we were the ones who found his stash, he got concerned. But I assured him that Ronny had warned Joey about getting even with us, and hopefully, we wouldn't have to worry about him, and his friend in the future.

When Joey, and Donnie finally came in, I grew a little uneasy because when they looked in our direction, the hatred in their eyes was almost physical in its intensity.

Tommy, and I knew we were going to have to watch ourselves around them, but they never laid a finger on us, although they bad mouthed us every chance they got after that.

About a week later, Tommy, and I went up to our fort, and found someone had wrecked it. We figured it was Joey, and Donnie, but it was hard to tell. I was kind of disappointed, but at least they didn't find our stash. We didn't build another one.

The nicest thing to come out of the whole situation, was that Ronny quit harassing me, and even the big guys didn't seem to get on me as bad as they had before.

Whenever they did, and I wanted to be by myself, I would retreat to the chow hall, and read. People rarely came in there between meals, and I enjoyed the peace, and quiet.

One of the books I read was called "Skippy." It had been made into a movie back in the 1930's, and was about a young boy growing up in a small town, and all his adventures and it made me laugh. There was one sad part though, when his best friend was killed in an accident. Jackie Cooper played the part of Skippy in the movie.

I really enjoyed the book, and read it several times during my stays at the camp.

The days began to swiftly pass by. We hiked up to the end of the Old Sawmill Road, and I was rather disappointed. There wasn't much to see, except for some old, dilapidated buildings. I'd expected more than that.

Then the final hike of the summer came. I watched enviously as the older boys got on the bus which Greenie would use to drive them to the starting point. I wished I was going with them.

After they left, we waited until he returned so that we younger kids could start our little trek. The youngest kids, of course, rode with Uncle Harry, and Aunt Alice.

It was a nice day for a hike, but I didn't care. I kept looking up at the mountain, and wished I was with Buck, and the guys, so I could search for the plane.

After we reached the park, I asked Tommy if we'd be able to see them, and he laughed.

"Hell no," he said. "Not unless ya got a big telescope."

"Well anyway," I told him. "I hope they don't find the plane. I want to be there when that happens."

Ronny overheard us, and we got into a discussion about the Mountain, and the hidden Plane. He felt the same way I did about wanting to be there when it was found. And to be able to get his hands on a machine gun.

"Hey!" I told him. "That's whut Tommy, and I have talked about. He says he'd like to use one on Joey, and make him crap his pants."

Ronny laughed at that, and I was glad that I wasn't on his shit list anymore. I don't know why he didn't like me when I first got to the Home, but it wasn't important anymore, because he seemed to be on my side now, and that was all that counted. Joey had done me a favor by stealing my chain.

The sky had clouded up, and I thought we'd get rained on, but there wasn't even a drop. I wondered if Buck, and the guys would run into any.

We returned to the camp, and we'd been back quite a while, when they finally showed up. There was no talk about finding the Plane, and I was glad.

The minimum age for climbing the Mountain was twelve, so I could go next summer. But that seemed like a long ways off.

That weekend was the last one at the camp, and when we had the final bonfire, I felt kind of sad. It had been a pretty, good summer, especially now that I'd made friends with Ronny. And that was nice.

Now, it was time to face the drudgery of the Home, and school. Hopefully the year would pass quickly, and then it would be summer again, and I would finally get my chance to climb the Mountain. It couldn't get here soon enough.

Part
5

Everything looked kind of strange, and alien at first. We'd been gone not quite three months, but it seemed much longer. And the odd feeling didn't go away after we reached the Home. The yard was over grown with weeds, and the building itself smelled musty and unused, and it didn't even seem to help after everything was aired out.

That night, lying in bed with the sounds of the busy traffic outside the windows, I tossed, and turned in the sticky, summer heat. I really missed the peace, and solitude of the mountains, and the infrequent, lonely roar of the semi-trucks, as they labored up the valley at night.

I didn't fall asleep until late, and when I awoke, it was to a wet bed. I was in a lousy mood that morning, but at least I was spared any insults from Ronny, and his friend. It was nice not to have to worry about them anymore.

School began that next week, and Dad, along with Bert, took Billy, and I to buy some new clothes. My current clothing fit tight, and I'd grown taller, although I hadn't noticed it that much, Bert had though.

"You know," she said. "You're going to grow up, and be just like your daddy. Just look at how you've grown."

"Where?" I asked, looking down at my body.

"He'll never be old enough to whip his Old Man, though," Dad joked, and punched me on the arm.

It stung, and I laughed, and rubbed my arm. I sure hoped she was right.

My dad was six feet tall, had broad shoulders, and weighed two hundred and fifty pounds. He was as tough as nails and you didn't want to get him mad.

If I ever got as big as my father, nobody would dare mess with me. Or so, I thought. To me, my dad was tougher than anyone I'd ever known, and that included Buck. My father's fighting ability was legendary amongst his drinking buddies.

When I was six, I'd seen my dad knock a man down outside a bar who'd been about Buck's size. I remembered how dazed the guy looked as he wiped the blood from a cut over his eye. I hoped I could turn out to be like my daddy.

School began, and we settled back in to the routine of the Home. And dad's routine with us continued also on our Sunday visits.

The bar, eat, movie, bar, then back to the Home. With an occasional dinner at one of our Aunt's houses. I'm not complaining, that's just the way it was.

About a month, and a half after we'd been back, my mom's sister, Aunt Marge, called dad, and invited Billy, and I out to the farm where she, and Uncle George lived. She had five kids of her own to raise, and we didn't get to see them very often.

I was really excited about visiting them, and I could hardly wait.

The following weekend, we drove out to their place, which was outside the city limits.

When we pulled into the driveway, our Aunt rushed out to the car. As soon as we got out, she gave Billy, and I a hug, and commented on how much we'd both grown.

She had dark hair, and eyes like mom had, and you could tell that they'd been sisters. Aunt Marge had the same pretty features, and was lightly tanned from living on the farm. She seemed to glow with good health.

It was so good to see her. Dad's family were good to me, and Billy, but there was a special quality about her, that made us feel really cared for, and worth while. I'd always especially loved Aunt Marge for that.

"Oh, it's so good to see you boys," she said. "How've you two been?"

"Good," we said one after the other.

Dad was still sitting in the car, and Aunt Marge bent over slightly, and peered inside at him.

"How're you, Frank?" she asked politely.

"Oh, okay," he replied the same. "How've you and your family been?"

"We're fine," she answered. "You need to come out more often, and bring the boy's"

"Yea," he said. "I've just been awful busy."

I knew that was a lie, and I sensed some tension between them, but I didn't know why. My father never had much to do with mom's side of the family, and it wasn't until years later that I learned the reason why that was so.

There was a momentary pause in the conversation, so I jumped right in.

"Where is everyone?" I asked excitedly.

"Oh, the kids are down at the pond swimming, and your Uncle George is out working on his tractor," she explained. "Let's go in the house, and we'll visit for awhile. Why don't you come in and have a glass of tea or something, Frank?"

"No, thanks anyway," he replied. "You boys be good now. I'll be back to pick you up after supper."

"We will," we told him.

He drove off, and we started for the house. Aunt Marge looked over at us as we walked in the front door, and she smiled.

"There's someone in the kitchen who really wants to see you two," she said.

"Who's that, Aunt Marge?" I asked curiously, and Billy perked up also.

When we went through the entryway from the living room, we saw Grandma Brewer sitting at the kitchen table, and both Billy, and I ran at, and hugged her.

She was a tiny lady whose gray hair was done up in a bun in the back, and she always wore printed, shift dresses that looked like they were from the 1920s and 30s.

Granny had a sweet, round careworn face, and she wore wire-rimmed glasses. She looked harmless enough, but that was very deceiving. She was tough, and had a temper. Grandpa Brewer had died of a heart attack the year previously when we were still with the Bryans, and we hadn't seen granny since his funeral.

Now, here she was, and it really added to the pleasure of being there with family. Like Aunt Marge, granny made us feel special and cared for.

We sat around the table and drank lemonade and talked.

"So how do you boy's like living at the Home?" Aunt Marge asked.

"It's okay," I lied for me and Billy. "the Camp up in the mountains was fun."

"What kinds of things did you do up there?" Granny asked.

They really seemed interested so Billy, and I told them all about the Camp, and our activities, and of course about the Plane, and how anxious we were to find it. When we'd finished speaking, both smiled.

"Well, it sounds like you kids are happy there, and we're glad," Aunt Marge said.

When she told us that, I was tempted to tell her that the Home was a joke, and we hated it, but then she said something that really threw me for a loop.

"You know," she said. "I called your father after your mom, and then, Mr. Bryan died and told him that you kids were more than welcome to come stay with us. He said that he would talk to you boys about it, and get back to me. But he never did, so I'm glad that things worked out okay for you there."

"Whut?" I said shocked, and Billy looked surprised too. "He never said nuthen about that to us."

"Didn't he?" she responded, and I saw her, and granny exchange knowing looks.

I was going to tell her how thrilled Billy and I would've been to stay with them, when suddenly my cousin Judy walked in.

We were the same age, and she'd always been my favorite. She had dishwater, blonde hair, a lightly, freckled, cute face, and a sunny disposition. Judy was wearing a swimsuit, and her long, skinny body was tanned a golden brown.

"Hi Tommy, and Billy," she said enthusiastically. "I haven't seen you guys in a long time."

"Yea, I know," I told her. "We've missed coming out here."

"Did you guys bring your swim trunks?" she asked.

"Yep," Billy said, and showed her the top of his, as I did mine.

We'd been told to bring ours, and we'd put them on under our jeans.

Aunt Marge had us slip off our clothes in her bedroom, then we joined Judy, and went outside. It was a beautiful Indian Summer Day, and we raced each other to the pond, and joined the rest of our cousins.

I'd always enjoyed visiting them. They always seemed to be glad to see, and make us feel welcome. When you talked to them, they listened, and appeared to really be interested in what you had to say.

At fifteen, Hughie, was the oldest. Then came Georgeanne, who was thirteen, and I thought was beautiful; Judy, then Alvin, and finally Carroll, in order of age.

We joined them in swimming, and laughing, and generally just having a ball. Being kids.

The afternoon passed too swiftly, and then it was time for supper, and Aunt Marge's fried chicken, I loved the way she cooked it, and there was mashed potatoes, and gravy, and veggies to go along with the meal, and I was starved, and devoured my serving. Then I helped my self to more.

I'd have never tried that at the Bryan's. The Old Man would've slapped the shit out of me. He was always slapping me at dinner for something. I had dreaded suppertime there. One of the things I'd learned not to do was stare at his wife when she was serving us our portion. That was worth a hard slap. Staring down at my lap or slouching was another way to earn one. I had to constantly be on my toes when I sat down to eat with the Bryans. So it was really nice not to have to worry about that anymore, and Aunt Marge smiled.

"My goodness," she said. "Don't they feed you at the Home?"

"Not like this," I told her contentedly.

I wished we didn't have to go back to that place, and when dad showed up, I was reluctant to leave. Especially now that I knew we could've been living with them all this time.

There were tears in my eyes after both granny, and Aunt Marge gave us hugs and kisses, and we said goodbye.

We got in the car, and drove off. On the way back, I wanted to ask dad why he'd never said anything about Aunt Marge's offer to let us stay with them, but I didn't. I guess it had to do with me being a child differing with an adult, and I didn't want to put him on the spot.

After we got to the Home, I was really feeling low. That always happened on the days I experienced the warm feeling of leaving people who cared, and then have to walk into the cold, and impersonal dump. It was especially true at this time.

When we went into the tv room, Donnie Abernathy was there, and he wised off, and called me Pissass.

"Please don't start in on me," I said sadly. "I can't handle it."

To my surprise, he dropped his arrogant attitude, and asked me what was wrong.

"Oh, this joint just gets me down sometimes, that's all," I told him.

"Tell me about it," he said. "I git the same way."

"Do ya really?" I asked stupidly.

"Sure I do," he answered in a nasty tone. "Whut? You think yer the only one who doesn't like it here? Grow up!"

He turned from me, and I walked away. I felt kind of foolish about my talk with him.

Not long after that, I finally had my first encounter with the Nightcrawler's. Up to then, I hadn't been bothered by them personally.

One night, I awoke, and felt someone's hand on my crotch. I looked, and saw this queer kneeling down beside my bed, and he reeked of alcohol.

"Does that feel good?" he asked, when he realized I'd awakened.

"No," I said, wishing he would just go away. I felt no fear, I just wanted to be left alone.

He continued to fondle me, but after getting no response, he finally moved on to someone else, and I was grateful, and went back to sleep.

Another time, I woke up, and had to pee. I sat up, and then noticed a Nightcrawler bending over somebody's bed. I didn't want to draw any attention to myself, but I really had to go, and I went ahead, and got up, and went out the door to the bathroom down the hall.

After getting there, I stood in front of the urinal, and peed, and then I heard someone come in, and I braced myself. Suddenly, I felt a hand caress my bare buttocks, (I wasn't wearing any shorts because I was always pissing in them) and I jerked.

I turned my head, and saw this molester standing behind me. He had a grin on his face. He must've been in his forties, short, and balding. He looked harmless, and I wasn't scared of him at all, just annoyed.

"Stop it!" I snapped at him.

"Hey!" he said, dropping the smile. "You don't have to be shitty!"

"Well, leave me alone then!" I told him irritably.

I'd finished peeing now, and I brushed past him, and went back to the dorm. I can't remember if he followed me back in or not.

I don't know why we never told Uncle Harry, or the counselors about these nocturnal visitors but we didn't. The two incidents with those clowns were the only times I came in contact with them. They only showed up once in awhile and were kind of like a cold. You never knew when you'd get one.

The months began to pass by becoming increasingly colder, and I longed for summer to arrive – Summer, and the Plane.

It was during that winter when I had a strange, and terrifying experience. One that I never told anyone about. Not even Billy, and Tommy, because I figured they wouldn't believe me anyway.

In February of 1955, I contracted whooping cough, which is highly contagious, and I was sentenced to the sick room. It was situated between the upstairs stairwell, and the back dorm. When you first entered, there was a short hallway along one side, and it opened up into a small, square room. There was a bed, sink, radiator, and a door on the back wall behind which there was a small bathroom.

There were two, double-paned windows side by side, on the outside wall, and the bed had been shoved into the corner underneath them. From there, if I wanted, I could look down on the small courtyard, and the alley, incinerator, etc.

I hated being put in there, and quickly grew bored. Uncle Harry brought me some books to read, and that helped some, and I was provided with a pencil, and a paper so I could draw. But I'd hear or see my friends laughing, and talking below, and I longed to join them.

I can't remember how long I was in there, but it seemed like forever. Uncle Harry had to change my sheets whenever I wet the bed, and I'm sure he didn't like that chore.

But surprisingly, I didn't do that more than one to two times. I guess it had to do with my not being so active, and I'd wakeup in time. That was nice.

One night, I woke up, but I didn't have to pee. I just couldn't go back to sleep, and I laid on my back, and stared up at the ceiling, and wished I could get out of here. I was sick of being cooped up. Tired of the terrible, whooping cough that plagued me, and I wanted to hurry up, and get well, so I could leave. As bad as the Home was, it was better than this. I wanted to get back with my friends, so I could run, and play.

Suddenly, in the middle of my reverie, the bathroom door near the foot of my bed, began to slowly open, and the hair on the back of my neck stood up. In terror, I rolled over on my side towards the windows next to my bed, and pulled the covers over my head. My heart was pounding furiously.

I could hear the soft, swish of bare feet going across the linoleum floor, which sent a chill up my spine. Then I heard the paper's rustle that were on the tray stand next to my bed. It was the kind that swiveled over so that I could eat my meals, and read, and draw my pictures.

Upon hearing that, I stiffened in fright, and tightly shut my eyes. My back felt naked, and exposed, and I expected to be yanked from the bed, kicking, and screaming. But nothing happened. There was just an eerie silence.

Eventually, I relaxed, but I didn't move a muscle. I don't know how long I laid there like that, but after the sun finally came up, I uncovered my head, and looked at the bathroom door.

It was closed, and I got up, and walked over, and slowly opened it. But there wasn't anything out of the ordinary to see.

I tried to figure out what happened. There was a window above the toilet, and being as I was on the second floor, maybe someone had gotten hold of a ladder, and had climbed up it to scare me.

But, I knew that was highly unlikely. The window was locked to keep out the cold air, and anyone trying to get in. And that ruled out the wind as the cause.

The rest of the time I was in there, I dreaded the nights, but nothing else happened. To this day I still get a chill when I think about it. Whenever I tell someone now, they just smile politely. I guess I can't blame them, because I sure can't explain what happened.

All I know is, it did. I wasn't dreaming. Something had visited me that night. It just confirmed my suspicion, that indeed, there was something somewhere out there in the creepy darkness.

A couple of months after that, I got into a fight with Timmy Miller. The significant thing about this event, was that for once, it wasn't one-sided.

Up to that point, as I've stated before, I avoided fighting, because I was always getting my ass kicked. But this time, it turned out different for once.

It all began as a result of my trying to imitate the big guys. Dad had bought Billy, and I a couple of jean jackets. They were nice, and were like the ones the older boys wore. I noticed the way they wore their collars up, and I thought they looked cool. So I decided to copy them, and turned mine up.

On the first day I wore my jacket to school, Tommy, and I were talking out on the playground before classes. I was feeling rather proud of the way I must've looked to the other kids in my new coat.

Suddenly, I saw Timmy approaching us, and I wondered what he wanted, because he was staring straight at me, and I began to get nervous.

Ever since last summer, when Ronny finally accepted me, Timmy had quit being so nasty. But he hadn't gone out of his way to be real friendly either. I think he just tolerated me out of respect for Ronny.

He was the same age, and size as me, and had blond hair, and green eyes. Like Ronny, he carried himself in a confident manner, and he could fight. I'd seen him in action, and I knew he was tough. Like a lot of guys at the Home, he looked down on me.

Now, as he walked up with a look of disdain on his face, I really began to worry. What was he up to, and what had I done?

"Hey, Pissass," he said flatly. "I 'choose' you." He meant fight.

"Whut!" I exclaimed "Whut for? I aint done nuthen."

"Becauz when you wear yet collar up," he said. "It means you think yer bad."

"But I don't think I'm bad," I told him. "I just like to wear it this way."

"Well, if you wanna wear it that way," he said. "Then yer gonna have to fight."

I thought he was being unfair, and I wished he'd lay off. I hadn't done anything wrong.

"Hey Timmy, I'm not botheren you," I pleaded. "Leave me alone."

"Look, Pissass," he sneered. "Either you put it down or else I'm gonna deck yer funny ass."

Some kids had begun to gather around, including Ronny, and I could feel my face flush at the mention of that hated name. It was one thing to call me that at the Home, but to do it out in public was something else. I felt a surge of anger.

"Don't call me that!" I told him with clenched teeth.

"Whut? Pissass?" he laughed. "Whutta you gonna do about it Pissass?"

I saw red, and lunged at him, wrapping my arms around his, and we fell to the ground. We rolled around a couple of times, and Timmy tried to get out of my grasp so he could hit me, but I held on tight.

Then Mr. Pennington, one of the teachers, came over, and broke us up, then grabbed our arms.

"All right!" he said. "What's going on here! You boys know better than to be fighting on school grounds. Who started this?"

When we didn't answer, he asked some of the kids there what happened, and Gloria Brumgardner spoke up. She was one of those girls who always seemed to know the answers to everything.

"Tim called Tommy a name, and Tommy jumped him, and they started wrestling around," she told him.

When we still wouldn't say anything, he took us to the principal's office, and Mrs. Glock. She was in her forties, wore glasses, and was thin, and stern.

She talked to Timmy first, and I sat on a bench in the outer office, and waited. I felt pretty good about what I'd done, but I hoped I wasn't going to get in a lot of trouble over it. One thing was for sure though. I knew Timmy would retaliate once we got back to the Home. But for now I wasn't going to worry about it. Taking him down had felt great, and I wanted to revel in it for awhile.

When Timmy came out of her office, he gave me a mean look, and I avoided his eyes. He stopped in front of me, and the good feeling disappeared, and I started to get scared.

"Yer next Pissass," he sneered. "And when we git back, to the Home. It'll he my turn."

One of the secretaries, who was sitting behind her desk, typing, looked up.

"You just never mind that, buster," she said harshly. "You get to class."

Timmy left, and then I got up and when I walked into Mrs. Glock's office, she told me to take a seat. I sat down anxiously in front of her desk. I was hoping she wouldn't call Uncle Harry, and tell him about our fight, such as it was.

"Allright Thomas," she said. "Do you want to tell me what happened out there? Timmy didn't say very much." I simply told her that we got into an argument and he called me a name, and I'd wrestled with him, because it made me mad. I didn't want to say too much so that he would think I was a rat.

"What did he call you?" she asked.

I lowered my head, and felt my face turn red with shame.

"I'd rather not say," I mumbled.

"Come now, Tommy," she said. "Don't be embarrassed for my sake. I've heard a lot of swear words in my time. Some that you've probably never even heard."

"It's personal," I told her, head still bowed.

"Please look at me when you are speaking," she said sternly.

When I raised my head, and she saw the miserable look on my face, her demeanor softened.

"Is it that bad?" she asked gently.

"Yes."

"Well, you're going to have to learn to accept it," she said, "or I'm going to have to expel you from school. Do you understand that?"

I nodded my head, and then she told me I'd better get to class. After I left her office, I started to worry. When I got back to the Home I knew I'd be screwed.

At recess, Timmy looked me up of course. He began to threaten me, but our teacher, Mrs. Andersen, started walking in our direction, and he turned to go. He looked back over his shoulder.

"I'll see ya back at the Home, Pissass," he said with contempt. "And we'll go behind the garage, and go Ratso, Fatso, and Japso."

I was filled with dread, and I wished that I'd put my collar down. But he'd really pissed me off. Now I was caught between a rock, and a hard place.

Tommy walked up, and he was grinning.

"Way to go, Tommy," he said. "You showed ole Tim. You shoulda seen the look on his face when you tackled him, and got him on the ground."

I didn't share in his delight in taking Timmy down a peg or two, and I told him what he had said about going behind the garage when school let out.

"Hey! That's okay," he said. "You've already given him a Ratso. Now, you need to finish him off with a Fatso, and a Japso."

His words failed to ease my mind, and I was fearful. I didn't want the school day to end, and when the final bell rand. I wanted to stay there. Reluctantly, I walked outside, and met Tommy. Then we headed slowly down the sidewalk. He was trying to pump me up, but I was too down.

"Hey! You'll be all right," he said. "Just do like ya did this morning. Git him down, and punch the shit outta him."

"Aw, I just got lucky," I told him. "I was mad, and I caught him off guard. I can't fight with my fists."

Despite my negative comments, he continued to try and encourage me.

The more I thought about it, the more I began to think maybe he was right. I'd already proven that I could take him down. With that thought in mind, a little glimmer of hope appeared. A small one, but a glimmer nonetheless. Maybe I could wrestle him down and tire him out. But the closer we got to the Home, the less unsure I became. By the time we got to the garage, I was filled with apprehension, and I wished I was anywhere but there.

Timmy was waiting along with Ronny, and some others, including Joey. When I saw Ronny, I hoped he would intercede, but I knew that wasn't going to happen. I was on my own. I handed Tommy my jean jacket, and he told me to give Tim hell.

I faced my opponent, and he looked at me with contempt in his eyes. "Are ya ready Pissass?" he said scornfully. "I'm gonna kick yer fucken ass."

I summoned up all the courage I could, and ran at him like I'd done that morning, but he stepped aside, and stuck out his foot, and tripped me. I fell to the ground, and scraped my elbows, and Timmy laughed.

"Git up, and fight, Pissass," he sneered.

When I did, he stepped in, and punched me right in the nose and I yelped in pain, and turned away from him. My eyes were watering, and blood began to pour down over, and inside my mouth, and it left a salty taste behind.

Timmy, in the meantime, came up, and rocked me with a couple of more punches, and I backed into the wall of the garage. I covered my head with my hands, and tried to protect myself while he beat on me. I begged him to stop, and finally he did.

"You fucken pussy," he said contemptuously. "All yer good for is to piss the bed, and suck yer fucken thumb."

For some reason that really set me off, and I was filled with rage. Then I flew at him, and struck out with my fists.

I have no way of explaining, but suddenly, throwing a punch felt natural, and not awkward like it had before, and I hit him two or three times, and drove him backwards.

Timmy had been standing there with his arms to his sides, and after I punched him, I saw the surprised look on his face. But, I don't think he was anymore surprised than I was.

"This was all right!"

Then he came back at me punching furiously, but I backed off, and got away from the garage. As he continued after me, I suddenly stopped, and punched him right in the spud (nose).

He stopped dead in his tracks, and blood began to drip from his nostrils. I paused for a moment to admire my handiwork, and then I went after him.

I could hear Tommy cheering me on, and I really felt good about hitting someone who had tormented me for, so long. The shoe was on the other foot now.

After that, neither one of us landed any real telling blows, and we grew tired, and finally quit.

When it was over, Tommy came up to me, and he was grinning.

"See Tommy," he said. "I told ya you could take him."

"Yea," I answered, out of breath.

I sure didn't feel like I'd taken him, but at least I'd put up a fight, and bloodied him, and that filled me with pride. At last, I could use my dukes to protect myself.

Ronny was talking to his friend, and now he walked over to me, and stuck out his hand, and we shook.

"All right Tommy," he said. "You done good. I didn't know you could fight."

"Me either," I told him truthfully.

"Well, great fight anyway," he said, then went back to Timmy.

Tommy, and I walked over to the side door, and went into the washroom, so I could clean up. A moment later, Ronny, and Tim followed us in. Timmy wouldn't look at me, and I thought about going over to him, and offer to shake his hand, but I didn't. The hell with him.

After our fight, he never bothered me again.

I got into a lot of fights in the years that followed, but none of them ever made me feel quite as good as that one did.

The spring of 1955 passed quickly with only a couple of events worth noting.

Elmer Lehr fell out of a tree, and landed on top of the fence, and it required eighty stitches to patch him up from his armpit to his hip.

The other thing was that I graduated from the sixth grade. I would no longer attend elementary school, and I'd go to Lincoln Jr. High in the fall, which was kind of scary.

But for now, all of my thoughts were on going to the camp. I'd be old enough to climb the mountain this summer, and at last I could begin my quest for the elusive plane. I could hardly wait.

Part

6

I loved the mountains, and returning to the Camp was just as exciting as the year before. Everything looked the same, but there were some differences.

One of them concerned the fact that some guys had left, among them Vernon. I was going to miss his innocence, and sweet smile, but the best thing was watching cruds like Danny Henderson and Dewey Ledbetter leave. With them gone, the old rules of big guys and little guys seemed to get lax. But, the one guy who moved on and had the greatest impact on my life was Timmy Miller. His mom had re-married and he went to live with her and his stepdad. After he departed in May, Ronny began to run around with Tommy and I, and that really me feel good. Ever since last summer, he had been friendly towards me, but now I could truly call him a friend. He really seemed to like me, and I often wondered what he saw in me that others didn't. We were complete opposites like Billy and myself. Ronny was tough, brave, and self-assured, all qualities that I lacked. I wished that I could be more like him. The only person he was afraid of was Buck, but that wasn't surprising, everybody was.

The biggest difference though, was that Greenie left. The guy uncle Harry brought in to take his place was named Dusty Rhoades. I liked his name, but I really came to dislike him.

He was compact, muscular, with dark hair, and eyes that seemed to bore a hole right through you. Dusty had been a marine during the Korean War, but unlike Buck, he didn't seem to mind talking about it. I heard him tell some big guys about his combat experiences, and as much as I found that interesting, I steered clear of him. He was scary.

Settling in that first night back, I again heard that lonely sound of the trucker's engine as they toiled their way up through the valley. I went to sleep with the familiar smells of the bunkhouse filling my senses. It was good to be back.

The next day, I finally got to see where the big guys had their fort at the end of the Indian trail. Ronny, Tommy, and myself, along with Jeff, Benny, and Billy, ventured up to it.

When we got there, I noticed there were a couple of forts, but someone had wrecked them, evidentially just before we'd gone back to the home last year. I don't know what I'd expected but was rather disappointing.

The surrounding terrain, and the babbling brook, made for a pretty setting though, and I told Ronny it was too bad we couldn't build some forts around there.

"Why not? Let's do it," he said.

"Yea, but won't the big guys be pissed?" I asked.

I knew they put up with Ronny because of his brother but I didn't think they'd like to see the rest of us being there.

"Naa," he said. "It'll be okay. There's enough room around here for all of us."

His words took some of the worry away, and we set about looking for wood to build our forts. They, of course, were just teepees.

We were in the process of doing that, when Larry, and some big guys showed up. I really got nervous, but with Ronny there, they didn't bother us. They worked on building their own forts, which unlike ours, were like the fort. It was nice to go up there, and not have to worry about getting beat up or thrown in the creek.

On my twelfth birthday, our relatives came up to celebrate with Billy and I. After we'd eaten, and opened our presents, Dougie, and my brother, and I, talked about the Plane.

"I'm going to be old enough now, to go on the climb this summer," I told him, "and I'm going to find it."

"All right," he said. "I hope you can do it. Don't forget to bring me back something."

"I won't."

I hoped that wasn't an idle boast, but I was confident because I knew it had happened before, and that gave me hope.

It wasn't long after that, when I got into trouble with Dusty.

One day, I was by myself going down Indian Trail, and when I got close to the end of it, I decided to cross over the creek and go to Queen's Chair.

It was an outcropping of rock, and in the middle of it, was an indentation that you could sit in, and your feet would dangle down. And down below it was a pool of water, made by this stream. Queen's Chair was a pretty spot.

The brook wandered off the trail a little there, and when I came out of the trees, I saw Pete Sanders taking a whiz off the top of the rocks. Pete was a tall, gangly, sixteen year old, and he had ahold of himself with one hand and a beer bottle in the other. I could see the heads of Dusty, and another big guy named Dwight Hollister, and I assumed they were drinking beer too. Pete saw me, and hollered:

"Hey! Git the fuck outta here!"

Startled, I turned, and headed back to the trail. I didn't know what to think of what I'd just seen. I couldn't believe that a counselor would drink with the big guys. They weren't old enough, and if Uncle Harry found out, Dusty could get into trouble.

But, I knew one thing for certain, he would never hear about it from me. I sure wasn't going to say anything.

When I got to the Camp, I joined in a game of softball at the field next to the bonfire area, and tried to forget about what I'd just seen.

It wasn't long after that when I spied Pete and Dwight, and they walked up and saw me out in the field. They just stood there watching. I dreaded our turn at bat, and when we came in, they got me off to one side. I was scared.

Dwight Hollister was a husky, mean looking fifteen year old who'd come to the home last fall. He was a carbon copy of Danny Henderson and he grabbed my arm roughly.

"You better not say anything about whut ya saw," he said.

"No," I told him, shaking. "I won't say nuth'en Dwight, honest."

"You better not," he threatened. "I'll stick my fist down yer throat if ya do!"

"Don't worry," I said sincerely. "I won't."

When they left I breathed a sigh of relief. I saw Ronny and Tommy watching, and they came over and asked what was wrong. I just gave them a lame excuse, because I didn't want to say anything more than I had to.

But, unfortunately for me, someone else saw what was going on and he told Uncle Harry. We heard Dusty got a royal chewing out, and upon hearing that, I was filled with dread and fear.

I knew they'd blame me, and would retaliate, and I was scared. There was no way to prove it hadn't been me, and I felt trapped.

That night, Dwight cornered me, and I cowered.

"I thought I told ya not to say anything, you little prick," he snarled.

"It wasn't me," I cried. "I didn't say nuthen."

"I don't believe ya," he said.

Then he hauled off, and slugged me, and I fell down. It really hurt and I hoped he wasn't going to hit me again and through fear filled eyes, I proclaimed my innocence. He just gave me a disgusted look, and walked away. What was I going to do? I couldn't handle being hit by guys like Dwight all the time.

I thought I'd talk to Dusty, even though I was afraid of him, and see if he'd believe me. I hoped so any way.

I went to the little bunkhouse the next day, and found him sitting at the small desk next to his bunk. He glanced up when I walked in nervously, and gave me a hard look.

"What do you want?" he asked harshly.

"I just wanted ya to know that I wasn't the one who told on you," I gulped.

"You'll have to come up with something better than that," he said. "You're on my shit list from now on."

I felt tears come to my eyes. It was so unfair. I hadn't done anything, yet was being victimized anyway.

"But it wasn't me, Dusty," I whined. "I'm tell'en the truth."

"I don't want to hear it," he snapped. "I don't even want to look at you! Now get the hell out of here!"

I hurried out the door, and then walked up past Crow's Nest, and thought about running away, but where the hell would I go? I was stuck here.

I found a fallen log, and sat down. The view from there was beautiful, but I could care less. I didn't know how I was going to get out of this mess, and felt sorry for myself. My life was so fucked up, and there was nothing I could do. I was just going to have to endure. I wished that I was dead.

I sat there for a long time, and then finally returned to the camp. I looked up Ronny, and Tommy, and told them what was going on. They knew I wasn't a snitch, and they were sympathetic, which made me feel a little better.

Of course, Joey, and Donnie, among others, got on my case, but I did my best to ignore them. Like I said, I was just going to have to endure.

A couple of days later, Ronny and I went down to use the joaners. I had to pee, and he was taking a dump, so when I was done I went outside, and waited for him to finish.

About that time, I saw a couple of guys walking in my direction and one of them was Butch Jessup. He was a new guy, and was thirteen, tall and thin, with jet black hair. We younger kids had quickly found out he was also a bully.

When he got close to me, he laughed sarcastically.

"Hey! Look who's here," He said. "The fucken pissass snitch."

I felt a spark of anger within me, but I didn't say anything.

"Whut're ya doen?" He went on. "Looken to rat on someone?"

About that time, Ronny came out of the joaner, and he gave Butch a dirty look.

"Hey! Lay off," he said. "Tommy's not a snitch."

"Oh, fuck you," Butch retorted. "Mind yer own fucken business."

"Why? Whutta you gonna do about it if I don't … Albert?" He mocked.

Butch's face turned red with anger because that was his real name, and he made it sound stupid.

"You son of a bitch!" Butch yelled, and took a wild swing.

Ronny moved his head then hit Butch with three or four punches and the guys head jerked with each blow. He stood there stunned for a moment then made a hasty retreat.

I watched him and his buddy hurry away, then looked over at Ronny.

"Thanks for stick'en up for me," I told him.

"Ahh, that's okay," he said, "He's a jerk, but you shouldn't let him talk to you like that. You need to tell him to fuck off."

"Yea, but he's bigger than me," I replied. "He'd beat the shit outta me."

"Naa, I doubt it," he said. "He ain't tough, you can whip him."

I didn't share his belief. Even though my fight with Tim had shown me that I could take care of myself, I still lacked self confidence. Ronny tried to encourage me to be tougher, but I just couldn't build up any nerve unless I was pushed, but the one thing he could make me do was laugh. He was always telling me jokes, and singing stupid songs.

One of his jokes was about country western star Tex Ritter (John's dad). Tex was walking down the street one day with his jacket slung over his shoulder and it fell to the pavement, but he didn't notice.

One of his fans did though, and he yelled out:

"Hey! You dropped your coat Tex!"

I of course, knew what feminine napkins were for, because in a place like the home you quickly learned about things like that.

Ronny was also good at making up lyrics to songs like Dewey had. One of them was to "My Country Tis of Thee."

"My country's tired of me,
I come from Germany,
My name is Fritz,
My father was a spy,
Caught by the FBI,
That's why I'm rich,
Oh, me, oh, my"

Another one was from the movie, "Three Coins in the Fountain."

"Three bums in a tavern,
Each one looking up her dress,
Three bums sitting in a tavern
Whose wiener will she caress?
Make it mine, make it mine, make ... it ... mine!"

He always lifted my spirits like Tommy did, and made me forget my troubles for a time. That was really needed now what with my problem with Dusty, Danny, and Pete.

After awhile, most of the guys let up on me, and that was a relief. But I knew one person who wouldn't, and that was Dusty. I tried to stay away from him, but sometimes that was hard to do.

I screwed up one day, and Dusty took me in the Little Bunkhouse for my punishment, and I was shaking with fear. When he started whipping me with his lanyard, he seemed to take great pleasure in my screams of pain.

Afterwards, I cursed him. Out of sight of course. I wished I was older and grownup, I'd kick his ass. If only that was true.

Whenever I wanted to get away though, there was always the chowhall and the books. Even though I'd read most of them the year before, I still enjoyed immersing myself in the stories again.

Especially Skippy, I found it charming, and sad. It was my favorite. If only I could lead the innocent existence he did, and have such a loving family. I would give anything to live like that. But it didn't seem to happen in real life.

I began to try my hand at smoking that summer. Most of the big guys smoked and I thought they looked cool, and tough, and I wanted to be like that.

Ronny had been smoking for awhile, and he coached me. My first attempts were spent coughing and choking. I didn't do too well, but kept trying.

One day, we were up at our fort, and I managed to smoke one without any problems, and I felt kind of proud, but then I began to feel ill. I kept getting sicker and sicker until finally I told Ronny I was going back to the camp.

"Whuttsa matter?" He asked.

"I'm not feelen too good," I told him, "I think I'll go lay down for awhile."

He smiled knowingly, and I'm sure I looked a little green around the gills.

I took off, and started walking down the trail and after I'd gone a ways, I really got sick and went over, and threw up behind a tree. After that, I felt a little better, and I got a drink of cold water from the stream. By the time I reached the camp, I was ok.

I swore I'd never smoke again, but I did. I never threw up again, but I still used to feel nauseous whenever I indulged. But finally though even that feeling went away, and I could smoke with no ill effects.

Now, I wish I'd never started, because I have breathing problems, and I owe it all to my stupidity. It's a lousy, stinking, dangerous habit.

When we first got to the camp, I went with Ronny down to the gully and took my first swing on the rope. It was exhilarating and I really enjoyed the rush I got whirling out over the ravine. We got Tommy to join in and he liked it too.

After that, I spent part of every day in the gully swinging, and I wished I'd have done it sooner. I couldn't get enough.

Unfortunately, I was only able to enjoy it for about a month.

One day, a new kid named Jimmy Marcus was swinging on the rope when suddenly it snapped in two and he landed on some rocks and bushes. He was pretty banged up, but didn't break any bones.

Elmer wanted to climb up, and attach a new rope, but Uncle Harry said "No." He didn't want anyone else getting hurt.

I was sorry to see the swing go, and kicked myself for not trying it long before Jimmy crashed and burned, Oh well.

Ronny, Tommy, and I used to sit around our fort, smoking, joking, and talking. I got to know a lot more about Ronny, and how he, and his brother came to be in the home.

We were talking about the war one time, and I mentioned the fact that my dad had been in the Navy.

"Really?" Ronny said, "so was my dad."

"What ship was he on?" I asked.

"He wasn't on a ship." He said. "He was stationed on Ford Island."

"Where's Ford Island at?"

"It's next to where the battleships were when the Japs attacked Pearl Harbor."

"Oh wow!" I exclaimed. "Did he shoot down any planes? My dad helped shoot down seven Jap planes!" I boasted.

"I dunno," he answered. "He never did say. He got wounded though."

"Was he hurt bad?" I asked.

"Naw, he just got some shrapnel in his shoulder," he said.

I was impressed. I thought that was really great and wished I could've been there. Then I'd really have something to brag about.

Of course, I had no concept about the horrors of war. I was used to seeing the way guys died in the movies of that time. They weren't blown to bits, there was no blood and guts, and they were killed without screaming in agony.

"Where's yer dad now?" I asked curiously.

"Oh, he's inna vet's home," he told me.

"Whut happened? Was he wounded again?"

"Naw, he was working for the railroad," he said, "and he fell between two boxcars and both legs got cut off.

"Oh Jeezus Ronny," I told him. "I'm sorry to hear that. Where's yer mom at?"

"Oh, she died when I was six," he said sadly. "She had cancer."

"Man that's a drag," I replied. "My mom died when I was eight."

"Did she?" he said. "I'm sorry to hear that."

"Yea, thanks."

We got off the subject because it was too depressing.

The summer began to pass quickly by, and anticipation was beginning to build up inside me for the upcoming trip to the Mountain.

Ronny and I would sit around and talk about the plane, and ponder it's whereabouts. The mystery intrigued us.

"I bet I can find that sucker," I told him. "I just know I can."

"I dunno," Ronny countered, "From what I've heard that ain't gonna be easy. It's hid some place good."

"Maybe we can come across it this year," I told him.

"I hope so" he said. "That'd be cool. Especially if we find a gun."

With each passing day the thought of the hike began to dominate my thoughts. I could hardly wait to get started.

Then just before the climb, fate dealt me a cruel blow.

We were playing around this one day up at our fort, and I was running through the trees beside the trail when suddenly, I stepped in a hole that I didn't see. I screamed in pain, and fell to the ground, holding my ankle. Ronny and Tommy ran up to me.

"Whut happened?" Ronny asked.

"Aah, I stepped in that fucken hole!" I cried pointing "son-of-a-bitch!"

I got to my feet and tried to walk, but it hurt too bad. Tommy and Ronny had to help me get back to the camp. I had a hell of time getting across the dam at the Old Mill Pond. I was forced to crawl over it.

When Uncle Harry saw my swollen ankle, he checked it out, and then told me I had a bad sprain, and I was going to have to soak it in hot water and Epsom salts.

Dammit! What a time for this to happen. I knew there was no way I'd be healed up enough to make the climb. I'd waited a whole year and now this.

On the day of the trek, I was with the little guys on their hike. My ankle was better now, and I could walk on it, but not without a limp. It still tinged with pain whenever I stepped wrong.

As we walked along, I kept looking up at the mountain and cursed. If it wasn't for this stinking ankle, I could be there with Ronny and the guys, looking for the plane.

The sky had clouded up and now began to rumble and complain. I thought we'd get rained on, but all it did was sprinkle. I wondered how Ronny and the others were doing.

After reaching the park, my ankle was sore, but not too bad. Tommy and I sat and talked and of course our conversation had to do with the Mountain and the Plane.

"Ya suppose they'll find it?" I asked him. "Dammit, I hope not."

"Yea me too," he said "I wanna get my hands on one of the guns before someone else does."

After we returned to the camp, Tommy and I sat on the porch of the big bunk house and waited for the guys to show up.

Finally, we saw them start straggling in and we spotted Ronny and went to meet him.

"Didja see anything?" I asked, meaning the Plane of course.

"Naw," he answered, "Just a lot of trees and rocks."

"Man," I said "I wish I coulda been with ya. We'd have probly found it."

"I dunno," he replied "There's so many places to look. I wouldn't bet on that. You'll understand better once you git up there."

"Hey, I'll be with you next year," I told him confidently "and together, we'll find her. You watch and see. It'll be different."

"Yea, well, I hope yer right," he said, rather dubiously.

You could tell he didn't share in my confidence, but I just had this feeling deep within me, that we were going to find the wreckage. It was just a matter of getting lucky and finding the right spot. I knew it could happen.

My ankle was still sore when we moved back to the home. As we drove away, I looked up at the Mountain, and there was an air about her that made it appear she was mocking me.

"Laugh now," I told her "next year I'm coming up there, and then we'll see who's laughing."

Looking back, the summer had been a mixture of good, and bad. The best thing, of course, had been the bond formed between Ronny and me. We'd had some good times, along with Tommy.

Dusty had been bad news, and missing out on the climb had really been a drag, but at least it ended with a high note.

Just before we were ready to leave, Dusty quit working there.

Part
7

Going back to the Home was much like it had been the previous year. Everything still looked, and felt strange at first. But, there were a couple of changes.

There was anew counselor names Paul Wetzel. He was nice enough, and seemed very mild-mannered compared to Dusty. I could handle being around this guy.

Another change was that I was put in the Back Dorm. That meant I was no longer a little guy. I had moved up in class. I still had a long ways to go before I was considered a big guy, but it was a start.

I was going to miss being with Tommy, and Billy, and the guys, but at least I wouldn't have to put up with the Nightcrawlers anymore. They didn't seem to bother the other two dorms.

Being next door to the sick room was kind of creepy at first, but after I'd been in the dorm a couple of nights, I forgot about it. It was something I didn't want to dwell on anyway.

Joey, and Donnie were going to be in there with me, and that was a drag, but so was Ronny, and I knew I had nothing to fear from them as long as he was around. All I had to put up with were their snide remarks.

Ever since Ronny, and I had become good friends, people had pretty much left me alone, and that was comforting.

When I walked into the dorm with my stuff, and began storing it in the locker assigned me, Joey, and Donnie started bad mouthing, but I ignored them. When I was done, I walked over, and began to make up the bed that was closest to the small bathroom we had in there. Ours was the only dorm that had one. In the meantime, the insults continued.

"Man, it's really gonna stink in here, Joey," Donnie sneered. "They should make him sleep in the bathroom."

"Yea, but then he'd probly piss all over the floor." Joey made a face. "We need to find a couple of beds as far away as possible so we don't have to smell him."

My face flushed with both anger, and shame. Why couldn't they just leave me alone? I never bothered them.

About that time, Ronny walked in with his things, and Joey, and Donnie busied themselves with their lockers. He smiled as me, then looked over at them, and his face grew mean. Apparently, he'd overheard.

"If they don't like it Tommy," he said coldly, "they can always find a bed so they can sleep together. They're queer for each other anyway."

Jimmy Marcus was in there, and he snickered.

Donnie turned towards Ronny, and his face was flushed with anger.

"Why don'cha mind yer own fucken business Collins?" he snapped.

"Why don'cha fucken make me Abernathy?" Ronny retorted.

Even though he was the bigger of the two, Donnie had gotten a taste of what a good fighter Ronny was, so he backed down. He was just a big, loudmouthed bully. I had to smile.

That night, the air was hot, and muggy, and there was no breeze coming through the open windows. I had a hard time going to sleep.

Now that the summer was over, I would start attending classes at Lincoln Junior High which I heard was kind of a rough school. They were mean to seventh graders, and called us "scrubs." During the first week there, if the older kids caught you after classes, they would write scrub on your forehead with lipstick, and then make you bow down to them.

Donnie had been a seventh grader last year, and I remembered how he'd come back from school one day with that word written across his forehead. I had really thought that was funny, but now the show was on the other foot.

Another change when we got back, was being able to go to the Majestic Theatre on Friday nights with the big guys. It was exciting to be able to go out at night, and stay up as late as nine o'clock.

The movie being shown that first week back, was "Blackboard Jungle," with Glenn Ford, and was about a bunch of juvenile delinquents at a school and how a teacher (Ford) tries to reach out to them. Sidney Poitier, and Jamie Farr (Cpl. Klinger from MASH) were in it.

The opening credits featured "Rock Around the Clock," by Bill Haley, and The Comets. I'd heard it played the previous year, and now because of the movie, they'd re-released it. It was a popular song, and I tapped my foot along with the beat.

I liked listening to music, and the radio in our dorm was always tuned to a rock and roll station. Some of the songs were by the usual artists such as Frank Sinatra, and Doris Day, but they paled in comparison to Elvis, and Little Richard. Their music gave me goosebumps.

I would go to sleep at night with songs like "Only You," by the Platters, or "Fever," by Little "Willie" John, playing in the background. There was a soothing quality in the melodies that helped lull me to sleep.

I know how lame those songs seem to kids now, but back then, they were pretty cool. You had to be there.

On the first day of school, we got our lunch of sandwiches from the kitchen, and then started out for the walk to Lincoln.

We younger kids had to stay back a ways from the older boys because it wouldn't look good for them to be seen with us.

It was a beautiful morning, but I was really uptight, and didn't care. I wasn't looking forward to this.

Ronny, and I walked with a couple of other scrubs. One of them was Jimmy Marcus. He was a chubby, good-natured kid with blonde hair, and I liked him.

We found out a lot of the kids from the school gathered at a place called Tony's, which was a couple of blocks from Lincoln. Tony served hamburgers, fries, malts, and pop. The jukebox played all the current songs, and the kids from the school liked to hang out there.

We stood around in front of the place, and I felt very self-conscious in my stiff, new clothes, and notebook under one arm. I had the feeling that the word "scrub" was branded on my forehead for everyone to see.

Ronny lit a cigarette, and after a couple of puffs, offered it to me. I tried to be cool, and took a puff, then inhaled, but I choked on the smoke, and coughed. I heard a couple of girls laugh, and I turned red with embarrassment.

Then most of the kids started walking towards the school, and we joined in.

Lincoln Junior High was one of those typical, two-story, brick schoolhouses. We stood around in front of it, and waited for school to officially begin. I was nervous.

Finally, the doors opened up and we started filing in. When I entered, the old, familiar smells of a school hit me. It was a mixture of books, chalk, cleaning fluid, and floor wax.

We all congregated in the auditorium where the principal welcomed us, and then after a brief speech, we were divided up into sections.

I found out I was going to be in 7A, while Ronny would be in 7B. Knowing we wouldn't be in the same classes together upset me.

I felt a little better when I saw some kids from Grant Elementary in my class. The teachers, and students seemed nice enough, and the day passed too quickly. I was dreading the walk home, and the thought of getting caught by the eighth, and ninth grades.

Ronny, and I had talked about meeting each other at one of the exits after school, and then we'd sneak down alleys, and side streets to avoid that.

Ronny was tough, and no coward, and he'd told me nobody was going to scrub him. Not without a fight anyway. But he wasn't stupid either. He knew he'd probably get his ass kicked. So we did our best to prevent that from happening.

We managed to make it back to the Home, without any problems that first day, and I'd never been so glad to see the place before. But I knew we were going to have to go through the same thing all over again the next day, and it was nerve-wracking.

I don't know why I was so afraid of getting scrubbed, but I was. Maybe it had to do with someone older singling me out. I didn't know what to expect when they did.

We got through the next few days without running into anyone, but then finally, one afternoon, our luck ran out.

This particular day, we came out of an alley, and just as we started down the sidewalk, four older students turned the corner, and began walking in our direction. We didn't have time to duck without being seen, and we stopped dead in our tracks. Because not only were they older, they were "Warriors."

Lincoln was situated between eighth, and ninth streets, and there was a gang of hoodlums there who called themselves the "Ninth Street Warriors." They were mean looking and they wore tight fitting jeans pulled down low, and penny loafers with white socks. They tucked their shirts in, and wore their collars up, daring anyone to "choose" them.

Even though I thought they looked cool, they scared the hell out of me, and that was especially true now. I knew we were in trouble. I glanced over at Ronny, and he looked pretty shook up too.

There were two Warriors along with their girlfriends. When they got close, they smiled, but they weren't what you would call friendly smiles.

"Hey!" one of them said. "Looks like we got us some scrubs."

They walked up to us, and I lowered my head. They were so scary, I couldn't look at them.

"You guys in the seventh grade?" One of the Warriors asked.

I nodded my head. I don't know if Ronny did or not.

"Okay girls," he said. "They're all yers."

They came at us, and the one across from me raised my chin, and I saw a tube of lipstick in her hand. She began to write on my forehead, and it felt silky smooth on my skin.

In the meantime, out of the corner of my eye, I saw the other girl start to do the same thing to Ronny, but he jumped back, and the girl writing on me quit.

"No fucken way," Ronny said stubbornly.

One of the Warriors walked up, and tried to grab Ronny, but he danced away, and put up his hands in a vain attempt to defend himself.

The guy was at least a head taller than Ronny, and I was afraid. He looked like he could devour my friend.

"You wanna fight, you little fucken punk?" he snarled, advancing on Ronny. "I'll kick yer fucken ass!"

"Wait a minute Johnny," the other guy said. "The kid looks familiar."

He got a little closer to Ronny, who had stopped backing away, but still acted defiant.

"You related to Larry Collins?" he asked.

"He's my brother," Ronny stated warily.

Larry was in high school now, but he'd been a Warrior before that.

The guy who was threatening Ronny eased up a bit.

"Oh yea?" he said. "I'll tell you whut. Since yer Larry's brother, I'm gonna let ya slide this time. But don't push yer fucken luck."

Then they turned their attention back to the gal across from me, and she finished what she'd started, and then they made me get down, and bow to them, after which they all laughed.

"You'd better get off your knees, kid," Johnny said. "Or else people'll think you're given out blow jobs."

The girls giggled, and I felt my face flush with embarrassment. They walked away and I slowly got to my feet. Ronny laughed when he saw my forehead.

"Hey," he said. "You look good in lipstick."

"Oh, fuck you," I told him. "Yer just lucky Larry's yer brother."

We got back to the Home, and I went into the washroom, and tried to get the word off, but you could still make it out when I was done.

While I was there, Tommy came in, and made fun of me.

"Go ahead, and laugh now asshole," I told him. "Cuz yer turn is cum'en."

Tommy would be in the seventh grade next year, and when I told him that, he didn't have much to say.

That night at supper, I got some funny looks, but I just ignored them. Next year I would be in the eighth grade, and things would be different. Then it would be my turn to humiliate someone. I was looking forward to that.

1955 was the year that I started to really take an interest in girls. There was one in particular that I fell in love with right away.

Her name was Barbara Stoner, and she was in Ronny's classes, so I didn't get to see a lot of her. She had short, dark hair, and blue eyes, and beautiful features. She reminded me of Annette Funicello on the Mickey Mouse Club.

In the afternoons, she, and her friend Michelle used to walk by a classroom of mine on the way to one of theirs. I started to stand in the doorway, and look at her reflection in the glass window, so I could watch her as she passed by. I was too shy to look at her directly. I was very self-conscious around girls.

Gawd, she was beautiful. I always felt a warm glow whenever I saw her. I indulged in that voyeuristic behavior every day, and the thought that she might notice what I was doing never entered my mind. I always acted like I was combing my hair.

One day, I was watching as she, and her friend were approaching me, and just before they got to where I was standing, Barbara turned her head, and smiled at my reflection in the glass.

I felt a surge of sweet emotion that was almost electric in its intensity, and I was thrilled clear down to my toes.

Then they were gone.

I stood there almost in a state of shock. I couldn't believe what had just happened. She had actually smiled at me. Was it possible that she liked me? I found that hard to believe. According to a lot of guys at the Home, I was pretty ugly.

But for whatever reason, she had, and I tingled all over. I wondered what she would say if I told her how I felt, and that I was in love with her.

But I knew that would never happen because I was too bashful. I would just have to be content with watching her in the glass, and hope that she would smile at me again.

When class started, I daydreamed about what it would be like to go with her. And to kiss her. I'd never kissed a girl, but I'd always wanted to try it. But deep down, I knew that I was just kidding myself. What made me think she would let me do that? Or be her boyfriend? I wasn't worthy of her. And besides which I was a pissass.

So I continued to dream, and worship her from afar.

One day, Ronny stopped by, and we were talking, when Barbara, and Michelle showed up, walking towards us, and I told him about my crush on her, and how I wished I could go steady with her.

"Why don'cha ask her then?" he said.

"I dunno," I told him. "I just … I dunno. I don't think she'd say yes."

He gave me a shit-eating grin, and I grew uncomfortable because I knew how ornery he could get.

"Wanna meet her?" he asked.

"Naw, that's okay," I told him, starting to panic.

"Hey Barb!" he shouted anyway. "Cum'ere! I wan'cha to meet somebody!"

"You asshole!" I hissed at him, although I wasn't really pissed.

I scurried into the classroom, and sat down at my table, my heart pounding wildly. I saw Barbara, and Michelle walk up to Ronny, and he pointed at me. I felt like crawling under the table.

"That's my friend Tommy," he told her. "This is Barbara, Tommy."

"Hi," I said, and glanced at her, then lowered my eyes. Gawd, I couldn't even look at her.

"Hi," she replied, and I lifted my head again, and saw her smile, and I gulped. Then he introduced me to Michelle, and afterwards, they left.

"Whut'd ya do that for?" I said, when they were gone. "That wasn't funny."

"Hey," he said. "You told me how much ya liked her. I just thought I'd help ya to git to know her better."

"Yea, well," I said. "I don't need any help from you."

He laughed at me, and left, and after he was gone, I thought about how foolish I must've looked to Barbara. Dammit! Why was I so sensitive around girls? I wanted to be like Ronny. It didn't bother him at all. He always acted cool around them.

But Barbara wasn't the only one I came to know that fall. There was a girl in my classes name Melody Schmidt, and she was almost as beautiful as Barbara. Melody had long dark, brown hair, and eyes, and she seemed to be interested in me. I liked her, but she didn't effect me the way Barbara did.

Of course I didn't know how to act around her. She was always trying to engage me in conversation, but I was so shy, I didn't know what to say. I was just a big dunce. But it still felt good to have someone that good looking show me some attention.

One day in Art Class, she asked me to help her with a picture she was working on, and I went over to her table. I'd always liked to draw, and it was one of the few things I was good at. So I was flattered by her request.

When I bent over, besides Melody, I could smell that faint, sweet odor of her perfume, and the fresh, girl scent of her hair. I got aroused, and it was very pleasant. I'd never experienced anything like this, aside from the rush I got from Barbara anyway.

In the meantime, I was erasing, and straightening out a line that she had drawn. I was telling her how that would make the picture look better. As I continued along, my hand was inching closer, and closer to her budding breast.

I began to get nervous. But what got me is she didn't try to move. It was almost like she wanted me to touch them.

Just before I did, I quickly moved my hand to another part of the paper.

"Here," I said blushing. "You need to do the same thing here."

She smiled up at me knowingly,

"Thanks Tommy," she said sweetly. "It's so nice of you to help me."

"Sure," I told her, and when I was done, went back to my table.

After that, Melody continued to try, and get me to open up, but I was a lost cause. I just couldn't get up enough nerve to ask her if she'd go with me. I know she would've said yes, but I didn't do anything.

Eventually, she lost interest, and she started going with a kid in our class, and I felt sad. She'd given me plenty of chances to carry on a relationship with her, but I'd blown it. I didn't have anyone to blame but myself.

Not only was I a failure with girls, it was the same way with my schoolwork. The change in curriculum from elementary to junior high was hard for me to comprehend and my grades were suffering as a result. I felt lost, and confused. Instead of applying myself, and giving it my best shot, I just gave up, and daydreamed, and drew in my notebook. The only classes I didn't have any problems with were Art and Music.

One thing I tried to work on was my attitude. I still wanted to be like the big guys. But I wasn't very good at it. Especially when it came to fighting. Although I knew I could handle myself in a fight, I had no guts, and was pretty much a chickenshit. I just lacked what it took to be a tough guy.

One morning, as all of us were walking to school, we noticed a beer truck sitting in front of a liquor store with the doors wide open. The driver was inside, and just as the older guys started to walk by, one of them reached inside, and grabbed a cardboard case of beer then started running down the sidewalk with it. His name was Dennis Carr.

He got about a block away, when suddenly, the case slipped from his hands, and hit the sidewalk. Some of the bottles broke, and he bent down, and ripped the box open. Dennis grabbed as many unbroken ones as he could, as did the others. Then they took off hurriedly, and we younger kids followed.

It had really been exciting, and I watched as they walked along, laughing and guzzling beer. I wished I had the guts to do something like that.

I was hoping they'd offer us young guys a beer, but they didn't. I just had to be content with being a part of the thievery, such as it was. All I'd done is watch what they did.

It wasn't long after that, when I got involved in some thievery of my own, but it didn't turn out very well. It was a repeat of the lock incident.

Ronny, and Jimmy, and I were going to Lincoln one morning, when we spotted some full, milk bottles on the front stoop of a house, and Ronny told me to go grab one.

Without even thinking, I walked up, and grabbed a bottle, then went back to my friends. We started to walk away, when suddenly, the front door of the house opened and a slender, middle-aged woman in her nightgown came out, and yelled at us.

Ronny, and Jimmy took off running, but for some reason, I just stood there frozen in my tracks.

The lady ran up, and grabbed my arm, then snatched the milk bottle from my hand.

"Just what do you think you're doing Buster?" she said angrily.

"I'm sorry," I told her guiltily. "I didn't mean to take yer milk."

"Then why did you do it?" she asked. "What's wrong with you anyway?"

"I dunno," I said. "My friend told me to."

"Do you do everything your friend tells you?" she inquired.

"No," I lied. "Yer not gonna turn me in are ya? Please don't."

"Well, I should," she said. "But I'm going to let you go this time. But if I ever see you pull another stunt like this, I won't hesitate to call the cops on you."

"I won't," I promised her, and she let go of my arm. I was relieved.

I took off, and went to Tony's where I met up with Ronny, and Jimmy.

"Whut happened?" Ronny asked. "Why didn't'cha run?"

I told him what took place, and as I talked, he kept shaking his head. When I was finished, he gave me a disgusted look.

"Man, I dunno about you," he said. "When ya do sumpthen like that, don't stand around wait'en to git caught. Run like hell."

"I will," I told him sheepishly.

I just wasn't very good at this stealing shit. Twice I'd tried, and twice I'd been caught. I didn't make for a very good hoodlum.

It wasn't long after that when I got involved in a "pantsing" incident.

Four or five of he Warrior's girlfriends were going around the school grounds looking for some young kid, who they would get on the ground, and then jerk his pants down.

They got a hold of one guy, and when they did that, he was screaming bloody murder. A bunch of us kids were following them around, laughing, and enjoying the moment, including me, and Ronny. But it wasn't long before my laughs got stuck in my throat.

That was because they singled me out. When they came after me, I began to titter nervously. I turned, and tried to run, but one of them stuck out her foot and tripped me. I fell, and they were all over me, trying to undo my jeans. They scratched my hands, but I had a death grip on my pants, and they couldn't get any further.

I surprised myself that I was as strong as they were. They finally gave up in disgust, and went in search of someone else. After they left, I looked up, and saw Ronny standing there laughing at me. I flipped him the bird, then got to my feet, and brushed myself off.

The Warrior's girls in the meantime, had found somebody else, and it just happened to be Cecil Meredith, who was the biggest pansy at Lincoln. He was in my classes and I kind of felt sorry for him. Cecil was one of those kids who wore glasses, parted his hair in the middle, and wore his pants way up high. It seemed like someone was always picking on him.

He was really screaming, because when they got him down, they completely took off his pants. Everyone was laughing as he got up in his shorts, and ran in to the school, crying all the while.

Then the girls went over to the school's flagpole, and lowered the flag, attached Cecil's trousers, then raised them up in the breeze. After that, they melted in to the crowd that had gathered, who were cheering, and saluting.

About that time, Mr. Peetz, the principal, came out, and some of the kids took off. He was a WWII veteran, and he didn't take shit off anyone, especially the Warriors, who hated him. Ronny, and I were off at a safe distance.

"Allright!" he roared. "Who's responsible for this?"

Of course, no one said a word, and he scowled.

"You people ought to be ashamed of yourselves!" he said in disgust. "Now get the hell out of here! Move!"

The crowd dispersed, and then Mr. Peetz retrieved the pants, and took them into the school.

Afterwards, Cecil refused to tell him who was responsible. He knew if he did, the Warriors would make his life even more miserable than it already was.

About a week later, the girls tried to pants another guy, but this time, they were caught by one of the teachers, and they were expelled. That pretty much put an end to the pantsing. It had been entertaining while it lasted.

Speaking of entertainment, the school put on a variety show, and Ronny asked me if I'd like to try out for it with him.

"Sure!" I told him excitedly. "Whut're we gonna do? Sing?"

"Naw." He said, although he was a pretty, good singer, and I thought we could do a duet together. But he said one of his teachers had told him about a neat stunt that involved a long rope.

We would appear on stage pulling on it, while one of the teachers would hold on to the other end behind the curtain. When we reached the other side, we would hand over the rope to another teacher, and then go behind the back drops. Once across, we'd take a hold of the rope, and then come out from behind the curtain, making it appear we were having a tug of war with ourselves. It sounded like a lot of fun.

The night of the show, I was excited, and nervous. Ronny, and I were pumped up, and when it came time for our turn, we gave it our all. So much so, that we nearly pulled one of the adults onto the stage.

The audience seemed to like our skit, and I really enjoyed myself. It was a blast, and I found out that I enjoyed performing in front of people. I was glad that Ronny had asked me to join him.

It was always that way with him. He made me feel worthwhile, and that meant a lot. He helped boost my ego.

That winter, we had a big snowstorm, and the streets were icy, and treacherous. Of course, that didn't stop us from having fun, pelting each other with snowballs, and sliding on the ice.

The best thing, though, was when Ronny, and Jimmy, and I would run up to cars at stop signs, and bend over, then grab a hold of the bumpers. Usually, the drivers didn't notice and when they drove off, we'd ski along behind them. After going a short distance, we'd let go, and glide to a stop. Then we'd head for the next intersection, and wait for another car to come along.

The thought that one of the cars following along behind might hit us, never entered our minds. We were having too much fun. Besides which, we were young and immortal. Nothing bad could happen to us.

We were doing this one morning, when a couple of teachers from Lincoln saw us. They stopped their car, and one of them got out. It was Mrs. Jamison, my math teacher. She was really a nice person, and always tried to encourage me in class. Math was my poorest subject, and I just didn't get it. Despite her help, I still failed. But I enjoyed the attention.

Now, when she saw what we were doing, there was a look of concern on her face. She was in her twenties, and had pretty features. I used to daydream in class about what it would feel like to be married to her. It made me horny to think about having sex with her.

"It's okay Mrs. Jamison!" I reassured her. "We're bein' careful!"

The other teacher, who I didn't know, got out, and gave us a shitty look. She was ugly to begin with, and it didn't help improve her features any.

"You little hoodlums get out of the street right now, and get to school!" she shouted.

We did as she said, but as soon as they drove off, we continued to engage in our risky sport. I had really liked being called a hoodlum, even though I was far from being one. But I could dream.

I could hardly wait to grow up, so I could kick ass like Ronny, and the big guys did. And look tough doing it. That was my goal in life.

Christmas came, and went, then New Year's Eve, 1956.

One night that winter, Ronny, Jimmy, me, and another kid named Mark Rogers, were sitting around the Back Dorm, talking, and listening to the music on the radio.

Suddenly, a new song came on, and all of us stopped talking, and Ronny told me to go turn it up, since I was closest. I walked over, and raised the volume. My spine was tingling as the music flowed over me in sweet waves of pleasure, and I started humming along with the melody. The other guys joined me in the meantime, and they seemed to be as swept up in the music as I was.

It was the most powerful, and beautiful song I could ever remember hearing up to that time. All of the guys seemed to feel the same way I did.

When the music ended, the DJ said the title of it was "In the Still of the Night," and was sung by The Five Satins."

"Man!" I told Ronny. "That was really a cool song."

"Yea, it was," he said, and the other two agreed.

It was among the first of the many "Do Wop" songs that were to follow, but it's always remained one of my favorites from the fifties.

After that, Ronny, and I kept our ears peeled and it didn't take us long to memorize the lyrics. Then, we would go in the big bathroom, and do our best to imitate the Five Satins. Singing in there seemed to make us sound better, especially when other guys would join in, like Jimmy, or Tommy. We used to sing other songs but, "In the Still of the Night" was my favorite, and I never tired of singing, or hearing it, and I really enjoyed harmonizing with Ronny, and the guys.

Then suddenly, one Sunday in February, my world was turned upside down by a tragic event that shook me to my very core. An event that left a deep, lasting impression on me, and was something that took me a long time to get over.

Billy, and I had returned from one of our visits, and when we walked into the TV room, I saw Tommy, and Jimmy sitting together, and I went over to them. I sensed something wrong, because they had sad expressions on their faces, and an uneasy feeling came over me.

"Hey guys!" I said. "Whut's going on?"

"Ronny got hit by a car today," Jimmy said sadly.

"Whut?" I exclaimed. "How bad was he hurt?"

"He's dead, Tommy." Tommy told me flatly.

When he said that, it felt like someone had hit me in the pit of my stomach, and I just stood there speechless for a moment. I couldn't believe what I was hearing.

"You've got to be kid'den," I finally said, not wanting it to be true.

"I wish I was," he replied sorrowfully.

Ronny was dead? This had to be some kind of cruel joke.

About that time, Billy walked up to me with a somber look on his face. Evidently, someone had given him the bad news too.

"Did'ja hear about Ronny?" he said.

"Yea," I answered, feeling numb.

Before he could say anything else, I brushed past him, and headed for the side door. I went upstairs to the back dorm, and sat on my bed and thought about what I'd just heard. It didn't seem possible.

On Sunday mornings, we boys from the Home, went to a church nearby, and in Sunday School class that day, he'd been joking, and laughing like always.

Now he was dead. I'd never him alive again, or hear his stupid jokes, and sing his silly songs. Or sing in the bathroom together.

I looked at his bunk next to mine, and then at his locker. Ronny was gone forever, and with that thought in mind, my eyes welled up with tears.

About that time, I heard someone coming down the hall, and I quickly wiped my hand across my eyes. I didn't want anyone to catch me crying.

I saw Joey walk in, and he was the last person in the Home that I wanted to see at that moment. But surprisingly, he came up to me with a sorrowful look on his face.

"I'm sure you've heard about Ronny," he started out.

"Yea." I wasn't sure what he'd wind up saying. I didn't trust him.

"Hey, he, and I didn't git along, but when he got killed today," he said, "I really felt bad. It was really a drag. I wouldn't wish that on anyone."

I asked him how it happened, and he said they were coming back from the movies. On Sunday's, the guys who didn't get visits could go to the show if they wanted. There were three or four theatres in the area to choose from.

Larry, and Ronny had gone along with some of the other guys. When the movie was over, they were walking back by themselves, when they came to the intersection that was half a block from the Home. It was always busy with traffic.

When the light turned green, Larry, and Ronny started to take off looking from one direction to the other to make sure everyone had stopped.

They were halfway across, when suddenly, a drunk driver turned the corner, and hit Ronny from behind, narrowly missing Larry. Ronny was thrown through the air, and he struck his head on the curb, which killed him instantly.

Joey was a couple of blocks behind, and didn't see the accident. When he got to the scene, a crowd had gathered, and he was startled when he saw Ronny lying on the pavement with a pool of blood around his head. Larry was standing there in a state of shock, and some bystanders were trying to comfort him.

The drunken driver in the meantime, had stopped, but he didn't get out of his car. He continued to sit there, until the cops showed up, and arrested him.

"Hey ... uh," Joey said, when he was done. "I'm really sorry he's dead. I know you guys were good friends."

"Thanks," I told him.

After Joey left, I couldn't get over how nice he'd seemed. I remembered the Bryan family treating Billy and I like that after our mother died. It had pretty much been the same.

It seemed like the death of someone you loved, or knew, brought people closer for a time, and the Bryans hadn't been any different. But, their sympathy only lasted for a short while, and then it was back to business as usual, with the beatings, and the molesting. I hoped it wasn't going to be that way with Joey, and his comrade in arms, Donnie, but I wasn't going to hold my breath over that not happening.

That night, in the dorm, after lights out, we talked about Ronny, and how fragile, and mortal we really were. It could happen to any of us.

"It makes ya wonder who's gonna be next," I said sadly.

"With my luck, it'll probly be me," Jimmy announced, and a couple of others echoed his sentiment.

The radio was playing in the background, and suddenly, "In The Still of the Night," came on, and without even thinking, I jumped out of bed, and took it upon myself to turn it off.

Nobody in the dorm seemed to mind.

I laid back down, and gradually, the conversation faded out, and the guys went to sleep. I remained wide awake, thinking about Ronny, and his sudden passing. I was reminded of how I felt when mom died.

Right after her death, the Bryans took Billy, and I to the mortuary for a private viewing. (We didn't get to go to her funeral. I didn't know why).

The mortician was very nice, and he took us to the room where our mother's body was. Mom was lying on a bed in a white nightgown, and she looked just like she was asleep. The gown she was in, and the alabaster look of her skin was in sharp contrast with her long, dark hair. Even in death, she looked beautiful: like Sleeping Beauty. Only in this case, it wasn't like the fairy tale where the Prince arrives, and awakens her with a kiss, and they then marry, and live happily ever after.

This was harsh, and real she was dead. I didn't know what to do or say, and felt awkward, and numb, and Billy looked like he was feeling the same way. We didn't even cry.

We only stayed a short while, and when it was time to go, the undertaker asked us if we'd like to kiss her goodbye.

When I bent over, and kissed her on the mouth, her lips were oh, so very cold.

Billy did the same thing, and then we left. On the ride back to the Bryan's house, I shivered in the back seat of the car, but it didn't have anything to do with the cold, November air outside the windows.

These thoughts continued to run through my head until finally I was able to go to sleep. As usual, when I awoke, it was to a wet bed. I really felt lousy, and depressed. I got up, and stripped my sheets, then went to the bathroom to do my thing. All the while, I was thinking about Ronny, and the heavy emotional loss I was going through.

When I was done showering, and rinsing, I went back to the dorm and got dressed, then carried my sheets out to the clothesline. I hated this chore, and it really sucked on this particular day.

And the fact that the sheets would be stiff as boards when it was time to bring them in from the cold, winter air, didn't help my frame of mine any. When I brought them back to the dorm in the afternoons, I had a hell of a time makeing my bed until they thawed out.

On the walk to school that morning, I dreaded coming to the place where Ronny had died. When we got there, I was afraid to look.

After I saw the blood-stained pavement, the reality of his death came over me. This was far worse than being told.

"Gawd Ronny," I mumbled, and tears welled up in my eyes.

Several of us had gathered, and Jimmy, who was standing next to me, put his hand on my shoulder.

"It's okay Tommy," he said gently. "He's in Heaven now."

When he comforted me, I almost broke down. Then we walked away. The rest of the way to school, everyone was kind of subdued. There wasn't a lot of joking, and laughing like there usually was.

The news of Ronny's death had spread throughout Lincoln, and a lot of kids were talking about it. Mrs. Jamison was very kind when we talked, and her caring concern almost made me want to cry, but I didn't.

At lunchtime, I saw Barbara, and Michelle walking towards me, and despite my sadness, I felt the thrill go through me that I always got at the sight of her. They stopped in front of me, and I was curious as to what they would say. They both had sad expressions on their faces. I felt very self-conscious.

"Hi Tommy," Barbara said softly, and I felt a sweet, burst of emotion when I heard her say my name.

"Hi," I replied, and had a hard time focusing on her beautiful round face. "Hi Michelle," I said to her companion.

Michelle was almost a carbon-copy of Barbara, except that her short, dark, brown hair was curly, and her looks paled in comparison to her best friend. But she seemed like she was really nice. Quiet, but nice.

"Hello," she replied sympathetically, and the concern in both their voices made my eyes mist, and I fought it back. I didn't want to cry in front of them.

"I'm so sorry about Ronny," Barbara said. "I can't believe he's gone. He was such a nice guy. I know you must really feel bad. You two were such good friends."

"Yea, thanks," I mumbled, not sure what to say next. I felt like such a clumsy, sad fool.

"What happened anyway?" she asked.

I told them everything I knew, all the while, fumbling, and stumbling over my words. Gawd, I was such a clod.

After I'd finish speaking, they left, and I kicked myself for being so bashful around her, but I couldn't help myself. That's just the way it was.

That was the only time I ever really talked to her.

When they held Ronny's funeral, I finally got to see his dad, and I felt sorry for him, as he sat there in a wheelchair. Not only had he lost his wife, and his legs, now he had to deal with the loss of one of his sons.

There were a lot of people there, including some of his classmates, and I noticed Barbara was among them, but this was such a solemn event, I didn't get any pleasure out of seeing her like I normally did.

When the service was over, we filed slowly past Ronny's open casket, and when I was in front of it, I briefly stopped, and reached out, and touched him for the very, last time.

After Ronny's funeral, Larry left, and things at the Home pretty much returned to the way it had been before Ronny became my friend.

With him gone now, it was open season on me for guys like Joey and Donnie.

One day Joey was hassling me in the dining room, and made a cutting remark about the relationship between Ronny, and I, and I saw red and slugged him.

He staggered back a bit, and then before I could move, he stepped up, and kicked me right in the crotch. I screamed, and fell to my knees, clutching myself. I was crying out in loud sobs because it hurt so bad. In the meantime, Joey was standing over me, cussing.

About that time, Uncle Harry came in with an angry look on his face.

"What in the hell's going on in here?" he yelled.

"He hit me Uncle Harry," Joey said fearfully.

The Old Man sized up the situation, then walked over to Joey who was cowering then he grabbed Joey's arm, and started slapping him.

"Gawdamm you!" he snarled. "I thought I told you to knock off that shit."

"I'm sorry, I'm sorry!" Joey wailed.

Uncle Harry finally quit, and after warning both of us to stop the fighting, he left.

When he was gone, Joey looked down, and gave me a dirty look.

"You son-of-a-bitch!" he swore, then took off.

After he was gone, I slowly got to my feet, and took a couple of deep breaths. I was still hurting, and I made a mental note to stay completely away from him and learn to take his shit or else like Ronny had said, I was going to wind up wearing my balls around my neck.

My problems with Joey though, finally came to an end that spring after he was arrested for stealing a car in broad daylight.

He walked onto a car lot, and found one with the keys in the ignition.

He got in, started it, then put the car in gear, and started to drive off the lot, with a salesman in hot pursuit.

It quickly became a comedy of errors. When Joey pulled out on to the street, he just about clipped an oncoming car, hit the accelerator, and wound up going over the curb across from the lot, and crashed into a light pole. He wasn't hurt. The salesman grabbed Joey, and held him until the cops showed up.

They sent him to the State Reform School, and after he was gone, it seemed like Donnie became less of a problem.

During that time, I got into it with Butch Jessup. With Ronny gone, he was like a lot of the guys who were free to pick on me whenever they felt like it.

This certain day, we were out in the yard, and we got into an argument, and he grabbed me by my shirt front.

"Hey, Pissass," he sneered. "Don't give me any of yer shit. You ain't got yer boyfriend Collins here to fight yer battles for ya now."

I lost it, and hit him right in the mouth, then followed it up with a series of blows that drove him back. He stood there for a moment, looking stunned, and then walked quickly away. Tommy came up to me, and he was laughing.

"That was purty neato keeno," he chortled. "You really kicked his ass, Tommy."

"Yea."

It had really felt good to punch him out, and it was nice to know that if someone put their hands on me, or really pissed me off, I would fight them. I couldn't tolerate anyone touching me in anger anymore. But I still didn't have a lot of confidence in myself. I was still afraid of guys who acted tough, and I'd usually back down when they called my bluff. I still had a way to go yet before I could consider myself a badass.

And I didn't always win fist fights. A couple of times I went behind the garage, and went Ratso, Fatso, and Japso with different guys, but all I did was fight them to a draw which was frustrating.

School ended, and I flunked the 7th grade, but I could've cared less. It wasn't that important to me.

My dad though didn't feel that way, and he told me I'd better try harder if I expected to get a decent job when I got older. He only had a ninth grade education himself, but he'd grown up in the Depression.

But now people liked to hire those who had a high school diploma, and I told him I'd try to do better.

Right now though, I was really looking forward to our move up to the mountain this year. I was bound, and determined to find the plane once we climbed the mountain.

I just wished that Ronny could be there with me when that happened.

Part

8

The summer of 1956, was a time of transition for me. I went through an awkward stage of growth. My voice started changing, and I grew taller, and gawky. I turned thirteen, and to my way of thinking, was no longer a child.

That thought brought about an attitude change I started to think I was tough, and whenever someone got on my ass, depending on how big they were, I would stand up to them. Butch Jessup did that one time, but I called his bluff, and he backed down. That really did a lot for my ego, and I began to believe in myself. But I was finding out that as soon as I took care of one clown, someone else would come along, and make me feel insecure. But, one thing I noticed is that I wasn't as afraid of Uncle Harry or Paul now. I started mouthing off to them, and surprisingly, I was getting away with it a lot.

But the one person I wouldn't mess with was Buck. Unlike the other two, there was no way I'd ever say anything bad to him. I was smarter than that.

One day, Tommy, and I were walking towards the camp. I was telling him about a run-in that I'd had with Donnie, and I was using some foul language.

Suddenly, Buck stepped out from behind a tree, and faced us. I don't know what he was doing there-whether he was taking a leak or what, but he was staring straight at me, and I froze in my tracks.

"Come here, Janicek," he said.

Fearfully, I walked up to him, and suddenly, he slapped me. I staggered from the force of it, and my ears were ringing. It really hurt, and my cheek was tingling, and I rubbed it.

"You've got a filthy mouth," he said. "And you're starting to get a little too big for your britches. You'd better knock it off."

"I'm sorry Buck," I told him. Hoping he wouldn't hit me again.

"Sorry don't get it pal," he said. "You've got a big mouth, and one of these days it's going to get you in trouble. Now move on."

After we walked away, I wished that I was as big, and as tough as my dad. I'd kick the shit out of Buck. I'd give it my best shot anyway.

When I grew up, nobody was going to put their hands on me, I vowed.

When we had first got back to the camp, Tommy, and I along with Billy, Benny, and Jeff, had gone up Indian Trail to see if our forts were still standing, and they were. We goofed around, and as we did, thoughts of the times I'd spent here with Ronny the year before, ran through my mind.

I remembered one day when we were sitting in our fort, talking, and a red, and black carpenter ant was trying to climb up on my tennis shoe. I raised my foot, and smashed it, and Ronny reached out, and grabbed my arm.

"Hey!" he said. "Whut'ja do that for? Don'cha know you just killed one of yer relatives?"

"Whut?" I answered. "Whut the fuck're you talk'en about?"

"You killed yer PissAunt," he laughed. "Git it? A-U-N-T? She was yer PissAunt, Pissass."

"Oh, fuck you Collins," I told him. "Yer about as funny as a dead puppy." Gawd, I missed him.

Our stay at the forts didn't last very long, because some big guys showed up, and ran us off, and told us not to come back. We had to build our forts elsewhere.

That summer, there were several, new kids. There were two of them my age, and they quickly became friends with each other, and just as quickly, became enemies of mine.

Their names were Ray Gillespie, and Scott Staman. They each had long, brown hair, combed straight back, and then pulled down in front in a waterfall. Ray, and Scott looked like young hoods, and acted like they were pretty tough. Ray was the bigger of the two.

Uncle Harry didn't like anyone's hair getting too long, so he got out his clippers, and gave them a going over.

They were sitting on a couple of chairs outside the chow hall, while the Old Man worked on them. He was cutting Ray's hair first.

Tommy, and I were walking by on our way to play softball, and we gave them sympathetic smiles. We knew how Uncle Harry's clippers pinched, and pulled.

Ray, and Scott just gave us dirty looks in return.

I hoped they didn't think we were laughing at them, but I forgot about it when we got to the ballfield, and got involved in the game.

After we'd been there awhile, Ray, and Scott showed up with their new haircuts. I was out in the field while Tommy, who was playing on the other team, was waiting for his turn at bat.

I saw them walk up to him, and say something. Then Ray shoved him, and Scott stuck out his foot, and tripped him, and Tommy fell to the ground.

I was playing first base, and when that happened I got mad, and took off, and ran up to them. They just looked at me with disdain, while Tommy got slowly to his feet.

"Whut'ja do that for?" I asked. "he wasn't both'ren you."

"Whut's it to ya Pissass?" Ray sneered.

I felt the familiar flash of anger at being called by my dreadful nickname. That always seemed to be the first thing new guys learned about me. Especially the ones I didn't get along with.

"Don't call me that!" I said briskly.

"Why? Whut the fuck're you gonna do about it, Pissass?" he asked me scornfully.

Some of the guys had wandered over to watch, and Elmer Lehr, who was pitching, walked up.

"Hey!" he said. "If you guys wanna fight, take it someplace else! We're try'en to play a game here!"

Ray laughed sarcastically, and I felt like punching him, but didn't. He had a confident air about himself that unnerved me. It seemed like I was always running into guys like him.

"I don't think this chump wants to fight me too bad," he said. "Do ya Pissass?"

"I said don't call me that!" I told him, trying to be tough,

"Make me," he challenged, and I didn't say anything in return.

"Make up yer mind, Tommy," Elmer said. "Either fight or play ball. We ain't got all fucken day."

I hesitated, because I wasn't sure about what to do. I didn't want everyone to think I was chicken, but Ray looked pretty man, and plus, he was a little bigger than me.

"I gotta go play ball," I said weakly, and walked away.

Some of the guys booed, and I felt my face turn red with shame.

"From now on, Pissass!" Ray hollered. "Keep yer fucken nose outta my business or else I'll break it for ya!"

For the rest of the game, I felt like everyone was staring at me, and thinking what a chickenshit clown I was.

Afterwards, Tommy walked up to me, and we talked about what happened. I told him I was feeling like a real pansy-ass.

"Hey," he said. "You ain't no pansy. You should'a fought him. I bet you could beat that son-of-a-bitch. You can fight better than ya think."

"I dunno," I told him. "He looks like he could be pretty bad."

After that incident, I tried to stay away from them, because they were always insulting me. The easiest way to do that was to go up into the hills behind the camp, and wrap myself in solitude. I would find a place to sit down, and think, and admire the beauty around me. That's what I liked about being in the mountains. If you wanted to get away from people; you didn't have to go very far. There were a lot of places to hide.

I'd gaze up at the Mountain, and I never tired of looking at her. She looked majestic despite the roundness, and there was a mystical quality surrounding her. Of course a lot of that had to do with the plane.

I always wondered where it could be, and why it was so hard to find. There was a sense of mystery about it, and I knew it would really be cool to unlock the key to the puzzle. I could hardly wait to get started.

The other choice I had about getting away from my tormentors was going into the chow hall, and read. That was my refuge from reality. I could shut out the world for awhile, and get lost in the stories.

I thought about reading Skippy again, but then decided not to. The part about his friend's death, reminded me too much of Ronny's, and I knew I wouldn't enjoy it like I had before. That was sad. It was like losing an old friend.

The summer passed pretty uneventfully, and there were only a couple of memorable moments.

Two twelve year old kids raided a campsite, and made off with a bottle of whiskey, which they drank. By the time they got back to the camp, they were stinking, falling down drunk.

They were sick as dogs, and were throwing up. Buck tried to talk to them, but they weren't making much sense.

Watching them was kind of scary. I'd always wondered what it felt like to get drunk. My dad used to give me a sip of his beer every once in a while, and I liked the taste, but I'd never felt anything. Judging from what I'd seen, I didn't want to find out.

That summer wasn't my favorite. I still enjoyed the activities, and being scared by Elmer on Sunday nights. But there were the negative things, like being hassled by Ray, and Scott. They ruined my good moods.

That's why I missed Ronny so much. He had made me fell good about myself, and I know that together we would've taken care of those two bozos.

Now I felt alone. It was me against the world, and my enemies. They took all the fun out of being there.

But it wasn't all that bad. There was always good, old Tommy to share a laugh with, and Jimmy Marcus too. At least, I had a few good friends there.

It wasn't long before August arrived, and the day of the climb was fast approaching. Barring another injury, I'd be going. At last I could begin my search. I was convinced that this would be the year we found the plane.

The morning of the climb dawned sunny, and bright, with hardly a cloud in the sky. Tommy was old enough to go this year, and we gathered around the bus with the other guys, and waited to be driven to the starting point, which was about five or six miles up the highway. I could hardly wait to get this show on the road.

Finally Paul, and Buck showed up, and we filed onto the bus. Then we took off. Tommy, and I were really excited, and we could hardly sit still.

After waiting for so long. I was finally getting my chance to go up there and see for myself why the plane was so hard to find. And hopefully be able to figure out where it was. Like those other guys had done years ago.

When we reached the place where the hike began, we got off the bus, and then Paul drove away.

"Okay guys," Buck said. "Let's try to stay together. I don't need any of you getting lost. Allright, let's go."

We set off on the trail through the woods that had been made there by countless hikers over the years. Tommy, and I were full of piss, and vinegar, and at first, the trek went pretty smoothly, but after awhile, it began to grow monotnous, and became hard work as we went up one slope, and then down, and then up another. We were attacking the mountain from the side. To go straight up would've been killer.

The thought of what lay ahead though, spurred me on, and Tommy, and I engaged in conversation, and that helped to pass the time.

"Whut if we find the plane wreck on the way up?" I said. "Wouldn't that be cool?"

"Man, that'd really be neato keeno," he agreed.

We kept our eyes peeled for any signs of the wreckage, but all we could see were trees, and more trees. And some rocks here, and there.

As the morning wore on, the sky began to cloud up, and we ran into patches of light, and dark landscape. Even with the cloudy conditions, we were still sweating. The incline, though, wasn't that bad.

At long last, we approached the huge, rock-strewn slope that led up to the summit of the thirteen thousand foot mountain. Now we were going to hike straight up.

When we passed the timberline, we began to make our way over, and around rocks. Some of them were pretty big, and we did our best to avoid them. It was slow going, and was the most difficult part of the hike.

I was in the process of going around a huge rock, when suddenly, something struck me between the shoulder blades. It felt hard, cold, and wet, and I jumped.

"Hey!" I yelled, and turned around.

Jimmy Marcus was standing there grinning, and then he reached down, and grabbed a handful of snow from a patch that was hidden from the sun in the crevice of a rock. He made another snowball, and threw it at me. I ducked, then looked around for some. Tommy in the meantime had found a patch, and I was pelted a few times until I found my own. Then it turned into a real free for all.

The novelty of winter in August was rather exhilarating, and it was fun. I noticed some of the other guys were doing the same thing.

We tired of our game, and then it was back to the rocks again. There seemed to be no end to them, and I began to bitch, and moan. Jimmy just smiled.

"Man," I told him. "These boulders just seem to go on forever."

"Yea," he said. "It sure seems that way, don't it?"

He'd been up here the year before with Ronny, and I quit complaining, and just concentrated on the rocks ahead of me.

After what seemed like a long time, they began to peter out, and then suddenly, we were on solid ground. We had reached the top! I was surprised at how level, and flat it was up here. You'd never have known it looking at it from the camp.

I saw Buck, and the guys gathered around a stack of flat rocks, and curious, I walked up to them.

There was a rusty, metal-covered book, and each one of them was writing their names in it.

When it was my turn, it suddenly occurred to me that I had done something that a lot of people hadn't. Namely, climb the mountain, and I was proud I'd been so wrapped up in my thoughts about finding the plane, I had forgotten about that.

I saw Ronny's name there from the previous year's climb, and that made me sad. It would have been great to have him here with me now.

I turned the pages back to some old dates, and saw that Uncle Harry had made some hikes up here in the 1930's. it was hard to picture him as a young man.

Buck did a head count to make sure everyone was there, then got our lunch sacks from his knapsack, and handed them out. Then we sat down to eat.

I wanted to forego lunch so I could begin looking for the plane. But once I got my hands on the sack, I realized how hungry I was, and devoured my two sandwiches.

When Tommy was done with his, we got to our feet, and walked over to the edge of the mountain that looked down on the scenery below, and we took in our surroundings. Some of the other guys had already beaten us there.

Tommy, and I stood silently, and stared. I had looked back over my shoulder several times on the way up, but I hadn't gotten a very good view of the landscape below. But now that we had reached the summit, we could see everything in sight, and it was awe-inspiring.

The cloud cover had taken a lot of the color out of everything, but there was still enough left to give the scenery around us a pretty, muted quality.

We gazed down at the dark, green valley below. The river, and highway were intertwined, looking like a long, thin, gray ribbon strewn carelessly along the entire length of the valley floor. The other mountains in the distance were covered in a haze of deep, dark blue, that gradually lightened as they faded away over the horizon.

It was really beautiful, and Tommy commented on it.

"Man, this is purty cool," he said.

"Yea, it is," I agreed.

"Hey! I wonder if we can see the camp?" he said.

We tried to pinpoint it, but were unable to. It was too far away.

Then we turned our attention on the terrain closest to us, and I was beginning to understand what Ronny had meant when he said it was hard to tell where the plane was.

From our vantage point, beyond the rocks, there was nothing to be seen, but vast acres of trees. Trees, trees, and more trees. Locating it wasn't going to be as easy as I had first thought; Far from it.

But we knew the plane was somewhere nearby. It was just a matter of looking in the right place. But there were so many trees, it was hard to tell.

Jimmy had joined us, and I turned to him.

"I wonder where the plane could be," I said. "I didn't think it would be quite like this. You can't see shit from here."

"I know," he replied. "That's whut Ronny, and I thought. It's a lot harder to find than you think. I don't know how those other guys found it."

As I gazed around, the peaks caught my eye, and that was when I found out they were connected to the mountain. You'd never have known that when you were looking at them from the valley floor below. They weren't as high as their sister, but they were a lot closer than I'd have guessed.

I stared at them, but it was the same down there. Nothing but more rocks, and trees.

Suddenly, we saw Buck and the other guys running towards us, and I wondered what was wrong.

"We need to get out of here!" Buck hollered. "There's a storm coming and I don't want one of you getting hit by lightning!"

The wind had been buffeting us, and there'd been the smell of rain in the air, but I hadn't paid that much attention, because I was so involved in trying to figure out where the Plane was.

Now, I noticed that over their heads, there were some dark, storm clouds that had snuck up on us. They were beginning to grumble, and complain, and flashes of light had begun to glow, and flicker within them.

I became alarmed, as did the others, and we turned around, and started to descend the mountain as fast as we could. It was a lot easier going down than up, and the threat of the storm helped to hurry us along. We made good time.

The rocks were starting to get spotted with raindrops, and faster, and faster they fell. I knew if this kept up, we were going to get soaked.

It wasn't very long before we approached the timberline, and as we did, I began to feel a little safer. At least I wouldn't be out in the open, feeling naked, and vulnerable.

But, suddenly, just before we got into the trees, there was a bright, white flash, and a tremendously loud crack of lightning that struck the mountain, and it knocked me off my feet. I think I fell more from the sound than anything else. I laid there for a moment trying to gather my senses. Then I sat up. I was stunned, and looked around, but I couldn't see anyone. I felt all alone, and scared as I sat there getting wetter by the moment.

Then I saw a solitary, gnarled pine tree, close to me. There was a long, blackened gash from a previous lightning strike, that ran all the way down it's trunk to the very roots. The tree's dying, reddish-brown branches, seemed to be waving sadly at me, as the wind, and the rain, lashed at it.

Suddenly, I realized that I'd better get my ass in gear or else I was going to be left way behind. I got to my feet, and just about that time, I heard Tommy hollering, and I took off in the direction of his voice, until I met up with him.

I noticed that Buck was going about, making sure everyone was okay.

When everyone was accounted for, we set out down the wet slope. It was still raining, but the thunder had let up.

"Man the son-of-a-bitch was loud," I told Tommy.

"Yea, it was," he agreed. "I must've jumped ten feet in the air, and just about shit my pants."

"I fell on my ass," I said. "I dunno if I shit or not."

"It's hard to tell," he smarted off. "You always smell like shit."

"Look who's talken wise ass," I retorted.

We joked around like that all the way down. We didn't really comprehend how close to death we'd come. We were young, dumb, and hung, as I like to say now.

The rain finally let up, but we were still soaked from the storm, and it didn't help matters any when we brushed up against the moisture laden branches of bushes, and trees. It didn't take as long to go down.

When we got back to the camp, Billy, Benny, and Jeff were waiting for us. As we changed to dry clothes in the big bunkhouse, they were full of questions, and of course the main one concerned the Plane, and if we'd seen the hide nor hair of it.

"Nope," I told them. "All we saw were a lot of trees. It's hard to tell where it is. We really didn't have much time to do anything because of the storm."

Tommy, and I bragged about our brush with death from the lightning strike, but I was really disappointed in regards to finding the wreckage. It was going to be a lot harder than I'd thought.

That next week, we headed back to the Home. It had been a rather shitty, forgettable summer. Especially the hike up to the Mountain.

I was discouraged, but there was always next year. Maybe the weather would cooperate then, and give us a nice, sunny day so that we could do some serious searching. I sure hoped so.

Part

9

Upon our return, I knew I was in for a rough time, because Scott and Ray were going to be in the back dorm with me, and I was going to have to endure their insults. With them in there, it wasn't going to be as easy to stay away as it had been in the mountains.

But there was one place I could go where I was pretty sure I wouldn't have to worry about them, and that was in the library. I doubted whether they could even read.

The best thing that happened though, was that my buddy Tommy moved in. He was going to start classes at Lincoln, and he was kind of sweating it like I had the year before, but I assured him it wasn't that big a deal.

When my dad took Billy and I to buy new school clothes. Bert again commented on how each of us had grown during the summer. I was now five foot seven and weighed one hundred and thirty pounds.

"If you keep on growing, we're going to have to start buying your clothes in the men's section," she said. "You're getting to be as big as your father."

"He's going to have to grow a lot bigger than he is now if he expects to be as tough as his old man," dad joked, then made a face, "When're you going to get your haircut? You look like a gawdammed zoot'suiter."

I didn't understand what that word meant, but knowing dad he wasn't paying me a compliment.

"Whut's wrong with my hair?" I asked uncomfortably. It had grown long during the summer, and I liked it.

"You look like that geek Elvis," he told me.

I'd taken to combing my hair straight back, then pulling it down in front like a lot of the guys did. I thought it looked cool.

When we got back to the home, my dad told Uncle Harry to be sure and have my haircut. That week, a bunch of us got crewcuts from the old man. I hated mine.

That first day of school, we all gathered at Tony's, talking and joking. I lit up a smoke, and proudly took a puff, then blew it out. Then I handed it to Tommy who just recently started.

He took the cigarette, inhaled, then started gagging, and chocking just like I'd done the year before. I was embarrassed for him, as well as for me.

When we got to the school, and filed into the auditorium, I felt self-conscious sitting with the scrubs. I saw Barbara Stoner with Michelle and my heart fluttered with that wonderful feeling that came over me whenever I was around her.

Tommy and I were in the same classes so that worked out cool. That first day after school, we snuck down side streets like Ronny and I had done the year before to keep from getting scrubbed.

Even though I was a second year student, I'd still have to go through the initiation if they found out I had flunked.

I just hoped we wouldn't run into any Warriors like Ronny and I had.

We didn't have any problems at first, but after a couple of days we finally got caught by two eighth graders. I knew them from the year before.

One of them was Eddie Felcher. He was big for his age, and was a bully, but he had a baby faced look about him, and I didn't find him very threatening at all, so I wasn't really worried. I'd never had any problems with him in the past, but I'd seen him throw his weight around with some other kids last year.

Now, upon seeing Tommy and I, he laughed sarcastically as he, and his friend walked up to us. He knew I was still a seventh grader.

"Hey," Eddie said grinning, "look what we got here. A couple of scrubs. You take that one, and I'll take Janicek."

"Fuck you, Felcher," I told him boldly, "you ain't fucken scrubben me, not without a fight anyway."

Eddie looked upset at first when he heard me say that, but to tell you the truth, I was rather surprised by how cool I had sounded, but he quickly regained his composure.

"Whut?" he snapped, "is that right? What're you? Bad or sumpthen?" When he said that, I thought of a smart remark Ronny had told a guy once, and I thought I'd spring it on Eddie, since I didn't feel any fear of him at all.

"No," I told him, "but I've seen bad, and believe me pal, you ain't it."

Eddie's face turned red and he walked up, and threw a punch at me that missed, and then I came at him, and hit him three or four times. His head jerked with each blow, and when I stopped, he put his hand up to his lip which was bleeding. Eddie looked at his fingers and then at me.

"You son-of-a-bitch!" he screamed. "You cut my lip!"

"I'll do more than that, asshole," I told him, "you keep calling me names."

"Hey," his friend said. "Were' just tryen to have some fun. You didn't have to git violent."

Yea, well," I told him. "Go find somebody else to have fun with."

We walked away, and Eddie shouted at me.

"I'll gitcha for this Janicek!"

I turned around, and laughed.

"Yea, talk's cheap, Felcher!"

Tommy laughed too.

"Man, that was cool, Tommy," he said. "He didn't know whether to fart or go shit."

"Yea, that jerk," I answered. "I've never liked that son-of-a-bitch."

I really felt good about it, and the way I'd handled myself. I'd sounded just like a big guy. Ronny would've been proud of me.

From now on, I wasn't going to take any shit off anyone. That included Ray, and Scott. I was sick of their crap. Things were going to change.

But unfortunately, this new found bravado quickly evaporated when we got to the home, and reality set in. After we went in the tv room; and sat down to watch the Mickey Mouse Club, and Annette, Tommy bragged me up to our friends about my fight with Eddie and the number I'd done on him. I blushed with pride.

Ray, and Scott were sitting nearby, and when they heard what I'd done Ray laughed sarcastically, which annoyed me.

"Big fucken deal," he said. "He wouldn't try that shit with me, would'ja Pissass?"

I grew angry, but all the confidence I'd felt before was gone now, and instead of standing up to him, all I did was stand up, and head for the back door. I heard Ray, and Scott laugh derislively, and my face burned with shame.

"Whut a fucken pussy," Ray said as I left.

I went out back of the garage, and found a foxhole to lay down in, and I lit up a smoke. Tommy came out right after that, and joined me.

"Hey Tommy," he said. "Why didn't ya stand up to him like you did that Eddie guy? I bet you could kick Ray's ass if you wanted to. He ain't even as big as Eddie."

"I dunno," I told him. "He looks pretty tough."

"Ahh," he said. "I think he's a lot of talk but no action."

I wasn't convinced, and I continued to take abuse from Ray, and his buddy. I just couldn't get up enough courage to face them, and call their bluff.

That fall, Miss Sarah left us. Her mother had a stroke, so she was going to stay with, and take care of her.

I was really saddened to see her go. She was the only adult at the Home that I liked, and I was going to miss her. It wasn't going to be the same. Another good person gone from my life.

She was replaced by a heavy-set, gray-haired lady in her fifties, named Miss Anders, who was the complete opposite of Miss Sarah. She was very cool towards us, and there always seemed to be a permanent scowl on her face. Miss Anders looked like one of those women who serve food in school cafeterias.

I guess you could say she was an old battle axe. She seemed to take an instant dislike to me, and I returned the favor. I sure didn't enjoy working in the kitchen after that.

Some guys left that fall, among them Jeff Russek, and his brother Jason, along with Jimmy Marcus. I was really going to miss them, and was sorry to see them go.

They were replaced by some new kids, two of whom became good friends with Tommy, and I.

Their names were Darren Shunkwiler, and Toby Garcia. They were like Mutt, and Jeff, with Darren the tall, skinny one, and squat Toby, the opposite. They were the same age as Tommy. People teased Darren about his name, calling him Skunkwiler, but it didn't seem to bother him. We had fun together, joking, and laughing, and we began to sneak out at night, and vandalize, car prowl, and generally, just raise hell.

I'd never really engaged in this kind of behavior before. I'd been caught stealing twice before, and I swore I'd never do it again.

But now, for some reason, all that kind of thinking just seemed to go out the window, and it was like I didn't care if I got caught or not.

One night, I got angry because I couldn't get into a locked car that had a package on the front seat. Frustrated, I looked around, and found a big rock that I threw at the windshield, and it went clear through, leaving a large hole.

It made such a loud, blast of noise, we took off running, the package forgotten, and all the while we were laughing excitedly at the wickedness of my deed.

As I said, I'd never indulged in this kind of thing before, and I found it to be great sport. As long at we didn't get caught of course.

Looking back now, I can't believe how uncaring, and thoughtless I was. But I was angry at my dad, and society for letting bad shit happen to me all of the time, and this was the only way I knew of expressing myself.

I was having problems at school too. Not only was I getting lousy grades, but I was beginning to mouth off to the teachers.

One day, I went too far, and was expelled for a week. I was given a lecture by the Old Man, and by dad. I told them I'd do better. Right.

One afternoon, during that week long expulsion, I was in the library reading a Tom Swift book. There were quite a few copies of the series, and I enjoyed shutting out the world for awhile, and losing myself in one of his fanciful adventures.

Suddenly, the doorbell rang, and after a moment or two when Uncle Harry didn't come out of his living quarters, I got up to answer the door.

When I opened it, there was a man in a suit, standing next to a tough looking kid, who eyed me up, and down with a slight smirk on his face, and I thought, "uh oh."

"I'd like to speak to Mr. Hawthorne," the man said.

"I'll git him," I told him, and just at that moment, the Old Man appeared. "Somebody to see ya, Uncle Harry," I said.

I went back in the library, and shut the door. I resumed reading, only now I couldn't concentrate. I kept thinking about that kid.

He looked pretty mean, and I hoped he wasn't going to become one of my enemies. But judging by the way he'd looked at me, the odd's of that not happening appeared to be very small.

I found out his name was Jake Spangler, and he was the same age as me. He'd just come from the State Reform School which was called the "Hill." The Hill. I don't know what it was about that name, but everytime I heard it, I was filled with dread. I hoped I'd never have to go there. I'd heard a lot of bad stories about the place.

Jake was dark complexioned, with jet-black hair that was combed straight back, and had brown, hooded eyes. They were cold, and unforgiving, and scared me. He was just one of those guys who looked, acted, and was mean. All without trying.

It was spooky.

Jake was husky in build, but the most striking thing about him were his hands. Not only were they big, but there were letters tattooed across his fingers that spelled out "love," on one, and "hate" on the other.

I thought they looked pretty cool, and I was reminded of Robert Mitchum having the same thing in the movie, "The Night of the Hunter."

My worst fears were realized when Jake became friends with Ray, and Scott. They had a lot of contempt for our little group, and whenever they got on us, me inparticular, Ray, and Scott did most of the talking, with Jake lurking in the background, the silent threat!

We tried to stay away from them as much as possible, but in a place like the Home, there were only so many places you could go.

The only time we didn't have to worry about them was when we snuck out at night. We had fun, and I always hated to go back after one of our nightly runs.

Tommy had told Darren, and Toby what a good fighter I was, and they asked me why I didn't take on one of these guys. I gave them some lame excuses instead of admitting that I was just plain chicken.

Those were the times when I really wished Ronny was still alive. Together, we could've take care of these bastards. I would've given anything to see him fight with Jake. That would have been so cool.

But that wasn't going to happen, and I continued to put up with their shit. It was just something I had to live with, like it or not.

That was the fall that my interest in girls went beyond the day dreaming stage.

There was a girl in my class who was kind of cute, and her name was Pat Ostrander. She had short, dark hair, blue eyes, and although she was only twelve, she was very well developed for her age. Pat had nice, big breasts, and a round, sexy bottom.

In science class, she used to sit at a table across from me, and I used to try, and look up her dress. But I never had any luck.

It was that way with all the girls in my class. Especially the ones who wore poodle skirts. But that still didn't keep me from trying.

Then one day, that all changed.

We were in class one afternoon, and as usual I wasn't paying any attention to the lesson in hand, and instead was looking around under tables for a peek. And as usual, I wasn't having any luck. There was nothing to be seen.

I was about to shift my gaze back down to the picture I was working on, when suddenly Pat, who sat across from me facing in my direction, parted her legs, and my eyes were filled with the sight of her pale, white thighs, and panties.

I felt a thrill of sexual pleasure go through me, and I got a hard on, and rubbed myself under the table. I couldn't believe it.

Pat, in the meantime, was staring at the teacher, acting like she was totally unaware, and unconcerned. After a minute or two, though, she closed the show, and I hated to see it end. It had been great while it lasted.

I decided to write her a note, and see if she'd be interested in letting me walk her home from school that day. I hoped she'd say yes.

I gave it to her after class, and she wrote me back, and said she'd like that. During the rest of the afternoon, I fantasized about what I was going to do to her once I got her alone.

When I met Pat after school, we started walking in the direction of her house. We talked, and shyly, I put my arm around her. I wasn't used to being with girls, and I wasn't sure of what to do or say. But that thought of what she'd done that day spurred me on.

I thought I'd lead her down an alley, but I was afraid she wouldn't let me, and I didn't want to scare her off. But, I decided to change it anyway.

"Let's go this way," I told her, and she didn't seem to mind.

We walked a short way, and then I took her between two garages, and we stopped. She looked up at me with a slight smile on her face as we faced each other.

"Would'ja mind if I kissed ya?" I asked her hopefully.

"No," she said.

Being as this was my first one, I didn't know what to expect, but it was great. Her lips had a delicate smoothness to them and I felt a warm glow inside, and couldn't get enough. She felt so soft in my arms.

While we were doing that, I thought about feeling her up, and I don't think she'd have minded, but I was still pretty bashful, and unsure of myself, so I didn't. After that first day, I continued to walk her home, and on Friday nights we'd meet at the theatre, and make out. Sometimes, the usher would catch us, and he'd flash his light at us, and tell us to knock it off, which was embarrassing.

We didn't go together for very long. I was the one who broke it off, and I know it hurt her, but she didn't thrill me like Barbara Stoner did. The only reason I'd gone with Pat was to see if I could have sex with her, but I was so dammed shy, I couldn't even get past first base. I was pathetic.

Looking back now, I realize what an uncaring, selfish bastard I was, and still am to a certain extent.

It wasn't long after that, when I got into it with one of Jake's gang, and I did pretty well. It helped to boost my self-confidence.

One night, about four or five of us were sitting in the dining room, listening to Little Richard on a record player. Tommy and my friends weren't there.

Ray came in from the tv room, and headed in our direction, and I grew tense. He walked up behindme, and I hoped he wasn't going to give me any grief, but from the way it looked, that wasn't about to happen. He put his hands on the back of my chair, and I braced myself.

"That music is too hip for ya Pissass," he said sarcastically. "Why dont'cha git outta that chair, and leave so I can siddown, and listen?"

I felt anger swell up inside me at how unfair he was being.

"Hey!" I told him. "Git yer own fucken chair. I'm not botheren you."

"You fucken pussy," Ray said. "Git the fuck outta here."

He pushed, and tried to tip the chair so I'd get up, but I held on to the seat, and he couldn't budge me.

That frustrated him, so he grabbed my shoulders, and began to shove, all the while cursing, and that's when I'd had enough.

When someone like Ray would pick on me, and call me Pissass, I'd get angry, but that was about as far as it went, and I usually never did anything about it. That's just the way it had always been.

But I was beginning to find out that when someone put their hands on me in anger, especially guys my age, they could expect a fight. When I got mad, I forgot about being scared. This was one of those times.

I stood up, and faced him, then moved the chair out of the way.

"Don't put'cher fucken hands on me!" I told him angrily.

"Why? Whutta you gonna do?" he sneered. "Pee on my shoe?" then he pushed me.

I pushed him back, and when I did, he took a swing at me but missed, and I backed away. He continued to come after me punching furiously, and then I stopped, and hit him flush on the chin.

It was like a scene right out of a movie. Ray flew backwards, went over my chair, and landed on his back under the table behind him.

One of the older guys who was sitting there laughed, and looked at me.

"Hey Tommy!" he said "Do that again! That was really cool!"

I watched as Ray crawled out from under the table, and stood up. There was a bewildered look on his face, and he averted my eyes as he scurried out the door. It had really felt good to hit him, and I think I was more astonished than he was about the outcome. I just wished I'd have done it sooner now.

Then I began to worry. I hoped Jake wouldn't try to get even with me because I hit his friend.

When my buddies heard about what happened, they were really upset because they'd missed out on it.

"Shit!" Darren said. "I wish I could've been there."

"Yea, me too," Toby added.

"I told'ja you could take him," Tommy said.

"Well, I hope Jake don't git pissed cuz I hit his buddy," I told them.

Thankfully he didn't, but any satisfaction I got out of my fight with

Ray didn't last very long. He claimed it was just a lucky punch, and the harassment went on. I would've punched Ray again, but with Jake around, I figured I'd better not push my luck. I just continued to put up with it.

Finally though, the shit hit the fan, and of course it hit me the hardest.

The trouble began when I was helping to clean up in the kitchen after supper one night. As I stated before, I didn't like to work there anymore, ever since Miss Sarah left.

Scott Staman was present that evening, and he didn't help matters any when he made some derogatory remarks, and I finally got mad. Scott was the least threatening of the three, and I really let him have it.

"Shut the fuck up or else I'll kick yer fucken ass!" I told him. "You ain't hiden behind Jake's skirt now!"

"Oh, fuck you Pissass!" he said. "Why dontcha kiss my dick?"

A flash of red anger went through me, and I punched him twice, and he fell down. Then he raised himself up in a sitting position, and looked at me, and started calling me names.

Before I could do or say anything else, Miss Anders came over, and tried to grab my arm, but I shrugged her off. Then she tried to slap me, but I grabbed her wrist. Angrily, she pulled away, and then told me to get the hell out of her kitchen.

"Gladly," I told her sarcastically, and started to leave.

Scott in the meantime, had gotten to his feet, and had found a spatuala, and was standing behind her. He was reaching around, and trying to hit me with it, all the while calling me by my lousy nickname.

"Yea Pissass! Git the hell outta here Pissass!" he was yelling.

I turned, and saw his head almost resting on her shoulder, and I let one go. My fist whizzed past Miss Anders ear, and caught Scott right in the mouth, and he went down again.

Miss Anders eyes got as big as saucers when she saw how close my hand came to hitting her, and she tried to slap me again, but I just stepped back, and she missed.

"Gawdamm you!" she yelled frustrated. "I'm going to tell Harry about this and then we'll see who's so tough, you little punk!"

"Big fucken deal!" I told her, and left.

I went outside in my shirt sleeves in the cold December air, and walked behind the garage, and lit up a smoke and thought about what had just happened. I was beginning to get worried because I knew I'd gone too far with Miss Anders, and the Old Man was going to be pissed. It had felt really good to kick Scott's ass, but I know there was a chance that I'd have to face Jake, and that was far worse than meeting up with Uncle Harry.

I stayed there for awhile, and smoked another cigarette, then decided I'd better go in, and face the music. I knew I was going to have to do it eventually anyway.

When I got to the washroom, I peeked into the tv room to see if Jake or his buddies were around, but they were nowhere in sight, which was a relief.

However Tommy, and Darren, and Toby were there, and I walked in, and joined them.

News about my fight had spread, and we talked about it. Of course they were disappointed that they'd missed it, but they were glad that I'd gotten even with Scott for being such a shithead.

About that time, Uncle Harry came in, and looked around. When he saw me, he called my name, and nervously, I got up, and met him by the door.

"Get to my office," he said harshly.

He followed along behind me, and when we got to his office, he bot out his belt, and then faced me. I was filled with anxiety about the upcoming beating.

"Just who the hell do you think you are, putting your hands on Miss Anders?" he bellowed.

Before I could say anything, he began striking me with his belt, and at first, I yelped in pain, but then suddenly I got pissed off.

I was sick of people always picking on me, and I felt like I hadn't done anything wrong when I hit Scott. I was just sticking up for myself, and Miss Anders shouldn't have tried to grab or hit me. She didn't like me anyway.

And now, here I was getting my ass kicked. I'd had it with this shit, and I snapped, and tried to grab the belt from him.

"Gawdammit!" I screamed. "Keep yer fucken hands offa me!"

The Old Man was startled at first, and he stopped for a moment. Then he started in again, but all the pain did was make me angrier, and again, I tried to grab the belt and, this time, I got a hold of his wrist.

"Gawdammit!" I yelled. "I said to keep yer fucken hands offa me; you old son-of-a-bitch!"

He jerked his hand away, and I could see he wasn't getting anywhere with me, and he ordered me out of his office.

"And don't you ever pull another stunt like this," he said. "You got that?"

"Oh fuck you, you old buzzard" I told him as I went out the door.

As I walked back to the tv room, I really felt good about what I'd just done. I could hardly believe it. I'd actually stood up to a grown man, and I'd done okay. I was feeling proud, and I was anxious to tell Tommy, and my friends about it.

Unfortunately, I never got the chance, because when I got to the tv room, Jake, Scott, and Ray, walked up to me, and any good feeling I had was quickly replaced with fear. Especially when I saw the nasty look on Jake's face.

"Hey Pissass," he said flatly. "I heard ya think Scott hides behind my skirt. Do I look like I wear skirts?"

"No, I'm sorry Jake," I told him trembling. "I didn't mean it like that."

"You must think yer a real baddass or sumpthen," he said.

Before I could say anything, he struck me twice, hard, and my head exploded in starry pain. I stumbled backwards, and landed against the wall by the door. I put my arms up over my face to protect myself, and I heard Ray, and Scott laugh, and I felt a twinge of anger, despite my fear of Jake. Scott walked up close and began to taunt me.

"Hey Pissass!" he sneered. "How'd ya like that? Yer not so fucken bad now, are ya, ya fucken Pissass?" there was such a nasty tone of contempt in his voice, I was overcome by rage, and I came out of my shell, and flew at him and I struck him in the face several times, which drove him back into some chairs, and he went down. Guys were scrambling to get out of the way.

Jake was behind me, and suddenly he reached around, and slugged me on the side of the jaw, and I fell into the tangle of chairs. My head was buzzing from the force of the blow, and I laid there stunned. I tried to get up, but then all three of them stood over, and beat on, and kicked me. They weren't really hurting me because I curled up in a fetal position, but it was scary, and I was begging them to stop.

Finally, they did, and after they left, I sat up, and saw my friends watching me. They had sad expressions on their faces, and they walked over to me. Tommy put out his hand to help me up, but I managed on my own.

"You okay?" he asked.

"Yea," I sniffed. I almost felt like crying, but that's the last thing I wanted to do. Especially when I saw Donnie Abernathy watching, with a shitty grin on his face. I felt that sharp, prick of anger, and hate that I had for him.

"Man, I just wish we coulda helped ya," Tommy told me.

"Aw don't worry about it," I said.

I hadn't expected them to jump in, because they weren't as big as my tormentors, and besides which, they couldn't fight anyway. But that was okay. At least they were my friends.

We walked out to the washroom, and I inspected my face in the mirror. I had the beginning of a black eye, and a fat lip, and various marks on my face.

About that time, Buck walked in. When he saw my face he laughed sarcastically.

"What's the matter Janicek? Did your mouth overload your ass again?"

"Nossir," I muttered.

"No? You could've fooled me," he said, then got serious.

"You better knock off the shit pal, Uncle Harry told me you put your hands on Miss Anders."

When I didn't respond, he grabbed me by the arm, and I winced. It felt like a vice.

"You pull any shit on me like that, and I'll stick my foot so far up your ass, you'll be shitting out of your ears!" You got that?"

"Yessir, I'm sorry Buck," I told him.

"That's the problem with you," he said. "You're always sorry, but you still continue to screw up."

"I know."

He gave me a look of disgust, and then left, for which I was glad, I didn't need anymore abuse.

After he was gone, we decided to go outside, and after getting our coats, we went behind the garage, and talked, and smoked.

"Man, I said. "One of these days, I'm gonna run off, and they can take this place, and stick it in their ass."

"Where would'ja go?" Tommy asked.

"I dunno," I told him. "Anywhere but here. I hate this fucken place."

"Me too," he said.

We didn't say anything for a moment, and then he spoke again.

"Hey Tommy," he said. "I know where we could go if we ran off."

"Where?" I asked curiously.

"My aunt, and uncle's place," he told me. "My cousin's got a tree house in the backyard, and we could hide out there. He could get us food and stuff."

We grew excited, and the more we talked, the better it sounded. The fact that what we were talking about was absurd never entered out minds. It just sounded like fun.

"Let's do it. You guys cumen along" I asked Darren, and Toby.

"Sure," they said.

We went over to the corner of the fence, and climbed up it, then quickly walked away. The novelty of what we were doing, was much more exciting than when we snuck away to raise hell.

The cold, winter air was chilling, but we didn't let that stop us. We were too pumped up. After awhile though, our enthusiasm began to wane. Our hands, and feet were getting uncomfortably numb.

I stamped my feet, and not having any gloves, I blew into my hands, then stuffed them down deep in the pockets of my coat. It was beginning to dawn on me that this wasn't such a good idea because the night was only going to get much colder.

"How much further we gotta go?" I asked Tommy. "I'm freezen."

Darren, and Toby said the same thing. Tommy looked a little the worse for wear himself.

"Not much longer," he said.

"Well, I hope so."

We were walking through an industrial area, and there weren't any houses around, so I knew we still had quite a ways to go yet. I wished we hadn't decided to run off now. It was just too damn cold.

There wasn't a lot of traffic, but as one vehicle approached us, I realized it was a police car. Tommy noticed too, and he panicked.

"Look out!" he yelled. "It's the cops!"

He, and Darren, and Toby took off running in the opposite direction.

"Hey!" I hollered. "Don't run!"

They ignored me, and kept going. I stayed where I was, and the patrol car pulled up, and a cop got out. Then his partner took off after my friends.

"What're you kids doing?" the patrolman asked me.

"Nuthen," I told him.

"Why did your buddies run then?" he questioned.

"I dunno," I replied. "We wuz just walken."

"You weren't trying to break into one of these buildings were you?" he asked.

"No!" I said, alarmed.

He didn't question me anymore until the other cop returned with my friends. I was crammed into the back seat with them, and then they asked us our names, and where we lived.

When we mentioned the Home, they seemed to be familiar with it, and I assumed that they had dealt with some of the other guys from there.

They drove us back, and I was nervous, and scared, and my friends looked like they were too. I figured we were in for it.

After the cops dropped us off at the Home, Uncle Harry got Buck to join us in the office. I know we were in deep doo-doo.

"Just what in the hell were you kids trying to prove by running off like this?" Uncle Harry asked angrily.

We were all standing facing him, and Buck, who was behind us, reached out, and smacked me on the back of my head, and I winced in pain.

"Why don't you tell him since you've got the biggest mouth here?" he said.

"I dunno," I spoke miserably. "We were just out walken."

We wound up getting a whipping (Buck punished me) and then Uncle Harry said our movie, and visiting privileges were going to be taken away for a week.

That Sunday, when dad came to pick up Billy, he told me I'd better straighten up my act. I was becoming a real problem, what with flunking school and talking back and putting my hands on adults.

I told him I'd try to be good from now on, but I knew the first time I lost my temper, I'd be back on everyone's shit list.

The only good thing to come out of the situation was that Uncle Harry never touched me again. I don't know if he was scared of me or not, but he always let the counselors deal with me after that. I thought it was pretty cool to be able to mouth off to him, and not have to worry about getting hit in return.

Since my grades were so lousy, they decided that I attend a private school. It was located in a large house, and was run by a kind, patient widowed lady in her fifties, named Mrs. Prososki.

The kids there were nice enough, and some of them were like Vernon. Her classes were easy compared to the ones at Lincoln, and with her tutoring, I did well.

One day, we had an assignment to write a short story about a certain subject, and then put it in our own words. When we were done, she had us read our version to the class. When I was through with mine, she praised me for how well written it was, and that I'd done a good job. That did a lot for my self-esteem. I really liked her.

Inspite of my success, with Mrs. Prososki, it didn't change my bad attitude at the Home. I continued to mouth off to the Old Man, and go out at night with my friends, and raise the devil.

In Feb of 1957, a family moved into the house next to the Home. There appeared to be three kids living there. One was a little boy, and his two older sisters. The youngest girl was about my age, and was really pretty. I started to wave at her, and she began to wave back, which made me feel good, but I never tried to talk to her. I was still kind of shy around girls.

One day after I'd waved, she mentioned to me, and I walked over to the fence in the small courtyard next to her home.

"Hi," she said.

"Hi," I replied shyly.

"What's your name?" she asked.

"Tommy," I told her. "Whut's yers?"

"Mine's Pam," she said. "Pam Ellison."

Pam, I liked that. I found out she was in the seventh grade. She had long, blonde hair, and blue eyes along with a cute, button nose. The longer

I looked into those eyes the more I knew I was going to fall for her. They only other one who'd had this effect on me was Barbara Stoner.

"What kind of place is that?" She asked curiously, pointing at the Home.

"Ahh," I said "It's just a lousy boy's home."

"Don't you like it there?"

"No," I told her.

"How come you're living there?" she inquired.

"Oh, when my dad works, he ain't got nobody to watch me, and my brother." I explained. "So that's why we're in here."

"Where's your mom?"

"She's dead," I said matter of factly.

"Oh. I'm sorry," she told me.

"That's okay."

"I hope you don't mind me asking," she said. "But how did she die?"

"Oh, I dunno," I told her. "They said she died in her sleep."

"I'm sorry to hear that," she said, then changed the subject. "What grade are you in at Lincoln?"

"I don't go there," I replied. "I … uh … I go to a special school."

"Oh."

Since she was being so nice, and seemed to be interested in me, I got bold and asked her if she'd like to go for a walk.

"Sure," she said. "Just let me put my notebook away."

When she went in the house, I waited anxiously for her return. I was excited. After Pam came back, I went to the big entrance by the alley, and met her there. I checked to see if anyone was watching, then told her we needed to hurry, and get out of sight of the Home.

"Why?" she asked curiously.

"Aw, I can git in trouble for leaven' the yard," I explained.

"Well, maybe we'd better not do this," she said.

"Ahh to hell with them," I cussed, then apologized for my language.

"That's okay," she said. "I just don't want to see you get in trouble."

"Ahh, it'll be alright," I told her.

We took off in a hurry, and once we were out of sight of the home, we slowed our pace, and made small talk. It really felt good to have a pretty girl walking by my side. She seemed to like me, and I really enjoyed being with her.

The time passed too quickly and soon it was time to go back. I asked her if she'd like to meet me after supper, and we'd go for another walk. Pam said she'd like that. We set a time, and then we parted.

I could hardly wait for supper to end, so I could meet her. After we'd eaten Tommy, and my friends asked me about going out, and getting into mischief.

"Naw, I've got a date," I told them proudly.

"Oh bullys," Tommy scoffed. "With who? Whut's his name?"

"Oh, fuck you Madsen," I told him. "How'd ya like a fat lip?"

After leaving them, I got my coat, then went outside, and walked cautiously through the entrance by the garage. Then I went down the alley until, I came to the rear of an office building where we were to meet. As I waited impatiently for her to show up, I hoped against hope that she hadn't changed her mind abut meeting me here.

So I was really relieved when I saw Pam come out of her house. As she walked towards me, I was so glad that I'd met her. Outside of Pat, I hadn't had a whole lot to do with girls. Some of that had to do with my trying to come across as a baddass. And I was so awkward, and uncomfortable around them anyway.

"Hi Tommy", she said as she walked up.

"Hi Pam," I told her with a smile.

"Shall we go walk?" She asked.

"You bet," I told her, and we took off.

"It's kind of cold, isn't it?" She said.

"Yea it is," I agreed.

"Would you like to hold my hand, and keep it warm?" she asked with a sly grin.

"Sure," I answered, and felt a glow inside.

I took her hand in mine, and despite the chilly air it was soft, and warm. We went a little further without talking, and feeling emboldened, I looked over at her.

"Can I put my arm around you?" I asked timidly.

"Yes."

I encircled her waist, and pulled her close. In return, she did the same thing, and I felt that sweet rush of emotion I'd only had around one other girl. Barbara Stoner.

Again we walked for a bit without saying anything. Then she spoke.

"How come you don't go to Lincoln?" she asked.

"Ahh, I had a hard time with my classes. Speshly math," I explained. "That's why I'm going to a tutoring school. The only classes I was good at, was art, and music."

"Really?" she said. "Those are my favorties. Are you a good singer?"

"I guess," I answered, not wanting to brag.

"Sing me a song," she told me. "I'd like to hear your voice."

"Okay," I said.

I started singing one of my favorites, the song was "Since I Met You Baby," by Ivory Joe Hunter. When I was finished, Pam told me how good I could sing. That really did a lot for my ego.

There was a tone in her voice that made me think she wouldn't mind if I asked her something. At least, I hoped she wouldn't.

"Pam?" I said uncertainly.

"Yes?"

"May I kiss you?" I asked hopefully.

"I'd like that," she said softly, and I was thrilled.

We stopped and faced each other, and then I took her in my arms. I was almost a head taller, and I bent over, and gently kissed her. The feel of her silky lips on mine was exquisite. I felt like I was melting in the marvelous sensation, and I didn't want the kiss to end. But I knew I had to come up for air sometime, and when I did, and leaned back, I saw that Pam still had her eyes closed, and there was a sweet smile on her lips. After a moment, she opened them. Gawd, she was pretty, and sexy. I knew from that moment on I was going to love her forever.

"Mmm, that was nice," she said. "You can really kiss."

"Thanks." That really built up my self-esteem. "So can you."

Then I kissed her again, and again there was the surge of excitement from the smooth, warm, softness of her mouth, and the way her body felt in my arms.

After that, we resumed our walk, but every block or so, we'd stop and kiss. I was caught up in the sweet moments of pleasure I was feeling, and

I didn't want them to end. But it didn't seem like it was very long before we had to return.

When we reached her house, I gave Pam a goodnight kiss, and told her we'd get together tomorrow if she wanted. She said she'd like that. Then I went over to the Home to sneak in. The doors were locked now, and I hoped I wouldn't get caught. I was in such a great mood, I didn't want it to be spoiled. But I got inside with no trouble.

I met up with my cohorts, and bragged about my date with Pam, and how we'd spent the night making out. They didn't have girlfriends, and they looked envious.

"I wonder if she's got a friend I could go with?" Tommy asked.

"Yea, maybe two," Darren said.

"I dunno," I told them.

After lights out that night, I laid in bed, and thought about Pam and the wonderful time I'd had. It was nice to know that she might feel the same way about me as I did her. She had made me forget about this stinking place for awhile. I felt wonderful, and I drifted off peacefully to sleep.

In the morning, I went through the ritual of stripping my wet bed, showering, rinsing, then take the sheets out to the clothes line so they could freeze-dry. While I was doing that, it occurred to me that Pam might see what I was doing. Gawd, I hoped not. I wouldn't know what to say if she ever found out I wet the bed. I swear I'd kill myself. I didn't want to think about it. Hopefully, that would never happen.

That day at Mrs. Prososki's, I could hardly wait to get back to the Home so I could see Pam.

When I returned, I hurriedly got my sheets off the line, and took them inside. Then I went out to the fence, and waited restlessly for her to showup. I didn't have to wait long. I saw her come down the sidewalk, and then she walked over to me.

"Hi," she said, smiling.

"Hi Pam," I grinned. "I've been thinking aboutcha all day."

"Have you?" she said. "I've been thinking about you too."

"You wanna go for another walk tonight?" I asked.

"Yes," she answered. "Here, I've got something for you."

She reached in her notebook, and took out an envelope. There was a gap between the bottom of the fence, and the ground, and she bent over, then slipped the letter under. I reached down, and took it from her hand.

"Don't read it until you get inside," she told me.

"Oh. Okay," I replied happily.

I knew what it was, and I could hardly wait to read it. We talked a bit, then she went in the house, and I headed towards the Home. When I got there, I went upstairs to the dorm, then sat on my bunk, and looked at the letter. Pam had sprayed it with her perfume, and I brought it up to my nose, and took a deep breath. The smell was heavenly. Then, I opened the envelope, and eagerly ready the contents.

Pam wrote that she thought I was cute, and that she'd really enjoyed our walk the night before. But the most important thing was that my sweet kisses had made her fall in love with me.

I felt a tingle go through me when I read that, and afterwards, I got a pencil, and paper, and went down to the library. Then I wrote her a love letter and put it in my pocket.

After supper, I went to our meeting place, and when she showed up, we walked again, and I kissed like we had the night before. I told Pam that her letter had meant a lot to me, and then I gave her my note, and told her to read it later.

"What did you think of what I had to say about the way I feel?" she asked.

"That's how I feel about you too," I replied and told Pam that I loved her.

"I love you, Tommy," she responded gently.

Just hearing her say that sent a thrill down my spine, and I kissed her passionately. I'd never been so happy, and like the previous night, I hated to leave her when it came time to part. But knowing that she loved me helped take some of thie sting out of going back. And it was nice to know that she was just a stones throw away. That was comforting.

It was on the following Monday morning that I suddenly realized Ronny had died on this date a year ago, and I felt lousy about it.

Whenever I passed the corner where he'd been killed, I always felt a twinge of sadness, and the feeling was really strong that day.

When I got to Mrs. Prososki's, I kind of forgot about it. I kidded around with some of the kids there, and I got involved in my studies.

But, on the way back to the Home, again I felt the sad feeling and it wasn't, until I saw Pam that I was able to shake it off. Thank God I had her to help me forget all of the negative things in my life.

That night before supper though, just as the sun was going down, one of my black moods came over me, and in the swirl of melancholy, I cursed. I didn't need this. Especially on a day like today. But, thankfully, the strong emotions didn't last long.

After I met Pam for our usual get together, I felt better. It was great to have her as my girlfriend. But, I was still a little down, and she noticed.

"What's wrong?" she asked. "You're kind of quiet."

"Oh a good friend of mine was hit, and killed by a car a year ago today."

"Oh, I'm sorry," she said sympathetically.

"Thanks," I told her.

I thought about showing her where Ronny had died, but then decided not to. I felt bad enough as it was.

Like I said though, Pam helped me to forget about my problems, and get through all the crap I had to put up with at the Home. It was so wonderful.

But, all good things must come to an end, and boy was that ever true in my case. My little dream world with Pam came crashing down after we'd been going together for about three weeks.

One day, Pam, and I were talking, and when we parted, we kissed through one of the links in the fence. Then I turned around, and headed for the Home. As I did, I noticed Donnie Abernathy standing by the steps of the side door, and he was staring at me. When I got close to him, I was expecting an insult. He was always doing that.

"That yer girlfriend?" he asked in a condescending manner.

"Yea," I answered nervously. "Why?"

"I was just wonderin," he said, and walked away.

When I went inside, I was kind of worried about Donnie. I didn't trust him, and I hoped he wasn't going to pull any shit on me with Pam. I didn't need his screwing around in my life, and I tried to put him out of my mind.

The next day, I was running late, and when I came out of the Home, I saw Donnie standing in front of Pam by the fence talking, and I was shocked.

Then I got angry. He'd better not be trying to take her away from me. Even if he was bigger than me, I'd fight him. I didn't care if I got my ass kicked or not. I wasn't going to let him screw up the best thing that had ever happened to me.

Just before I got to them, Donnie turned around, and started walking in my direction. When he saw me, he grinned evily, and I wondered what he was up to.

After he passed by, I saw Pam reading a letter, and I knew something was wrong. She had a sad expression on her face. Then she looked up at me as I got to the fence.

"Whuttsa matter?" I asked worriedly.

"Look atthis," she said, and slipped the note under the fence.

As I read it, despite the cold air, I could feel my face burn with the hot flames, of shame, and embarrassment. Donnie had written that I pissed the bed, and if she didn't believe it, all she had to do was look out her window in the mornings, and she'd see me hanging up my wet sheets.

I ripped up the letter, and then turned around, and hurried away. I'd never been so humiliated in my life. I was almost sick to my stomach.

"Tommy!" Pam called. "Don't leave! It's okay! I don't care!"

I just kept going. When I got inside, I went up to the dorm, and sat down on my bed. Gawdamm him! That son-of-a-bitch! I'd never be able to face her now. That creek. That fat bastard! I should look him up, and punch him out. But I knew I was just kidding myself. If I tried that, he'd just kick my ass, then laugh at me. That jerk off.

Then I started to cry. Dammit. Why couldn't people just leave me alone? I wasn't hurting anyone. Now I'd lost Pam. It wasn't fair. All because I couldn't be like normal people who didn't have to wake up, and find out they had pissed all over themselves.

I was still sitting there with tears streaming down my face, when suddenly I heard someone coming down the hall, and I quickly wiped at my eyes. I saw it was Tommy.

"Hey Tommy," he said. "Pam said she'd like to see ya. She's waiting at the fence."

They were in classes together at school, and she'd told me that she thought he was funny and cute. Evidently, she seen him just now.

"Yea. Well I don't wanna see her," I told him.

"Whuttsa matter?" he asked. "Did you guys git inna fight or sumpthen?"

"Naw," I replied. "That fucken Donnie told her I wet the bed."

"Whut?" he said. "That son-of-a-bitch!"

"Yea, I know."

"You should kick his fucken ass," he told me.

"Naw," I said. "He's too big. He'd beat the shit out of me."

"Ahh, I don't think so," he replied. "I've never seen him fight. Have you?"

"No," I had admit.

"I think he's a lot of talk but no action," he said. "Like Ray."

"Yea, well, all I know is, I can't face her now," I told him. "It hurts too much."

"Hey, she didn't act like she gave a shit," he said. "You should go talk to her."

"I dunno," I answered uncertainly.

He kept prodding me, and I finally decided I'd try. My love for her was strong, and I didn't want to give it up just because Donnie was a prick.

When I went back outside, Pam was still waiting at the fence. I really felt self-conscious as I walked up to her. I averted her eyes, and looked down at the ground.

"Hi," she said gently.

"Hi," I mumbled.

"I know you feel bad about what that jerk wrote," she said, "but it doesn't matter to me. I still love you."

"Thanks," I told her. At least she still cared from the way it sounded.

"You shouldn't let it bother you," she said. "My brother Gary does the same thing. It's just something that happens to people."

"Yea." Somehow that didn't make me feel any better.

"You're going to meet me tonight, aren't you?" she asked.

"Sure."

"Okay. I'll see you then." She said.

After she left, I then went back up to the dorm for some peace, and quiet. Thankfully, nobody was there, and I laid down on my bed, and thought about how Donnie had screwed up things Pam, and I. That fat bastard!

I wished there was a way I could get even, but outside of attacking him, there wasn't much I could do.

At supper that night, I saw Donnie, and he gave me one of his shiteating grins, and I wanted to get up and go over, and wipe it off his face. But I knew that would never happen. That smug bastard!

When I met Pam later on, she was very kind, and sweet, and that made me feel a little better, but I was still uncomfortable. We walked, and talked, and kissed as always, but it just wasn't the same.

After I got back to the Home, and then went to bed, I felt like I'd lost something. Something precious that I could never get back, and that made me feel like crying. That fucking Donnie!

Pam, and I continued to go together, but like I said, it just wasn't the same after that. Gradually, we began to see less of each other, and then one day it all ended.

We met at the fence as usual, and on this particular afternoon, she was acting rather distant, and I sense something wrong.

"Hi," I told her.

"Hi," she said, then pulled out an envelope, and slipped it under the fence. "Here you need to read this."

I bent down, and took it, then started to open it, but she told me to wait until I got inside the Home. Then she left.

I went to the library, and sat down to read it. As I did, I felt my heart break. Pam wrote that she had fallen for a boy in her class, and that she didn't want to see me anymore, and tears came to my eyes.

I blamed Donnie. If it hadn't been for him, this might not have happened. But, deep down inside, I knew that things probaby would've turned out the same anyway. He just hadn't helped the situation. Gawd, I hated him.

Our breakup really hurt, and it took me quite awhile to get over Pam.

I plotted revenge against Donnie, but that was as far as it ever got.

Finally, though, in April, he got his come uppance, and I loved it.

It came as the result of a gang fight between the Ninth Street Warriors, and their rivals, the Morrell Cobras. Morell Junior high wasn't that far from the Home. There must've neen fifty or sixty of them altogether.

A bunch of kids, including Tommy and I gathered to watch. He'd heard that they were going to fight, and he came, and got me, and we walked back to the lot a couple of blocks from the Home.

The two gangs were taunting, and calling each other names, and just when it looked like things were going to heat up, the cops arrived. That put a damper on the festivities, and the police told everyone to disperse, and go home.

As Tommy, and I walked away, we talked about what a drag it was that the cops showed up when they did.

"Man! That would've been something if all the guys started fighting," he said.

"Yea," I agreed. "I wanted to see that."

When we got about a half block from the Home, we stopped, and waited as some of the gang members came along behind us.

Donnie had been walking ahead of Tommy, and I, and he just picked that moment to stop also. Of course we ignored him,

Most of the Cobras wore black, leather jackets, with their collars up in the back, and we were scared to look at them. But fascinated, we stared anyway.

Four of them approached us, and then they stopped. The biggest, and meanest looking one of them all faced us, and I, gulped in fear.

"You guys from Lincoln?" he asked.

Tommy nodded, and even though I wasn't now, I did also.

"Whut grade'er ya in?" he asked roughly.

"Seventh," we both replied.

When I said that, the Cobra fixed his gaze on me because I'm sure he thought I looked a little too big to be just a scrub, and I grew more tense. But then he eased up much to my relief.

"Ahh, you guys are too young to fight," he said, then looked over at Donnie who had started to creep away. "Hey you! Cumere!"

Donnie stopped, then turned around, and walked up nervously to the Cobra. He really looked scared.

"Whut grade'er ya in?" the hood growled.

"Ninth," Donnie gulped, and the Cobra gave him an evil smile.

"Yer old enough," he said.

Then he hauled off, and punched Donnie in the mouth, who stumbled backwards. The Cobra came after him, punching him on his head, and Donnie tried to protect himself, but he was still getting hit.

He took off running, trying to get away, and he went up on the porch of a house in a panic. The Cobra followed and the beating continued until he finally knocked Donnie over the railing of the Home, and he landed with a thud on the lawn below.

He didn't move at first, but then he finally got slowly to his feet. His face was full of blood and he looked so pathetic, I almost felt sorry for the jerk, but I didn't. He was such an asshole.

In the meantime, the Cobra had joined his buddies, and now they were standing around, talking, and laughing, and smoking.

Tommy and I walked up to Donnie, who was wiping his nose, which was bleeding with his arm. His shirt was spattered with red spots.

"Are you okay?" I asked him politely, although I really didn't care if he was or not.

"Whut's it to ya?" he snarled. "Mind yer own fucken business."

"Okay," I said, and Tommy and I walked away.

"That was really neato, fucken, Keeno," Tommy told me. "I loved watchen Donnie git his ass kicked."

"Yea. Me too," I agreed.

When we got to the Home, Buck came out on the porch with a scowl on his face. From the looks of things, someone must've told him about the fight with Donnie. Either that, or he was just pissed off at somebody. As long as it wasn't me, I didn't care.

When Tommy, and I came up the steps, Buck asked us what had happened.

"One of those guys from Morrell beat up Donnie," Tommy said.

"Which one?" he inquired.

"That big guy there," I told him, pointing out the Cobra. I didn't mind snitching on him.

About that time, Donnie showed up, and Buck asked him if he was all right.

"Yea," he mumbled.

"Well, go wash up," Buck told him. "You look like hell."

Donnie went on in, and Buck kept on eye on the group of Cobras. When they finally started walking in our direction, he went down to the sidewalk and then stood in the middle of it with his hands on his hips, and waited.

The Cobras approached him, and they were staring at Buck curiously and when they were within reach, they stopped. They didn't seem to be the least but intimidated. The fools. In the meantime, some of the guys from the Home joined us.

Buck gave the guilty party a hard look.

"Did you just hit one of our boys?" he growled.

The Cobra looked over at the Home, and it must've dawned on him that was where Donnie lived. Then he faced Buck again with a smirk.

"Yea," he said insolently. "Why? Whut the fuck's it to ya?"

Buck reached out, and slapped him, and it sounded like a gunshot. They guy's head snapped to one side, and he staggered backwards, and held his cheek with one hand. There was a shocked, and hurt look on his face, and I knew how he felt.

When Buck did that, the other Cobras gathered around him and started calling his names. When one of them got too close, Buck grabbed him by the face, and showed. They guy flew backwards, and just about fell on his ass.

In the meantime, some cobras were coming down the sidewalk across the street, and when they saw what was happening, they ran over to our side. There were six or seven of them, and I was kindof worried about Buck. What if they pulled some weapons on him? That was known to happen. A kid had been stabbed to death in a gang fight not that long ago, in the city projects. And shootings weren't that uncommon. But Buck just stood there unconcerned.

They were hurling insults at him, but he never said a word in return. He just stared at them with contempt in his eyes.

Suddenly, a short, husky Cobra came at Buck with a long, choke chain in his hand, and he hit him across the chest with it. Buck made a grab at him, but the kid danced away from his grasp. Buck followed, trying to get his hands on him, but the guy was too quick. He kept eluding Buck, and striking him with the chain while his buddies cheered him on.

It was almost funny. The kid looked like a horsefly pestering a big, old water buffalo.

Finally, though, the guy made a slip, and Buck got his hands on him.

He jerked the chain from the Cobra's hand, slapped him, then picked him up by his jacket, and threw him into his friends, who jumped out of the way. The kid landed on his ass, and then the Cobras started badmouthing Buck again, who just held out his hands, and motioned for them to get it on.

Uncle Harry had come out while all of this was going on, and now he told Buck they'd better call the police. When the Cobras heard this, they called the Old Man an "Old Bastard," but then finally after some more name calling, they walked away.

When it was over Tommy, and I looked up Toby, and Darren, and told them what'd happened. They'd been downstairs playing pool, and they were pissed because they'd missed out on all the excitement. But they were glad to hear about Donnie finally getting his. It sure did my heart good to witness that.

One night shortly after that, my buddies and I left the Home for one of our nightly prowls through the surrounding area. When we came back, we climbed in one of the windows in the tv room.

I was the last one, and just as I was pulling myself inside, Paul Wetzel showed up at the back door of the room, and he yelled. I was startled, and just about fell back out on to the ground below.

"Hey, what the hell are you doing?"

He rushed over, and grabbed my arm, then jerked me inside. I landed on all fours, and just about hit my head on the floor. I flew into a rage and jumped to my feet.

"You son-of-a-bitch!" I screamed, "what the fuck you do that for, you bastard?"

"Don't you cuss me, you little punk," he said, and slapped me.

I turned around, and went over, and grabbed an empty chair, then threw it at him. He moved aside, and the chair clattered across the floor, and hit the back wall. Paul was startled for a moment, then he got mad.

"Gawdamm you!" He cussed, "I should kick your ass. Now, you just march yourself into Uncle Harry's office! Right now! Move it, you little jerk!"

I was sullen, and we went to see the Old Man. When Paul told him what had happened, Uncle Harry gave me a dirty look.

"You are really getting to be a real pain in the ass," he said disgustedly.

"I'm going to call your father, and see what he wants to do. We can't have this kind of behavior."

"Go ahead," I said bravely, "I don't care."

I sulked on the bench while he called my dad. I figured he'd be pissed, but if people would just leave me alone, and keep their hands off me, I wouldn't act like I did. The fact that I was in the wrong didn't occur to me at first. I just hated this place and the people in it.

But, the longer I sat there, the less angry I felt, and the more worried I got about what I'd done. I wasn't looking forward to seeing my dad. All of my bravado was slowly draining away, and I hoped my fit of rage wasn't going to cause me to be thrown in Juvenile Hall.

I shuddered when I thought about that, and I started to get scared. Dad had warned me that I could be put in there if I didn't start knocking off the bad behavior.

It was a holding facility for young offenders, and depending on how bad you screwed up, there was the possibility that you could be sent to the Hill. I sure didn't want to go there.

When my father finally showed up, he looked angry, and I braced myself. I was full of fear about what might happen to me. I really regretted what I'd done now.

"Hi dad," I said meekly, "how're you?"

"Don't give me that shit," he said gruffly, and I knew I was in trouble. "Just what the hell're you trying to prove, throwing a chair at an adult? What, you think you're tough or something?"

"No," I answered truthfully, "I didn't mean to do it. I'm sorry. I just got mad."

"That's the only answer you seem to have anymore," he said "I'm sorry, but you continue to act the same, and cause trouble and talk back to the people in charge of you."

When I didn't say anything, he looked at Uncle Harry, and asked him if there was some place private where we could be alone.

"I think it's about time he got an old fashion whipping like the one my father used to give me." He told the Old Man.

Uncle Harry said we could use the basement. As we walked there, I hoped my dad wouldn't be too rough on me. He was awful strong.

When we reached the basement, Uncle Harry unlocked the door, then left. Dad, and I stepped inside, and I was really nervous. He took off his belt, and I gulped. I wasn't looking forward to this, and I was filled with uncertainty and fear.

As far back as I could remember, my dad had never laid a finger on me in anger. When it came time for punishment in our family, my father always left it up to mom. She could be wicked with a belt.

One time when I was about six, I told my mother that she must not love me. She asked me why Id say that.

"Becuz yer always whippen me, and it hurts," I told her.

"That's because I'm doing it for your own good," she explained.

I didn't understand what she meant. I just knew it was really painful when she whipped my butt.

Of course, it wasn't like I didn't deserve to be punished. I was always getting into shit.

I remember when I was about four or five, I took a bunch of newspapers and stacked them on the middle of the linoleum floor in the kitchen of the tar paper shack we lived in. Then I set them on fire with some matches, I had found.

After I lit the papers, the flames shot up in the air, and I got scared. Billy and I were alone because mom was next door at grandma and grandpas. I ran across, and told her the house was on fire. She rushed over, and put it out. Afterwards there was a big black spot on the floor.

I can't remember if mom spanked me or not, but knowing her, she probably did.

Now it was dads turn, and he began to hit me with the belt. At first I flinched, but then I almost laughed. I could barely feel the stinging sensations.

"You know, this is hurting me more than it is you," he said, stopping for a moment, after he'd struck me four or five times.

Then I did laugh, and he gave me a dirty look.

"What the hell's so funny?" he asked.

"Shit dad," I told him. "You aint hurt'en me. I git worse beatings here all the time."

"Whatre you talking about?" he said surprised. They don't beat you here.

"The hell they don't," I retorted.

"Well, we'll go talk to Mr. Hawthorn about that," he answered with a scowl.

"That's fine with me," I told him.

We left the basement, and when we got to his office, Uncle Harry was sitting at his desk. He looked up when we came in.

"How did it go?" he asked. "Did you get him squared away?"

"We've got a problem," dad said, rather awkwardly.

"What is it?" Uncle Harry queried seeming to sense something was wrong.

"Tommy told me that he gets bad beatings here," dad answered "Is that true?"

The Old Man looked guilty at first, but then he put on an innocent face, and I realized how much I hated him.

"Why Tommy," he said. "how could you say such a thing. You know that we don't do that here."

That was such a bold faced lie, I gave out a loud snort of disgust and then dad slapped me across the chest with the back of his hand and that did hurt, unlike the belt. "Knock off the bullshit," he said. "If you get out of line again, he's got my permission to kick your ass. You keep up this shit, and I'm going to have you thrown in Juvenile Hall. You got that?"

"Yes," I told him fearfully. "I'll be good. I promise."

"Well you better think about that the next time you pull another stunt like you did tonight," he said.

"Okay, dad," I told him. And I was really serious. Anything but Juvie.

After my father left, I went to the tv room, and met up with my buddies. They were all grinning.

"Hey Tommy," Tommy said. "Way to go."

"Yea Tommy," Darren jumped in. "You should'a seen the look on Paul's face when you threw that chair at him. I thought he was gonna shit his pants.

"Yea" I had to admit it was kind of funny.

Now that it was over, I felt pretty good about what I'd done. But I was going to have to watch myself. I didn't want to wind up in the Hill.

"Where'd you go with yer dad?" Tommy asked curiously.

I told them what had happened with him, and how the Old Man

had tried to act like I didn't know what I was talking about as far as the punishment here went.

"That lying sack of shit," Tommy said "Whut a prick."

"You got that right." I told him. I vowed I'd be cool for awhile. But my vows never lasted long. One night, after that, me, and my friends were sitting outside the small courtyard fence smoking and talking. There were some lilac bushes there, and we were using them for cover. Uncle Harry's quarters were close to us, but the traffic going by made a lot of noise.

"Hey Tommy," Tommy said, "Let's play some chicken."

"Okay," I told him.

"You guys wanna try it?" Tommy asked the other two, although he pretty much knew what they'd say.

"Naw," Toby said, "you guys go ahead. We'll watch."

Our version of chicken consisted of going down to the street, and then standing on the curb, and waiting until a slow moving car came along. Then the trick was to run out, and slap the side of it with your hands, and fall down. The driver would screech to a stop, and when they got out, you'd jump up laughing, then run off.

"I always got a thrill when we did that. We didn't do it alot because it was dangerous. Fun, but dangerous. Toby and Darren were too scared to try.

Tommy and I went down to the curb, and watched. I decided to go first and cars were passing by, but they were moving too fast, so I continued to wait.

"Whuttsa matter?" Tommy asked, "you gitten yellow?"

"Hell no," I told him, "I'm just waiten for a good one."

Finally, I spotted a slow moving car coming towards us, and I steeled myself. Then hoping I had the timing right, I took off and as the vehicle started to pass by, I reached out and slapped the side of it, and fell down.

The driver slammed on his brakes, and stopped. Then he started to get out.

He was an old guy, and when I jumped up, and joined Tommy, we ran off laughing, and hid behind the lilac bushes.

The driver cussed at us, then got back in his car, and drove off Tommy and I grinned at each other.

"Man, he was pissed," Tommy said.

"Yea, he was," I agreed.

"Man, you fucken guys are crazy," Darren told us, and Toby echoed his sentiment.

"You guys should try it," I told them, "It's fun."

"No thanks," Darren replied, "I wanna die a ripe, old age."

"Chicken's," Tommy said.

"Yea, well" Toby answered, "I'd rather be alive than splattered all over the street."

"Aah," I replied bravely, then looked at Tommy, "well, let's go see if we can find you a good one."

We sauntered back down to the curb, and began to look for another slow driver. There were a lot of cars to choose from, but most were going along at a pretty good clip, and we waited patiently.

Finally, an old Hudson approached us at a fairly low speed, and it was being driven by a lady who looked to be in her fifties. There was another woman in the car with her, and they were engaged in conversation.

They were a perfect target for our stunt, but there was only one problem. The car was coming from the opposite direction, and Tommy would have to cross the lane closest to us. We checked to make sure there was not traffic coming that way, and seeing no one, he took off running towards the car.

After that, it seemed like everything just became a blur. The woman driving, didn't see Tommy, but her friend did, and she yelled. The driver was so unnerved that she hit the gas instead of the brakes, and they whizzed past my friend.

Tommy in the meantime, tried to slap the car but he missed and stumbled, almost falling down in her lane.

Meanwhile a pickup being driven by a guy, who looked to be in his twenties had turned the corner in the lane and he started to speed up, suddenly he saw Tommy ahead of him, and he hit his horn, and brakes which really caused his tires to screech.

Tommy saw him coming but he froze before he could jump out of the way. The truck skidded, before he could stop, and it hit Tommy who went on up on the hood, and almost landed against the windshield.

Then the pickup finally came to an abrupt halt and Tommy slid back down and hit the pavement in a heap. The driver just sat there stunned.

I was horrified and my heart was in my throat. I started to run across the street to him, when suddenly, Tommy jumped to his feet, and ran back towards me. He wasn't watching and luckily there weren't any cars coming from the other direction.

I did see that the ladies in the Hudson had stopped, and then Tommy pushed past me. The guy in the pick up was yelling something at us, but we ignored him, I thought Tommy would stop at the bushes, but he kept going, and passed between the fence, and Pam's house.

We ran until we got to the big entrance to the Home and then he slowed down and I caught up to him.

"Jeezus Tommy!" I told him. "I thought you was dead! Are you okay?"

"Yea," he said shakily. "I think so."

We didn't speak again until we had snuck back in the Home, and gone into the washroom. Tommy checked himself out, but aside from some small cuts and abrasions he seemed to be okay.

"Hey Tommy," he said. "Ive got an idea."

"Whut?" I asked.

"Let's don't ever do that again," he answered.

"Yea," I said "I think that's a good idea."

Darren and Toby came in right after that, and they looked shook up.

"Man" Darren said. "Like I said you guys are fucken crazy to do that kind of shit."

"You got that right," Toby added. "and stupid too."

Tommy, and I never did try it again the rest of the time. I was in the Home. It was too painful a reminder of Ronny.

During that time, Buck finally left the Home. He was going to get married, and try to raise a family.

Now that he was leaving, I was almost going to miss him. Even though he was a mean SOB, one thing you could say about him was that he was fair. When he meted out punishment, it was usually deserved.

The day he left, Tommy and I told him goodbye, and he smiled. I was surprised, because he'd never done that before.

"You kids take care," he said. "Especially you Janicak. You'd better work on that temper of yours before you really got in to some serious trouble."

"I will," I told him, but I always said that after I'd gone off on somebody, I kept up the same old attitude and nothing ever changed."

After he left, Uncle Harry hired a man named Herman Reinhardt. If ever anyone was unlike their name, it was him. He was as tall as Buck, but he had the build of a basketball player, which I learned he'd been in high school. Herman was rugged-looking, and like Buck, we found out he didn't take shit from anyone.

He had brown hair, and eyes, and he wore glasses. Despite his outward appearance, he was very friendly, and seemed interested in us. I liked him right away.

I engaged him in conversation and I found out that like me, he was fond of the mountains also. I told him all about the camp and the neat places like Queens Chair, and the beautiful setting upon which the fort sat and of course about the mountain and the plane and the tailgunner who survived, and how badly I wanted to find it.

"That would really be cool," I told him enthusiastically.

"Yea it sounds pretty interesting," he replied.

After talking to Herman, I could hardly wait for the day of the hike to be upon us. Maybe with his help, we could find the hiding place of the plane.

Going to the tutoring school paid off, and I graduated to the eighth grade. My father was pleased, and I felt pretty good about it. Maybe I wasn't so dumb after all.

When school let out, Donnie Abernathy left, which really did my heart good. At last, I wouldn't have to look at his smirking face, and put up with, or listen to the garbage coming out of his mouth.

With Donnie gone, and a new counselor who seemed like he was nice enough, maybe this would be a good summer.

I just hoped Herman wasn't going to turn out to be like that crud Greenie. I didn't really trust male adults. Especially the ones who acted friendly past experience had shown me that was a bad sign.

I prayed it wasn't going to be that way with Herman. Only time would tell.

Part

10

Herman Rhinehardt helped make the summer of 1957, the most memorable, and enjoyable one of them all. My putting him in the same class as Greenie turned out to be a joke. He was all man. Herman was a natural storyteller, and he filled our heads with stories of King Arthur, and The Knights of The Round Table. I could listen to him all day, and night.

Elmer Lehr had moved on, and I missed his scary act, but Herman made up for it by telling us ghost stories around the bonfires on Sunday nights, which gave us goosebumps. Especially me, because of my experience with the spooky visitor in the sick room.

Although he was an adult, Herman had a boyish enthusiasm for life. I really liked him, and followed him around, becoming some thing of a pest, but he didn't seem to mind. He was a nice guy, and I trusted him.

When I first told him about Indian Trail, and the forts up there, he said he'd like to see it. I thought it was pretty neat that an adult was going to visit the place. None of the other counselors had ever done that.

Herman strolled along with us, and when we reached the end of the trail, we found out someone had wrecked the fort, which wasn't unusual. I asked him what he thought of the setting.

"It's an awful pretty spot," he said. "It'll take some work, but we'll find some more poles, and put it back together even better than before."

"We can't," I told him. "Especially the little guys."

"Why's that?" he asked.

When I told him that the older boys considered it their domain, and didn't like for the younger kids to come up here, he just laughed.

"Well they're wrong," he said. "There's plenty of room here for everyone, and they're just going to have to learn to share."

We began to build some forts, and about that time, here came some of the older guys; Jake, and Ray, and Scott among them. You could tell they were pissed, but with Herman there, they didn't try anything.

He invited them to join us in building some forts, but they declined, and took off. I was kind of worried, because I wondered what they'd do when Herman wasn't around.

But they didn't bother us, and instead, built some forts on the hills around us. We called them "Hill People."

In the meantime, most of the little guys joined in helping, and with all of the teepee forts, we named it Indian Village.

Herman said we should build a fence around it to protect ourselves from our enemies. We set about doing that, and it really looked neat when we were done.

The best part of it though, was when Herman, and I built a treehouse in the middle of the compound. There were three, tall aspens grouped together, and we started out by building a ladder. Using short lengths of wood, we tied them onto two of the trees with wire. When we were up about fifteen feet, we built a three sided platform with a railing. After we had finished it, you could see a long way down the trail. I really felt good about what we'd done. I'd never been a part of something that cool.

We got caught up in Herman's tales about Sir Galahad, The Castles and Dragons, and battles from long ago, and I really enjoyed our little pretend world. For the first time in quite a while, I felt like a young child again. I'd been working so hard at becoming a big guy, I'd lost sight of what I actually was. Which happened to be a big, fourteen year old kid. It was nice to just let go, and float away on a cloud of fantasy. I didn't want the summer to end.

We began to carry around long sticks like swords, and we'd engage each other in mock combat like the Knights had.

Sometimes, the Hill People would come down, and attack us, and we'd have sword fights. The idea was to break your opponent's sword in two. Once that happened, you were declared "dead," and could fight no more.

We weren't supposed to hit each other, but accidents did happen and guys got bumps, and bruises, and sometimes fights broke out. But, for the most part, it was pretty harmless.

We out numbered the Hill People, but most of them were older than us, and so they always won the battles. But they never wrecked our village, or tried to run us out of there. All because of Herman, naturally.

Even though we always lost, it was still fun. Especially if I came across Ray, or Scott. I'd single them out, and really goat them, and they'd take off in the opposite direction. I always got a chuckle out of that. I was the oldest guy in our group.

But it wasn't so funny when Jake showed up, or was with them. Then I was the one who ran or hid.

Herman noticed this, and finally, one day, he asked me what the problem was, and I told him how mean Jake was. And how hard he could hit, and that he scared me.

He smiled when I was done talking, and I wondered what was so dammed funny. I didn't see any humor in the situation.

"From what I've heard, you're a pretty, good fighter yourself," he said. "You should stand up to him."

"Naw," I told him. "He'd beat the shit outta me."

"Oh, I don't know about that," he said. "I don't want you kids fighting, but if it came to that, I could show you how to defend yourself against him. Even beat the pants off his funny ass."

"Could'ja really?" I asked him excitedly.

"Sure," he answered. "I can show you how to box. I used to do that when I was a kid."

"Did'ja really?" I questioned. "Did'ja beat up a lot of guys?"

"Oh, I fought in the Golden Gloves when I was seventeen, and I was the Novice Middleweight Champ," he told me matter of factly.

I was impressed. I didn't know what Novice meant, but I knew what a champion was. Like Rocky Marciano.

"Could'ja teach me now?" I asked.

"Sure," he said. "Okay. Show me your fighting stance."

I gave him my best impression of how I thought a boxer would pose, and he looked me over for a moment, and then told me to move my left foot forward, and crouch down a bit. Then he moved my arms around until he was satisfied. Then he told me to throw some left jabs.

Tentatively, I threw a few, and he stopped me.

"When you throw a jab," he said. "Snap it out there. You want to keep the other guy off of you. And after you throw one, bring it straight back. You don't want to let him have a clean shot at you. So you need to protect yourself with your gloves at all times."

I continued to do as he said, and then he told me to move around, and not stand in one spot. I did that for a while, and after I felt a little better, he stopped me.

"Okay," he said. "Now, I want you to throw some combinations."

He held up his hands with his palms to me, and told me to throw some lefts, and rights at his outstretched arms. I did so, and then he stopped me, and showed me how to do it correctly.

"When you throw a right hand after a jab," Herman said, "put your shoulder into it, then follow that up until you're back in your fighting stance. And remember to move around so that you don't become a sitting duck. And try to keep your hands up for protection."

I did as I was being told, and some of the guys were watching, and now they joined in, looking like a bunch of crippled kangaroos as they danced around, flailing their arms.

Herman told me to practice doing that every day, and the next time Jake tried to get physical with me, boy would he get a surprise.

I didn't share in his confidence, but I did continue to practice. I liked the fact that I could fight, even if I was too chicken to mix it up with guys like Jake. But at least I could take jerks like Ray, and Scott.

That's when Herman decided to put on a boxing tournament. He came up with some old boxing gloves, a scale, and then he encouraged us to sign up. Especially me. I let him talk me into it.

When he weighed me, I was surprised at how heavy I was, and so was he. (I came in at one hundred forty-five). I found out I was going to be in the Welter Weight Division (140-147 pounds). Jake, and Ray were just over the limit, but Herman included them in our division, because they were the only Middleweights.

Scott just barely made 140. There were two light-heavies, Bill Snodgrass, and Dave Geist, but they wouldn't fight each other.

As soon as I found out Jake was going to be in my weight class, I wanted to quit, and Herman was disgusted with me. I didn't like that, but I was fearful.

"What are you concerned about? If it comes down that you're going to face him, you just do like I taught you, and I think you'll be surprised. Don't let him beat you before you even get in the ring with him," he said.

His words failed to make me feel any better, but I decided to stay out of respect for him. But I vowed that if I had to fight Jake, I was going to fall down the first time he started hitting me, and that's where I was going to stay. I knew that was the coward's way out, but I didn't care.

The fights started, and Scott got knocked out by a kid named Bobby Grassell. (I think he just laid down, like I was going to do with Jake).

Billy joined up, and he won his first bout. I was impressed. I'd never seen him fight before, and he seemed to have as hard a punch as I did, and I was proud of him.

Toby went out, but he got his ass kicked, and I felt bad for him. But at least he tried. Which was more than I was going to do if I had to go up against Jake. I was relieved to find out that my first opponent was going to be Ray, and I could hardly wait to get my hands on him.

He acted like he wasn't concerned, but I knew better. It was going to be nice to beat him up without having to worry about Jake.

When it came time to fight him, I forgot all the things that Herman had taught me, and just wildly pounded on Pay, who kept going out of bounds.

Finally, in the second round, Herman stopped it, because Ray just wouldn't fight back, and I was declared the winner.

Afterwards, I felt pretty good, but then I saw Jake with Ray, and he gave me one of those cold, hard looks of his, and I gulped nervously. I didn't know what I was going to do if I had to face him. Well, actually I did, but I didn't want to think about it, because it made me feel like such a chickenshit.

Jake won his first bout by stopping a sixteen year old guy named George Kelso, which I thought was impressive.

There were only six of us in our weight class, and I had to fight a second time, while Jake drew a bye. He would fight the winner of my bout for the Welter Weight crown.

My opponent was Bobby Grassell, who had stopped Scott. He was freckled faced, red headed, and a little older. Like most of the guys, he had a lot of contempt for me, and liked to call me Pissass. I was nervous about fighting him, because I knew if I won, I was going to have to face Jake.

But I figured Bobby could take me anyway, judging from the way he had beaten Scott.

He'd called me out several times in the past, but I'd always backed down. Now, I was going to have to step into the ring with him. But I wasn't worried about it. I was planning on letting him win anyway, by taking a dive.

But when we squared off, Bobby had this smirk on his face, and after he landed a couple of hard punches that really smarted, I decided that the hell with it. I was going to fight back, I'd worry about Jake later. Right now, I just wanted to wipe the wise-ass look off this guy's face.

I had backed up when Bobby hit me, and now, when he got within range, I punched him a couple of times. He stopped, and looked confused, then pissed, and then he ran at me, arms swinging away, but I avoided him. Then I stopped, and hit him again.

I continued to do that kind of thing throughout the rest of the bout, and although Bobby put up a decent fight, I was declared the winner. At first I felt good because I'd beaten up another jerk who'd tormented me in the past.

But then came the realization; What had I done? I must've been crazy. Now I was going to have to face Jake, and I shuddered.

Herman praised me on my bout with Bobby, but I told him that I wished I hadn't won because now that meant I was going to have to fight Jake.

"Just let him be champ," I told him. "I don't wanna get in the ring with him."

He sighed, and shook his head.

"I don't know about you," he said. "Jake's already won before the fight's even started. You've all but given up. Hell, anybody can quit. That's easy. The winners keep going."

"Yea, but he's tougher than me," I argued.

"Hey," he said. "Give yourself some credit. You just fight him the way I taught you, and you'll be amazed at what you can accomplish. You're just as good as he is."

I doubted that. Despite his efforts to bolster my self-confidence, I was dreading the upcoming bout, and I was trying to think up excuses to get out of it. But aside from jumping off a cliff, and breaking a leg, or stepping in a hole, and spraining my ankle, I was stuck. But at least I still had my original plan to fall back on, even though it was shameful.

And that was to go down, and just stay down.

Better to be a live chicken, than a dead one.

The bouts were being held once a week, so I had plenty of time to stew about the upcoming fiasco.

The day of the championship bouts arrived, and I stood around anxiously and watched the other fights, and waited for mine to begin.

The only thing that made me feel good was watching Billy fight, and I cheered him on and saw him win and be crowned Featherweight Champion. But afterwards, it was back to worrying about my confrontation with Jake. I was dry-mouthed, and scared to death.

I was with Tommy, Darren, and Toby, and they were really trying to pump me up, and be supportive, but all that did was make me feel bad. They wanted to see me do well, and all I was planning on doing was going through with my cowardly act.

Jake, and his company, were standing nearby, and I kept my eyes off of him. I just wanted to call it quits now. Fuck it.

Then it was time for our bout.

I nervously walked into the ring, and Tommy helped me put on my boxing gloves – the insides of which were damp with the sweat of the other guys who had fought before.

"Our ring" was nothing more than deep lines drawn in the dirt. If you stepped over, or were knocked over them, the referee – in this case, Herman, would stop the action, and have you start over in the middle of the ring.

He, and Uncle Harry, and Paul were the judges, with Paul the timekeeper, and there were three, two minute rounds.

As I stood there, staring across at Jake, who was talking to Ray, and Scott, there was a knot of fear in my stomach. I wanted to take off my gloves, and walk away into the hills behind the camp. I'd have given anything to be anywhere but here. Why had I let Herman talk me into this? Now it was too late to back out.

Herman walked into the middle of the ring, and motioned us to him. I was shaking, and felt weak in the knees as I joined him, and Jake. I looked down at the ground.

"Okay guys," Herman said. "This is for all the marbles, so let's put on a good fight. Now, touch gloves, and may the best man win."

Jake hit my gloves, and then we went back to our corners. I was really afraid now.

Paul told us to start, and warily, I came out. Jake wasted no time, and rushed at me, and started throwing punches. I covered up, and backed away, as he followed doing his best to knock my head loose from my shoulders. But, all he was able to hit were my gloves, and forearms.

Jake finally drove me out of bounds, and Herman stopped the action, and had us start over in the middle of the ring. Again Jake rushed me, and again I covered my head, and avoided him as he stalked me around the square, and did my best to keep from getting hit.

I didn't even try to throw any punches, and I know I must've looked pretty pathetic, as for the second time, Jake drove me out of bounds. Guys were starting to boo me, but I didn't care. Let them get in here with him. I was just trying to survive.

Before the first round ended, I'd been driven out of the ring a couple of more times, and when I went back to my corner after it was over, Herman walked up to me. I couldn't look him in the eye.

"Come on Tommy," he said. "What are you doing out there? You didn't throw one punch. You can do better than that, and you know it. If you don't start fighting back, I'm going to stop the bout. You don't want that do you?"

"No." I really meant that. I just didn't want to get hurt.

"Well you better start boxing or else," he said. "Okay?"

"Yea," I replied uncertainly.

I decided I'd at least try to put up some semblance of a fight, and hopefully I wouldn't get hit too hard in return. I didn't want to look like a complete pansy-ass. I could fight. It was just a matter of getting up enough courage to do it against this guy.

When the second round started, I came out cautiously, and of course Jake rushed me, and threw punches, and I in return, backed up as usual.

But, this time, instead of covering my head with my gloves to protect myself, I stopped, and stuck my left hand out, which caught Jake right in the mouth. That stopped him dead in his tracks, and we both stood there, frozen for a moment.

The shocked look on his face was gratifying, and it really felt great.

But then, I got scared because his mean features turned even more menacing, and he came at me, throwing haymakers furiously. I retreated, and a couple of them landed on my shoulders, and I wound up going out of bounds again.

But I could hear my buddies cheering, and that helped boost my confidence a little. At least I'd hit him, and been able to get away without being hurt in return.

When we started over again, I repeated what I'd done before, and there was that moment of pleasure on my part, and consternation on his. I backed away, and he followed, throwing punches like before.

Only this time when I tried to excape, he was able to land a hard blow which made the stars square dance around in my head.

But I didn't let that stop me, and I was able to land some more punches before the round ended. Jake landed a few on me too, but aside from that one punch, they didn't hurt that bad, and I managed to stay out of trouble.

This time, when I went back to my corner, my buddies were really happy, and they were telling me what a great job I was doing. I felt pretty good about it too, especially when Herman came up to me with a grin on his face.

"Damn Tommy," he said. "Did you see the way he looked when you hit him?"

"Yea." I'd really liked that.

"Okay, now you need to put some combinations together," he told me. "Don't be afraid to throw your right hand at him. Just remember to follow it up with a left, so that your back in position. Got all that?"

"Yea."

"And keep your hands up to protect yourself at all time," he reminded me. "Okay?"

"Yea." I'd give it a try anyway. It was hard to think about all that with things happening so fast.

When the final round started, I came out of my corner, expecting Jake to attack me like he had before, but instead, when he got close, he seemed a little wary, and we circled each other at first.

"Hey!" I thought. "He's actually worried about me hitting him again."

That really boosted my confidence, and I flicked a jab out at him which missed, and he stepped in, and caught my cheek with his right glove and it hurt.

I instantly backed away, and covered up, and he followed, trying to catch me again. I managed to avoid getting hit, and then I stopped, and caught him with another left, but this time I followed it up with a right hand that landed squarely on his nose. Then I threw my left behind it, and hit him for the third time in a row.

He backed off when I did that, and his eyes were watering, and then a trickle of blood began to flow from one of his nostrils. I pressed my advantage, and took after him, trying to land some more blows. I drove him out of bounds for once, and when Herman had us start over in the middle of the ring, I thought to myself: "Hey! I can take this guy!"

I decided to throw caution to the wind, and slug it out with him, which wasn't a very good idea. I did pretty well at first, but then he rocked me with a couple of good punches, and I decided discretion was the better part of valor, and went back to what had worked before, and I managed to stay out of trouble for the rest of the fight.

When it ended, I walked back to my corner, and Tommy and the guys were really happy, and they slapped me on the back. I was panting heavily.

"Allright Tommy," Tommy said. "You held yer own, and bloodied his fucken nose. That was really cool. I told'ja you could do it."

"Yea," Darren told me. "Jake found out he's not as tough as he thought he was."

"Thanks," I told them breathlessly.

Tommy helped me take off my gloves, and then we waited for the adults to pick the winner. I already knew it wouldn't be me, but that was okay. At least, I'd put up a fight, and landed some good punches.

Finally, we were called to the middle of the ring, and of course Jake's arm was raised in victory. Herman shook my hand afterwards.

"I'm proud of you Tommy," he said. "You really did well."

"Whutta ya mean?" I told him. "I lost, didn't I?"

"Yea," he said. "But if you'd fought him at first, like I taught you, you'd have probably whipped him."

"Yea." He may've been right. I could've made it closer anyway.

"Why don't you go shake hands with him?" He said. "See what he has to say."

My friends, and I walked over to where Jake was talking to his buddies and he was dabbing at his nose with a handkerchief. When I stuck out my hand, he slowly shook it, and there was a hint of respect in his eyes, and that was nice.

"Congratulations champ," I told him. "Good fight."

"Thanks," he said, and I looked at his bloody nose.

"You better go wash up," I told him, trying not to sound flippant.

"Ahh, this is nuthen," he said. "My nose bleeds real easy."

"Well, anyway, congratulations," I repeated.

He, and his friends walked away, and Tommy gave me a pained look.

"Congratulations champ," he mocked. "Fuck him. If you'd have fought back with him from the start, you'd have won."

"That's whut Herman said," I answered. "But I dunno about that. He caught me with some pretty good punches even after I started fighten back."

Despite the loss though, I still felt pretty good about myself. I'd put up a pretty decent fight, and the nicest thing was, I didn't have to fear him anymore. He knew that I could hold my own against him, and that was comforting.

I was finally beginning to feel like a big guy.

Unfortunately, that good feeling didn't last very long.

One day, not long after that, Billy, and I got into it, and I wound up slugging him. We were in the big bunkhouse when this happened, and as I went out the door, he was crying.

It happened just before supper, and as I headed towards the washroom to clean up, I began to feel bad about hitting him. That was something that happened once in awhile, and I always regretted it. Billy was a good kid.

Whenever I apologized to him afterwards, he never seemed to accept it. Or at least that was the impression I always got. We didn't talk a lot so I never knew for sure. But I still planned on telling him I was sorry.

When I got to the washroom, Tommy, and Darren, and Toby were there. We were talking, when suddenly, I saw Jake, and his gang come out of the bunkhouse, and start to walk in our direction.

I began to get nervous because I knew that Jake liked my brother and I hoped he didn't know that I'd hit him. But judging from the mean look on his face, he did, and as he walked up to me, I felt that old, familiar fear of him take over my senses.

"Why'd you hit Billy?" he asked harshly.

"I'm sorry Jake," I told him fearfully. "I didn't mean to. Honest."

He didn't say anything, but hauled off, and punched me twice, and my head exploded in pain with each one. I put my arms up to protect myself, and when I did, he hit me right in the pit of my stomach. It really hurt, and all the wind went out of me, and I sagged to the floor, gasping for air.

Jake turned around, and left, and Ray came up with Scott, and stood over me.

"How'd ya like that Pissass?" he sneered. "You ain't gotcher buddy Herman here to protect ya now."

Then he, and Scott walked out, and Tommy came over, and helped me to my feet. I leaned against the sink, and tried to get my breath back.

"That son-of-a-bitch!" Tommy said. "Why didn't cha hit him back?"

"I dunno," I told him miserably.

Now it was back to the same old shit. Always have to watch myself around him. And of course, putting up with Ray, and Scott.

I never told Herman about my run-in with Jake.

The lazy, idyllic summer began to flow by, and before I knew it, August was upon us. Thoughts of finding the Plane started to run through my mind, and I was really looking forward to the hike this year simply because of Herman. I had a feeling that with his help, we could find it.

One day, my friends, and I, along with Billy, and Benny, were sitting around on Crow's Nest, and we were talking about the upcoming climb. And the plane.

"I wonder why nobody is found it in such a long time?" Toby asked.

"I dunno," I answered. "Wherever it is, it's hidden purty good. Last summer, we didn't have much time to look because of a storm, but if it's nice this year, maybe Herman will let us search for awhile."

"I bet I can find it," Billy said confidently.

"Yea, right," I told him. "That's whut I thought when I was up there last time. When you reach the top, you'll understand. There's a lot of ground to cover."

Despite my words, I hoped Billy was right. I was still determined to find it. Last year's failure hadn't lessened my resolve at all.

"Maybe we'll git lucky," Tommy said, "and find it this year."

"Yea, and maybe if we do," I told him, "there'll be enough of it left so we can git inside, and see where the tailgunner sat! And maybe the machine gun will still be there!"

As we talked excitedly, Darren said something that brought our conversation to an abrupt halt.

"Maybe the reason nobody's been able to find this plane wreck, is cuz it ain't up there," he spoke out.

After a moment of shocked silence, I jumped in angrily.

"Whut?" I retorted. "Whut the fuck're you talken about? Of course there is! Too many guys have said there is!"

"Hey!" he said. "I'm not tryen to piss you off. All I'm sayen is, whut if there ain't? Maybe somebody made it up."

"Yer full of shit!" I told him. "It's up there!"

"Hey," he said. "I hope I'm wrong. I'd like to find it too."

"Well!" I said. "Take my word for it, yer wrong!"

I wanted to believe that, but now Darren had planted a seed of doubt in my mind, and that really made me angry. Damm him anyway. I wished he'd have kept his mouth shut. I'd dreamt about finding the plane for too long, and I didn't want to have it snatched away from me now.

I mulled about it, and then I had an idea. If there was one person who'd know about the plane, it would be Uncle Harry. At least, I was pretty sure, he would. As much as I disliked him, I was going to ask the Old Man.

That night, after supper, I walked up to the table where he, and the counselors sat in the chow hall. He looked at me curiously.

"What is it?" he asked.

"Uncle Harry," I said. "Is there really a plane wreck on Mt. Baldwin?"

"Yes there is," he told me." A B-17 crashed there in the winter of 1944. We read about it in the press."

I breathed a sigh of relief, and I was glad that I'd decided to talk to him. That stupid Shunkwiler. What a bozo.

"Has anyone from the camp ever found it?" I asked.

"Yes," he said. "But it's been quite awhile since that happened."

"Well, thanks Uncle Harry," I told him, and turned to go, but he spoke, and I stopped.

"I'd like to compliment you on your change of attitude," he said. "I know Herman's played a big part in that. Keep it up."

I really didn't know what to say. We'd never gotten along, and this was the first positive thing he'd ever said to me.

"Thanks," I told him, and walked away.

When I met up with the guys, I told them what the Old Man had said about the plane. That got them worked up, and Tommy turned to Darren.

"See," he gloated. "Whut'd we tell ya?"

"Yea, I was wrong," Darren admitted. "Now all we gotta do is find it."

About that, he was right.

That night, after lights out, I lay there thinking about the plane. I was glad that I'd talked to Uncle Harry. It really was up there, and now like Darren had said, it was up to us to find it. I wished with all my might, that we'd be successful.

Not long after that, I had an experience that really upset me.

One day, we were up at Indian Village, and I got into an argument with a twelve year old kid named Cecil Becker, and he called me Pissass. I hauled off, and slugged him, and he fell to the ground, then jumped up, and began to call me names.

I was going to hit him again, but he turned around, and took off running. I started after him, but suddenly Herman appeared, and he grabbed my arm. It really hurt, and I struggled to break free, but his grip was strong, and I began to cuss in anger.

"Gawdamm you!" I screamed. "Let go of my fucken arm, you son-of-a-bitch!"

Herman did, and then slapped me hard across the face, and a bright, flash of pain rattled my senses.

I cried out, and then hurriedly took off down Indian Trail. My eyes were filled with tears, and I was having a hard time dealing with what had just happened. I was almost in shock.

Just before I got to the Old Mill Pond, I left the trail, and went over to

Queen's Chair, and climbed up on the rocks. Then I sat in the hole there, and stared down at the water below.

I couldn't believe that Herman had slapped me. We were supposed to be friends. He was the last one I thought would do something like that to me.

But the more I went over it, the more I knew that I'd been wrong. Even though Cecil had called me that hated name, I was bigger than he was. I shouldn't have hit him.

And I couldn't blame Herman for slapping me. I'd deserved it.

A wave of self-pity came over me, and I felt sad. No wonder, people were always on my case. I was a pain in the rearend.

Now I'd fucked up the best thing to come along in awhile. I wished I was dead. Nobody'd give a shit anyway.

I sat there for awhile, feeling sorry for myself.

Finally though, I snapped out of it, and I climbed down, and went back up the trail to our village, and faced Herman. I felt remorseful, and full of regret.

"I'm sorry Herman," I told him. "I didn't mean to swear at you."

"That's okay Tommy," he said. "You just need to curb that temper of yours."

"I know it, I will," I answered, and as usual, I meant it. Until something set me off again.

"You need to think before you act," he said. "or else you're going to continue to have problems."

"Yea," I told him. "I just don't like being called Pissass."

"Oh, it's just a word," he said. "Words can't hurt you unless you let them."

"Yea," I'd never get used to being called by that name.

"I'm sorry that I slapped you," he said. "but you were way out of line especially with Cecil."

"I know I deserved it," I told him.

"Well, you need to go apologize to him," he said. "In the meantime, we still friends?"

"You bet," I told him happily.

He stuck out his hand and we shook, and that really lifted my spirits.

I looked up Cecil, and told him I was sorry, and he was okay with it.

I felt better after that. The nicest thing was that I was in Herman's good graces again, and things returned to normal.

Then that very next week, the day of the climb finally came, and that morning Tommy and I, along with Darren, Toby, and Billy, and Benny, stood around the bus, and talked. My brother, and our friends were really pumped up. Just like Tommy, and I had been the year before.

It was a beautiful, sunny day, and I turned to Tommy.

"I sure hope we don't run into any thunderstorm this time," I told him.

"Yea, really," he replied.

"Oh man," Toby said fearfully. "Don't even mention that word."

"We almost got hit by a bolt of lightning last year," I said. "It knocked me on my ass."

"Shit!" he said. "I wish you wouldn't have said that."

Toby was scared of the storms, as were all of us. But his fear was almost comical. Whenever there was a loud clap of thunder, he would jump, and cringe, and we would laugh at him. But it really wasn't all that funny.

After we loaded up, and headed out, I looked up at the Mountain, and hoped it wouldn't rain on us, and spoil our chances of looking for the plane. The sky was bright blue, and cloudless; but I knew how quickly that could change. Maybe we'd catch a break this time, and that wouldn't happen.

After being let out of the bus, we set off on the seemingly, endless hike up to the Mountain. The trail began to lead us on the wooded rollercoaster of hills, and glades. The only time we stopped the ride was to take a leak, and then we'd continue on.

We talked, and joked, and that helped to relieve the boredom. I'd forgotten about how much time, and effort it took to reach the top of the mountain.

"Whut's it look like when you git up there?" Toby asked.

"It's really somethen," I told him. "Wait'll ya git a load of the view."

"I'd sure like to see that plane wreck," he responded wistfully.

"Hey Tommy," Darren said. "I wonder if those other guys who found it took all the machine guns."

"Man," I told him. "Let's hope not. That'd be a drag."

As we toiled long, I kept an eye on the sky to see if any clouds were building up like they'd done previously, but there wasn't any in sight, except for a few smudges here, and there. And that was good.

I had a feeling we were going to find it this year, although I'd pretty much felt this same way last August. But this time was different. I don't know if it was because of Herman or what, but I could hardly contain myself. I was in a hurry to reach the top.

We trudged along through most of the morning, until finally, we reached the place where the trees, and the huge round mound of rocks began. There were some lightning scarred trees, here, and there, and I pointed one out to Toby.

"Hey Toby," I said. "How'd you like to've been under that tree when it got hit?"

"Oh fuck you," he told me. "That ain't funny."

We started to make our way up the boulders, and I kept my eye out for hidden snow. I was hoping that Darren, Toby, Billy, and Benny wouldn't see any before Tommy, and I did.

Finally, I spotted a patch in the darkened cranny of a rock, and I bent down, made a snowball, then flung it at Darren who was ahead of me. It struck him in the back, and he jumped, and turned around, just as I'd done last year when Jimmy Marcus had hit me with one.

"Hey! Whut the fuck!" he yelled, and felt his back. "Where the hell'd you git that?"

"Right here," I told him, and bent over, and made another one which I threw at Toby, who ducked.

Tommy, in the meantime, found some, and he pegged one at Billy. At first, we were using them for target practice, but after searching around, they got their own, and then it became a real melee with us ducking, and dodging, and laughing all the while.

Then I threw one at Billy, and it hit him right in the face, and he turned away in pain, holding his cheek. I really felt bad, and I ran across to where he was standing.

"Are you okay?" I asked, concerned.

"Yea," he said, staring at me with a blank expression, rubbing the side of his face.

"Im sorry." I told him. "I didn't mean to hit you in the head."

"That's okay," he said. "I'll live."

"Oh. Okay then," I told him, and started back over to where I'd been.

Suddenly, a snowball hit me right in the back of the head, and it burnt. I turned around, and Billy was giving me a shit eating grin. I started to chase him, but he got away before I could retaliate.

Finally we stopped, because the guys ahead of us were out of sight, and we figured we'd better move on. We started out again, going over one rock after the other which really became monotonous.

"Jeezus," Darren said. "There must be fifty billion rocks up here."

"Yea," I told him. "It takes a while to git there. You just hafta take yer time."

I felt like a seasoned veteran even though I'd only been up here once.

We continued to climb, and Darren continued to bitch. Even Toby seemed irked. But Billy was his usual patient self.

Finally though, the rocks did end, and we reached the summit. Darren, Toby, Billy, and Benny couldn't get over how flat it was.

"Yea," I told them. "You'd never guess that when ya look at it from below."

We saw Herman, and the other guys standing around the rock pile signing the book, and we joined them. After we'd done that, I saw Herman taking in the scenery from the edge of the Mountain opposite that of the camp. I didn't look from this vantage point the year before.

Maybe the wreckage of the plane was on that side, and I rushed over to join him.

When I did, and looked down, everything was almost a carbon-copy of the other side, except there were no more mountains, just hills. There was nothing to be seen, but rocks, trees, and more trees. No sign of a plane wreck though.

But despite that, the blue-green scenery was gorgeous to look at.

"Isn't it purty up here?" I told him.

"It really is," he agreed.

"Hey Herman!" I exclaimed. "Look! You can see the city from here!"

"Yea," he said. "You sure can."

Below the Mountain, the beryl colored foothills began to unfurl downward, until they merged with the mottled flatlands. On the edge of the horizon, through a veil of bluish haze, you could just see the outline of the city.

Several of the kids joined us, and we all gazed at the view.

Then we went back to the rock pile, where Herman had his knapsack. He doled out our lunches, and we sat, and ate, and talked.

The wind was blowing pretty good, and I glanced around, but there was hardly a cloud in the sky. I looked over at Tommy.

"It looks like we're gonna git lucky this year," I told him. "No fucken rain."

"Yea," he said. "Maybe Herman'll let us go explore for awhile."

After we were done eating, my friends, and I walked up to the edge of the Mountain, overlooking the Camp, and took it all in. a few other guys wandered over also.

The surrounding terrain was bathed in bright sunlight. Last year, I had thought the view was spectacular, but this time there was no comparison.

The valley was etched in verying shades of deep dark, and lightgreens and the river glittered like a tiny, swirling chain of diamonds. The hills, and smaller mountains around us began to take on a lovely shade of misty blue, as they receded into the distant reaches of the landscape. It was breathtakingly beautiful.

"I wonder where the Camp is?" Toby asked, peering down.

"Shit," I told him. "You can't see it from here. We're too far away."

"Man," Darren said irked. "Look at all these fucken trees. No wonder it's so hard to find that plane."

"You got that right." I replied, then turned to Billy. "Well, you still think you can tell where it is?"

He shrugged his shoulders, and I smiled. Now he knew how I felt last year when I'd been so sure we could spot the wreckage. It wasn't going to be that easy.

I was thinking about asking Herman if he'd let us go down into the trees surrounding the mountain, and let us look for the Plane for a while.

That way, when he and the other guys were ready to go, all they had to do was join us when they came down off the top.

Suddenly, I saw something out of the corner of my eye, and when I looked, I felt a tingling sensation go up my spine.

I'd seen some Western movies where the Indians would signal one another with mirrors whenever the calvary was approaching. The blinking lights could be seen for several miles.

Now, there off to the side, and down in the trees below the nearest peak, was something that was shining steadily in the sun at us. Something made of metal.

"Hey! Hey!" I hollered excitedly. "Look! Look over there!" There's the plane!"

"Where?" Toby said, looking around wildly. "Where?"

"Right there!" I said pointing.

"Jeezus Tommy!" Tommy yelled. "We've finally found it! We've found it!"

We were beside ourselves, and some of the other guys came over to see what all the fuss was about. Even Jake, and his cohorts seemed to be caught up in the excitement of the moment.

I looked around for Herman, and saw him walking towards us with the rest of the guys evidently they'd heard the commotion.

"Herman!" I yelled. "We've found the Plane! Come look!"

He strolled up to us, and looked down at the flash of light in the woods. Then he turned and looked at me.

"Yea," he said. "There's something down there alright. But that doesn't necessarily mean it's the Plane wreck. It could be almost anything."

"But it has to be," I told him, unconvinced. "Whut else could it be?"

"Oh, I don't know," he said, with a slight smile. "Maybe we'll take a stroll down there, and see."

"Yea!" I shouted, along with just about everyone else.

Herman turned around, and walked back to the rock pile to get his knapsack, and we fidgeted, until he returned. I could hardly wait to start.

"Okay," he said. "Let's go!"

We set off down the slope, jumping from rock to rock, yipping with excitement. I was filled with elation. At long last, my wish was coming true.

The peaks were quite a ways down from the mountain, and it took us awhile to reach the area where we thought the Plane was, but the spot of light had gradually disappeared. I tried to memorize the location, but it became difficult. There were too many trees.

At last we reached the rocks above the treeline where we thought we had last seen the bright reflection of what I prayed was the wreckage.

When we got there, for some reason, instead of having everyone look,

Herman chose six or seven of us to go down into the forest to search while everybody else waited up above.

I was lucky enough to be one of the chosen, and we spread out, so as to cover as much ground as possible. Tommy was on one side of me, and Billy was on the other.

We began to climb down to the timberline, and when we got there, we quickly lost sight of each other. I was really pumped up and excited about what lay ahead of me. This was going to be great, and I was almost shaking in anticipation of what was to come. Now, my dream was about to be realized, and I was looking from side to side. I sure hoped we were in the right place. I didn't know how long Herman would let us search. I knew we couldn't screw around all day, because we'd have to start back down before it got to be too late. But all around me were just trees, and more trees. As I continued along through the forest without seeing anything, I began to get concerned, and doubt began to settle in. What if Herman was right? Maybe it was something else. But what?

No. it was the Plane. I was convinced of that, and I kept going.

Suddenly, I heard Billy yell, and his words thrilled me to my very soul.

"I've found it! I've found it! Over here! I've found the plane!"

"Tommy!" I hollered. "Tommy! Billy's found it!"

I turned, and began to run in the direction of my brother's voice. I could hear Tommy yelling at the other guys as I brushed past bushes, and trees. The branches acted like hands, grabbing at my clothes, as if trying to hold me back.

Finally, I glimpsed Billy up ahead, darting around, and then I came to a break in the trees. I stopped running, and stood there for a moment, shaking with excitement, my heart pounding wildly.

There, in a barren area, was the wreckage of the Plane.

Or what was left of it. Pieces were strewn about like large bits of silver-grey and olive, green colored confetti, and it was hard to tell that it had once been a plane. The only things that gave it away were the engines – great, hulking, rust-stained – and the big, silver propellers, all bent, and twisted.

Billy ran up to me, and I'd never seen him so excited before.

"We did it Tommy!" he said. "We found it! Isn't it great? I told ya I could find it!"

"Yea, yer right!" I told him, and he took off.

I'd dreamed about this for so long, and even though there wasn't a trace of the tail section left. I was thrilled beyond compare, and I began to walk across the crash site, looking for anything of interest. Like a gun for instance.

I turned over some debris, but found nothing. There was a lot of stuff to go through, and I hoped we could find some neat things before we had to leave.

Then I saw Tommy, and he rushed up to me.

"Jeezus Tommy!" he squealed. "Isn't this cool? We did it!"

"Yea," I told him. "I just wish part of the Plane was left."

"Yea really," he said. "Have ya found anything yet?"

"Naw," I told him. "I just started looken. Hey! Let's split up, and see if we can find any guns or anything before the other guys git here. You take that side, and I'll take this side."

"Okay," he said, and left.

After he was gone, I continued to turn over debris, but I kept coming up empty. The only things I found were some heavy pieces of string. I wondered what they were for. Maybe a parachute.

But, despite the fact that I couldn't find anything, I still took great pleasure in being able to touch, and be in the presence of something from the WWII era. I don't know why the war fascinated, and held such a spell over me, but I always got a sense of bittersweet nostalgia, and yearning, whenever I thought about it. Almost like my black moods. But much more pleasant.

I wished that I could've been old enough to remember it, or best of all, to have been able to have served in the armed forces. That woud've really been something to be proud of. Especially if I won some medals for bravery.

While I continued to search, kids began trickling in, and pretty soon Herman, and the rest of the guys showed up. I walked over to him, and he smiled.

"Well, Tommy," he said. "You were right. What do you think of it?"

"It's great," I told him. "But there ain't nuthen left. I hoped there would be a solid piece of the back of it, so we could explore inside. That would've been cool."

"Oh, that's usually the way it is when a plane crashes," he replied. "Although I will have to admit at least the tail sections usually left. It's hard to tell. From the look of things, I doubt very much that anyone survived this crash. (He was of course referring to Tommy's story of the tailgunner). "Have you found anything of interest yet?"

"Naw," I said. "I've been looken for the machine guns, but I ain't found nuthen." Not even any bullets."

"That's probably because there weren't any on it when they crashed." He explained. "I'll bet the only people aboard were the pilots, navigator, and radio man. And even if there were any guns on the plane, I'm sure the men from the government who came to retrieve the bodies, took anything of value."

"Oh," I replied, disappointed to say the least. "I wonder what made them crash?"

"Oh, the wings were probably iced up from the storm," he told me. "Or they may have just been off course. It's hard to say."

"Yea."

About that time, I saw Darren, Toby, and Benny, pawing through some stuff, and excused myself, and walked over to them.

"Well, whutta ya think?" I asked.

"Man!" Darren answered. "This is really cool! You guys seen any of the machine guns?"

"Naw, just a lot of this shit," I told him, and kicked a piece of debris.

"We have to just keep looken," he said. "They gotta be around here someplace."

"Yea, really," I replied.

I wasn't going to hold my breath about that happening. Since my talk with Herman, but I didn't want to ruin it for them. So I kept my mouth shut.

There was one, large part of the plane, that took a couple us us to turn over, and when we did, we discovered that it had the old, Army Air Corps insignia on it.

The sight of the round, circled star, outlined against the drab, olive-colored background, looked rather pathetic, and suddenly, it stirred something deep inside of me.

I was reminded of when I first saw Ronny's blood on the street, and how that had made me feel. Even though I'd known he was dead, it hadn't seemed real. But after I'd come to the place where the accident had happened, the harsh reality of his death had swept over me. Just like when I'd seen mom's lifeless body.

This was similar, and the ugly spectre of death seemed to rise up out of the wreckage. Men had died here, and although I knew that, I'd never given it much thought. I'd been so preoccupied with finding the Plane. I'd always thought of it as being just an object that I wanted to find, and that was as far as it had gone. The fact that the Plane had contained human beings didn't really register.

Now, their deaths were upon me.

The poor bastards. How terrible it must've been for the pilots as they struggled to keep the ice-covered B-17 high enough, so they wouldn't hit the Mountain. Since there weren't anymore mountains on the other side, if they'd just been a little bit higher, they might have made it over the peaks safely.

But despite their best efforts, the swirling whiteness ahead had suddenly ended when the Plane slammed into the trees on the unforgiving side of the peak.

I felt sorry for them, and for their families, and friends. I knew what it felt like to lose both a loved one, and a good companion.

Herman was standing nearby, and when he saw me staring down moodily at the piece of fuselage, he walked over.

"What's the matter Tommy?" he asked.

"Oh, I was just thinking about the people who got killed here," I told him. "Whut a drag."

"Yea it was," he said. "The only good thing is, they probably didn't even know what hit them."

"Yea."

"Well, I guess we'd better be heading back," he said.

He hollered at the guys to get their butts in gear, and everyone started to leave.

Suddenly, my cousin Dougie, and my promise to get him a souvenir when we found the Plane, flashed through my mind. I looked around for something – anything. Then I spied a small piece of control panel with a toggle switch on it. It had gone unnoticed until now, and I was glad that nobody else had seen it. From the looks of things, it had been under the section of the plane we'd turned over.

I bent down, and picked it up, and put the piece in my pocket. Then I walked away.

After I'd gone a short distance, I looked back over my shoulder at the crash site, but it had already disappeared behind the curtain of trees, and bushes.

As we came down, I thought about how great it had been to have finally found the Plane even though there hadn't been much of it left. The only bad part about the whole thing was when I'd thought about the men who had died on the peak. That'd been a bummer.

But I tried not to dwell on that. It felt too good to have finally accomplished what I'd set out to do, and it had been exciting and was something I'd never forget.

And we owed it all to the sun. that had been the key to the puzzle all along. No wonder the Plane was so hard to find.

I remembered how during the hikes in the previous three summers the skies had become overcast. Evidently, that's the way it had been on some of the other ones in the past. And even when the sun was out, maybe it hadn't been in the right position to show the way, or else nobody had paid any attention to it.

But we had, and I was really feeling great about the discovery.

I was glad that Billy had found it when he did, because he was the last one on our end of the line, and if he hadn't come upon the wreckage, we would've walked right past it. To be that close, and yet not find it. What a drag that would've been. Then Herman wouldn't have had any choice but to make us head back to the Camp unsuccessful. But we'd done it!

I just wished Ronny could've been there to share the moment with me. That would've been so neat. Maybe he'd been there in spirit. I sure hoped so. Judging by what had happened to me when I had the whooping cough, there was no reason to think he hadn't walked beside me through the debris field.

When we got back to the Camp, we boasted about our adventure to the younger kids, and they were envious. They really liked the souvenirs that we brought back. Especially mine. They all wanted to touch it like it was a magic charm or something. I guess in a way it was.

Now, I wished that I'd brought back something for myself. I thought about keeping the part, and just tell Dougie I'd forgotten. But then I decided that wasn't fair. A promise was a promise. I'd get something for myself next summer.

When dad came up that Sunday, I gave him the piece of the Plane, and asked him if he'd give it to Dougie. He said he would.

One afternoon, just before we were scheduled to go back to the Home, I walked into the big bunkhouse, and saw Herman packing his things, and as I went up to him, I knew something was wrong.

"Whattsa matter?" I asked half-jokingly. "You inna hurry to git back to the Home, Herman?"

"No Tommy," he replied. "I haven't said anything before now, but I've decided to go back, and finish my college education. So … uh … I won't be seeing you after today. I'm going to miss you, kid."

I couldn't believe what I was hearing, and my heart sank. I tried to hide my disappointment.

"Oh."

"Hey look," he said. "You hang in there Tommy. You've got the potential to make something of yourself. You're a good kid. Just try to control that temper of yours, and you'll be surprised what you can accomplish. Don't let it get the best of you. Okay?"

"Yea."

"Hey, this has been a lot of fun," he said. "I'll never forget this summer."

"Me neither." That was true.

"Well, you take care, Tommy," Herman said, and stuck out his hand.

"Yea, I will," I told him, and we shook.

Then I hurried out the door. I thought about looking up Tommy, and tell him about the situation with Herman, but I didn't. instead, I went up the Old Sawmill Road, and as I walked along, I was feeling kind of numb, but then I started getting angry.

That fucken Herman! How could he do this to me! Fuck him, and his education! That son-of-a-bitch! He was the best thing to come along in awhile and now he was leaving, and deserting me! Dammit!

These thoughts, and others, ran through my mind until I got to the path that led down to the fort. As I walked across the glade, I began to feel sorry for myself.

When I got to the fort, I kept going, and went on up the small hill above it, and sat down on a big rock, and lit a cigarette.

I thought about how screwed up my life was, and how it was all my fault. I was a troublemaker, and a pain in the ass, and the reason my dad wouldn't take Billy and I out of this stinking place.

I wasn't worth a shit. I was ugly, and stupid, and a Pissass. Nobody cared about me. I couldn't blame them.

Even God didn't seem to care. He was always taking the people I cared about from me. Like Mom, Ronny, Miss Sarah, and now Herman. The last two might as well be dead, because I'd never see them again.

Gawdammit! I wished I was dead! Nobody'd care! They'd just say "good riddance."

Then I gazed up at the Mountain, and the peaks through an opening in the branches of the trees, and I got no pleasure, looking at them now.

Ever since the climb, and we'd found the Plane, I'd noticed a change. Something was different. A vague kind of difference that gnawed at me, and I didn't like the way it felt.

Frustrated, I stood up, flicked the cigarette away, then got behind the rock I'd been sitting on, and began to push on it. I continued to do this until the boulder broke free, and began to tumble down the slope.

The fort was right in it's path, and the rock hit the back wall with a thud. I stood there for a moment, looking down. I usually got a thrill whenever I rolled a boulder, but this time, I felt nothing.

I went down to inspect the damage, but the rock had hardly made a dent, because it didn't have much time to build up any steam. And the fort had been built pretty solid anyway.

I felt kind of bad about it at first, but then I thought, "Fuck the fort! Fuck Everything."

Then I left, and went back to the Camp. When I got there, Herman was gone, and I was glad. Fuck him!

That night, after lights out, I stared up at the bunk overhead, and I felt empty inside. It had been a shitty day, and I'd lost another friend. Someone who had made me feel good about myself, and now he was gone.

When we left the Camp a few days later, I stared out the window of the bus at Mt. Baldwin, and Twin Peaks. They looked the same as always, but they no longer had that special aura about them like before.

They were just mountains.

I had no way of knowing that would be my last look at them for a very, long time.

Part II

When we got back to the Home, there were a couple of changes as usual. I was put in the front dorm, which officially made me a big guy now, although I didn't feel any differently than I had when I was a little guy. I was just a bigger, and older, chickenshit version of what I'd been before.

The nicest thing about being in the front dorm though, was that Tommy, and Billy were going to be in there with me because the back dorm was full. My brother had the bed next to mine, and I liked that.

Of course my "friend" Jake, and his pals were in there also, but there wasn't much I could do about that. I was just going to have to live with it whether I liked it or not.

The counselor Uncle Harry hired to take the place of Herman, was named Kelly Stander. He was in his twenties, had red hair, wore glasses, and was stocky in build. Kelly was also an asshole. He didn't seem to like me from the start, but that was okay, because I didn't like him either. I did my best to stay away from him.

I started attending classes at Lincoln again, and now that Billy was a seventh-grader, I offered to walk with him after school that first week, but he turned me down. As a result, he, and his friend, Benny Martinez, got scrubbed twice. I could have scrubbed some kids, but I didn't because I knew how it felt.

Now that I was going to regular school, I got back into my habit of daydreaming, and doodling in class. One day, I mouthed off to a teacher, and when I was sent to Mr. Peetz's office, he, and I got into it, and I was expelled for a week. And as usual, I received a warning about my behavior. And, naturally I told them I'd watch it. Just like I always did.

But then finally, of course I really screwed up.

There was a kid in my classes names Clarence Wentzbarker, who was a real pansy-ass. I thought his name was stupid, and I liked to torment him. I was bigger, and older than most of the kids in my class, and I'm ashamed to say I'd become something of a bully at school, and the Home, even though I sure didn't like it when that happened to me.

Clarence liked to carry a briefcase instead of a notebook, unlike the rest of us. I used to try, and knock it out of his hand in the hallways, and he'd get pissed.

"Stop it!" he'd whine. "Leave me alone!"

"Stop it! Stop it!" I'd mock. "Whut the fuck you got in there anyway?"

"None of your business," he'd snap, and stomp off.

I'd laugh at him, and I continued to tease him. Finally though, in class one day, I went too far.

He used to sit behind me in one of our classes, and I wished it was the other way around so that I could fuck with him without the teacher seeing me.

On this certain day, I was sitting in class, doodling, and I got bored. The teacher was droning on, and then I thought of some mischief. Clarence always put his briefcase on the floor beside his desk.

I thought I'd try, and get a peek inside it. I waited until the teacher had turned around to the chalkboard, then I looked back over my shoulder at Clarence. He was watching Mr. Graham, the teacher, write on the blackboard, and when Clarence saw me, looking at him, he made a face.

I turned back around, and then waited a few moments. When I glanced back at him again, he was engrossed in writing, and I figured now was as good a time as any.

I reached back with my hand, and grabbed the top of his briefcase, then began to slowly slide it towards me. Clarence wasn't aware of that at first.

Suddenly, he looked up, saw what I was doing, and dropped his pen. Then he hauled off, and slugged me in the back. It really hurt, and I was surprised I didn't think a pansy like him could hit that hard.

I sat there flabbergasted for a second, while he reached down and pulled his briefcase back to him. He had an angry look on his face.

Then I turned halfway round in my seat, and punched him in the mouth. He was still bent over, and when I hit him, he fell to the floor. Then he scrambled to his feet, and his face was flushed red with anger.

"You son-of-a-bitch!" he screamed, tears in his eyes. "Leave me alone!"

I got up, and started to go after him, but Mr. Graham yelled at us, and I stopped, as he walked up.

"Allright!" he said. "What's going on here? Who started this?"

"He hit me!" Clarence blubbered.

"Yea, cuz he hit me in the back," I told him,

"He was trying to steal my briefcase," Clarence retorted.

"I wasn't stealen it," I explained. "I just wanted to see whut was inside of it."

Then Mr. Graham sent us to the principal's office. When Mr. Peetz reprimanded me, I mouthed off to him.

"Don't you get smart with me you punk," he said angrily. "I've had it with you. You're nothing but a troublemaker. I'm kicking you out of here for good."

"That's fine with me," I told him. I didn't care.

The upshot of it all was that they sent me back to Mrs. Prososki's school, and that was okay with me. I liked her, and her studies were a lot easier than the one's at Lincoln, and she was so nice, and patient with me.

Attending her school really did a lot for my self-esteem. I wasn't used to having people praise me like she did. But, despite my success with her, I still wanted guys to think of me as someone you didn't want to mess with, and, I continued to have behavioral problems at the Home.

The fact that I was basically a coward, didn't stop me from trying, and I continued with my act. What helped keep it going was the fact that I could fight. Especially if pushed.

But, one day in that regard, I really surprised myself.

Tommy, and Darren, and I were standing in the tv room, talking, when George Kelso came in from the dining room, and headed in our direction. He was the sixteen year old guy Jake had knocked out in the tournament at the camp.

George was tall, and lanky, with a long, pimpled face. He combed his dark, brown hair to the side, instead of straight back like most of us did, and he was one homely kid.

He walked up to us, and I didn't see him. We were standing behind the rows of metal chairs by the side door, and I kind of had my back to him. Tommy, and Darren were across from me.

I'd had a few run-ins with George, but I'd always kept my mouth shut, when he wised off to me. He must've been in a bad mood that day, because when he got within striking distance, instead of just going around, he shoved me hard, and I nearly stumbled, and almost fell down by the door.

"Git the fuck outta the way!" he growled, and started to walk out the doorway.

"Hey!" I yelled, pissed off. "Don't be fucken pushen me asshole!"

George stopped, and came back to me. He had a nasty look on his face.

"Why? Whut the fuck're you gonna do about it Pissass!" he snarled, and threw a punch at me that missed.

I was mad, and I forgot all about him being bigger, and threw a punch in return, which also missed. Then we began swinging in earnest, and he tagged me a few times, but they didn't hurt, and then one of his punches sailed past my head, and I stepped in, and caught him solidly on his left cheekbone with my fist.

When I did that, he fell to the floor on his back, and began to roll from side to side, moaning, and holding his face with both hands.

I stood there watching him, and got kind of scared. I hadn't meant to hit him that hard, and I hoped he wasn't hurt.

In the meantime, Tommy, and Darren had cleared the area, and now they came back, and like me, watched George, fascinated.

Finally, he stopped, and got to his feet. There was a big, ugly, bluish knot under his eye, and I felt bad about it.

"Man, I'm sorry George," I said honestly.

"Ahh, don't worry about it," he mumbled, and went on out the door.

"Jeezus Tommy!" Darren told me in awe. "You really nailed that son-of-a-bitch!"

"Man, I guess," Tommy agreed.

"Yea, I did, didn't I?" I told them.

Now that I knew he wasn't really hurt, I began to feel proud of myself. I saw the way some of the guys in the room were staring at me, impressed, and my ego really fed off that. If I kept up this kind of thing, nobody was going to mess with me. Maybe even Jake, although I wasn't going to bet on that.

About a week later though, George, and I got into it again and this time we were in the front dorm, but things didn't turn out the way I thought they would.

When I tried to punch him out like before, he ducked, and got a hold of me with those long arms of his, and we fell to the floor. We rolled around a bit, and then he got me in a half-nelson, and I was screwed. I struggled to get free, but couldn't, and finally just went limp.

"You give up?" he asked.

"Yea," I said sheepishly.

He let go, and got up, then walked out. I laid there for a moment, and felt rather foolish. Old George had showed me that I wasn't as tough as I thought I was.

After that, we pretty much stayed out of each other's way.

In the meantime, my dislike for Kelly grew with each passing day. He didn't hit me or anything like that at first, but he'd correct me, and make snide remarks every chance he got.

Finally though, one night he caught me, and my friends sneaking back in the window of the tv room after one of our nightly jaunts, and we all wound up getting whippings by the Old Man, and him. Kelly used a lanyard on me.

Being as I was fourteen now, I felt like I was too old for this kind of shit, but he let me know otherwise. I found myself begging for mercy, and crying before it was over, just as I had in the past.

Gawd, I hated him.

Then finally, one night, it all came to a head.

The guys in our dorm were wound up, and we were engaged in horseplay. Everybody was pretty much involved, except Jake. We were being pretty loud, and obnoxious.

Suddenly, Kelly came roaring in, and he was in a bad mood.

"Hey!" he yelled. "What the hell're you kids doing?"

Billy just happened to be the closest one by the door, and Kelly slapped him, and he flew backwards into a locker with a thud. When I saw that, I was filled with rage.

"Hey!" I shouted. "Keep yer fucken hands off my brother, you bastard!"

"Don't give me any of your shit, you little prick!" he said. "If you'd been closer, I'd have slapped you."

"Like hell you would've," I said defiantly.

He walked over to where I was standing between two beds, and put his hands on his hips. Kelly glared at me with an angry look in his eyes, but for some reason, I felt no fear.

"You don't think so huh?" he said.

"No."

He hauled off, and slapped me, and the force of the blow jolted me. I recovered, then drew back my fist, and punched him as hard as I could. I got him right between the eyes, and his glasses snapped in half. One of the lenses dug into his skin, and left a red mark under his right eye.

There was a moment of dead silence in the dorm, and you could've heard a pin drop. Kelly stood there for a moment with a look on his face, that let me know he was having a hard time dealing with what I'd done. Then anger filled his features.

He punched me with his fist, and it really hurt, and I slammed into the wall behind me. Then he rained blows on my head, and I tried to protect myself, but it wasn't doing much good, and I got scared.

I decided to make a run for it, and I turned, and jumped across the bed next to me, and headed for the door with Kelly in pursuit.

Once I reached the hallway, I ran down the front staircase in a panic. I didn't know where I was going, but I had to get away from Kelly. When I got to the bottom of the stairs, I decided to go to Uncle Harry, and see if he'd get Kelly off me.

I ran to his door, and banged on it, shouting his name. In the meantime, Kelly came rushing in, and I backed off into the corner by the front door, behind the roll top desk and he advanced on me.

"Git away from me," I begged him.

Then the door of Uncle Harry's quarters opened, and he came out. There was a scowl on his face, and he looked annoyed.

"What the hell's going on?" he asked, then noticed me in the corner. "What are you doing down there like that?"

I was stark naked, but I wasn't concerned about that. I just wanted him to keep Kelly off my ass.

Kelly explained what had happened, and Uncle Harry gave me a disgusted look, and then warned me that if I kept this up he was going to call my father, and recommend that he have me put in juvenile hall.

Of course, when I heard that, I told him I'd watch my P's, and Q's.

On the way back to the dorm, I apologized to Kelly, although I really wasn't sorry, just humbled.

"Well, I'll tell you right now," he warned. "You better never pull another stunk like that on me, you little punk."

That made me angry, but I didn't say anything. Screw him.

When I walked back in the dorm, Tommy came up to me smiling, and told me how much he enjoyed watching me hit Kelly.

"Yea, well," I told him. "I dunno if that was such a good idea or not. He really kicked the shit outta me."

But despite that, it had still felt good to punch him.

Most of the guys, including Ray, and Scott, were looking at me as if they couldn't believe I had the balls to pull a stunt like that. As for me though, I was beginning to feel more like a big guy all the time, and I was starting to gain more confidence in myself with each passing day.

There were only two people there who I wouldn't mess with. One, of course, was Jake. The other was big, sixteen year old Bill Snodgrass. Dave Geist, and Bobby Grassell had left, so it was kind of nice to know I was one of the biggest, and oldest guys in the place. Billy, as usual, didn't mention anything about me sticking up for him against Kelly. He never liked it when I did that with other guys because he said he could fight his own battles. But this time was different, I'd fought for him against a counselor, and I'd gotten my ass kicked. I felt like the least he could've done is tell me he appreciated my effort. But he didn't, Oh well. After that, I managed to stay out of trouble for awhile. Kelly didn't seem to get on my ass as much, and it was the same way with Jake, and his cohorts. During that time, I went with a couple of girls, but aside from that, the months passed pretty uneventfully.

That all changed in January of 1958, however.

A guy showed up, and like Jake before him, he'd just come from the Hill. His name was Dan Camacho. He had dark hair, and eyes, was tall, slender, and sixteen. Dan was arrogant, and had a condescending attitude towards us. Jake was the only one he could relate to.

He dominated the front dorm from the beginning. The only guys his age were Bill Snodgrass, and George Kelso, but they wouldn't challenge him.

I was scared of him from the start, and I prayed he wouldn't single me out, but I should have been so lucky. As soon as he found out, I wet the bed, he cornered me in the dorm that first, night, and I cowered in fear as he fixed me with those dark, merciless eyes of his.

"I hear you piss the bed, asshole," he sneered.

"Yea," I gulped.

"I'll you what asshole," he threatened. "You better learn how to stop right now. Cuz if ya don't, I'm gonna kick yer fucken ass every time that you stink up the dorm. You got that, you son-of-a-bitch?"

"Yea," I answered, close to tears.

"You just remember what I said," he told me, and walked away.

After he left, I didn't know what to do. I felt doomed. His threat wasn't going to stop me from wetting the bed. What he was asking of me was impossible. I had no control over my bladder, and no amount of threats was going to change that.

I wanted to run off, and hide somewhere, but where, I didn't know. This was totally uncalled for, and unfair.

The only thing I could think of was to try, and stay awake as late as I could. I'd be sleepy in the morning, but at least I wouldn't get my ass kicked.

Of course, that didn't work, and I awoke to a wet bed around dawn. I quickly, and quietly got out of bed, and checked, but everyone seemed to be asleep. I stripped off my sheets, then went to the shower room, and went through my routine of bathing, and rinsing out my bedding.

Then I snuck back to the dorm, and got dressed, arranged the blankets so as to make it appear the sheets were on my bed, then headed down the hallway so that I could make my way outside to hang them up.

As I did all that, I realized how futile it was to try, and keep Dan from knowing that I had wet the bed. It wouldn't be hard for him to find out.

When I got downstairs, I went to the tv room, and took one of the folding chairs, and propped the outside door open, so I could get back in after I'd hung up my sheets in the cold, winter air.

Afterwards, I went, and sat in the tv room, and waited for people to start moving around, and getting up. I was filled with dread, and I just didn't know how I was going to live like this, day after day.

Dammit anyway!

That morning at breakfast, Dan was giving me the evil eye, and I figured he knew I'd wet the bed. I didn't know if he was going to jump me afterwards, so I hid from view until we left for school. Of course, I knew I was just postponing the inevitable.

All day at school, I was in a constant state of anxiety, worrying about what was going to happen that night when I got back to the Home.

After supper, I kept waiting for Dan to do or say something, but nothing happened, and I tried to hang on to the illusion that nothing would. But I knew I was just kidding myself. Especially when we went upstairs to bed. When I entered the bathroom to relieve myself, Dan, and some of the guys from the dorm followed me in. When I looked back over my shoulder at him. I started shaking with fear. I turned around, and he walked up, and put his face close to mine, and I was filled with dread.

"I thought I told you not to wet the bed, asshole," he snarled.

"I'm sorry, Dan," I whined. "I can't help it. I tried not to."

He didn't say anything, but just hauled off, and punched me. To my surprise, it didn't hurt. I thought he could hit harder than that.

Dan continued to punch me, and I covered my head, and backed up until I was against the wall between the urinal, and one of the toilets. Like I said, his fists didn't hurt, but he was scaring me, and I pleaded with him to stop.

Finally, he did, and then he threatened to do this every time I pissed the bed, so I might as well get used to it until I stopped. Then he left.

After he was gone, I looked through tear-filled eyes at the guys standing there watching, and most of them were staring at me with disgust. But the one who I was surprised at was Jake. He was looking at me like he couldn't believe that I hadn't fought back with Dan.

Tommy had been hanging around in the background while all of this was happening, and now he walked up to me, after everyone had left.

"Are you okay?" He asked with sympathy.

"Yea," I sniffed. "He didn't really hurt me."

"Why didn't ya kick his fucken ass then?" he queried.

Judging from the way Dan hit, there was probably a good chance I could accomplish that, but he looked and acted so mean, it was hard to tell what he would do to get revenge. Knowing him, he'd probably use a chair or a club.

I tried to explain that to Tommy without sounding like the pussy I really was.

"Yea, but you can't let him keep beaten on ya," he said. "He's just gonna keep it up unless ya nail him, and make him pay."

I knew he was right, but like I said, I was afraid to retaliate. I just wanted to crawl into a hole, and die. Why was I a Pissass Lord? Why couldn't I be like most of the guys? I wanted to wake up in the morning, and feel warm, and comfortable in a dry bed. I envied my little brother.

That next morning, I'd wet the bed again, and this time. Dan caught me in the tv room before breakfast, and punched me, then told me I could look forward to more of that when we went upstairs for bed that night.

All day long at Mrs. Projoski's, I was miserable, and wracked my brain about finding a way out of this mess.

But I was only able to come up with one answer, and it was something that was very alien to me.

As much as I hated the idea, I was going to have to tell Uncle Harry. There was no way around it. I had to do something. I couldn't go on like this.

I knew I'd be labeled a snitch, and I'd really get harassed, and have my ass kicked a lot, but that was happening anyway. Maybe, hopefully, after a while, Dan, and the guys would lay off me. I sure hoped so.

I decided to go see the Old Man after supper that night. I waited until the little guys went up to bed, and then I made my way to his office. I felt like everyone's eyes were on me, and they knew exactly what I was up to. But nobody was around when I knocked on his door, and he opened it.

After I'd told him what Dan was doing, he acted like he didn't really give a ratsass. I guess I couldn't blame him. I'd been pretty shitty to him in the past.

"Well," he sighed. "I'll have a talk with him. We can't have this kind of thing going on."

After I left his office, I really felt ashamed of myself, and my self-esteem was pretty low. I had sunk to the depths. I was a lousy fucken snitch, and it didn't feel good.

I went back to the tv room, and watched a show for a while. I couldn't concentrate on the program, because I was waiting for the bomb to go off from the fuse I'd just lit.

Suddenly, I saw Kelly come through the room with Dan in tow, and my heart seemed to jump in my throat with fear, and I was having a hard time breathing.

Tommy was sitting next to me, and I asked him if he'd like to go out behind the garage and have a smoke. I had something important to tell him. He acted like he didn't want to be bothered at first, but when he saw the distressed look on my face, he came along.

After we'd got our coats, and headed outside, I told him what I'd done, and he stared at me like I was crazy.

"Whut?" he said. "Whutta you stupid? He's gonna really git on yer ass now, along with the other guys. Man, I don't know about you."

"Yea, I know," I muttered, and was sorry I'd told him now.

We snuck back in the Home, and I sat in the tv room, and wallowed in self-pity. I knew I was in for a rough time, but there wasn't a dammed thing I could do about the situation now.

We hadn't been sitting there long, when suddenly a snowball hit me right in the back, spraying snow all over. Tommy, and Darren, who were sitting on either side of me.

I looked back, and saw Ray, and Scott standing in the doorway of the washroom. We'd had a recent snowstorm, and they'd found some left over snow.

"You fucken snitch!" Ray said. "Yer ass is grass, Pissass!"

Evidently, word of my telling Uncle Harry about Dan had spread, and now I was in for it. But I didn't see Jake around, and I stood up, and started towards them, but they took off.

When I sat back down, I felt like the weight of the world was on my shoulders. The harassment had begun, and there wasn't anything I could do about it. I felt trapped in a lousy world of my own, and I was all alone, and lost. There was no way out.

Even my friends seemed to be disapproving of me, although I'm sure a lot of that was in my own mind, and not theirs.

When it was time for bed, I trudged reluctantly upstairs. I wished it would hurry up, and get over with. I was trembling when I walked in.

Dan had Ray, and Scott keep an eye out for Kelly, and then he came at me. I pleaded with him for mercy.

"Please Dan," I told him tearfully. "I'm sorry, man. Don't do this."

"You fucken snitch," he snarled, and the attack began.

Like I've said, his assaults never really hurt me physically. They just scared me, and this one was no different.

Or the one that came after that, and so forth. The beatings went on for about a week, but then eventually, he began to do it less often, and finally it got to the point where he would just walk up, and without saying a word, haul off, and hit me, then leave.

It was something that was a part of my everyday life at the Home, and there wasn't much I could do about the situation, except exist.

Dan was always picking on, or pulling dirty tricks on people, and one night he chose Billy, and I'm ashamed to say I did nothing to prevent it.

The incident started when Billy got up, and went to the bathroom after lights out. When he left the dorm, I saw Dan get up, and walk in my direction. I wondered if he was going to the toilet also. But when he reached the foot of my bunk, he turned and walked between my brother's bed, and mine, and I braced myself for another one of his assaults.

But I was surprised, because he turned towards Billy's bed and stood there for a moment. I couldn't figure out what he was doing.

Suddenly, there was the rushing sound of water, and I realized he was pissing on Billy's sheets.

Several guys started laughing, including myself, but mine was more out of nervousness than anything else. I knew I should've at least said something to this asshole, but I didn't.

To this day I regret the fact that I just didn't get up, and smash that moron's face in. I'm pretty sure I could've if I hadn't been such a coward.

When Dan was gone, he, and some of the guys were giggling. He went back to his bunk, and laid down, and waited.

There was an air of anticipation in the dorm when Billy returned, and I wanted to warn him, but I remained silent, just like the big chicken that I was.

Poor Billy. He walked between our beds, then turned, and sat down and swung his legs over, and started to lay back. That must've been when the wetness hit, because he started flapping his arms, and legs around in his haste to get out of the piss-filled bed.

The guys were laughing at his effort, and he was finally able to clear himself of the soaked bedding. He stood there for a moment, with piss running down his legs from his wet underwear. I couldn't make out his face in the dark, but I knew he must've been pretty upset.

I really felt sorry for him, and in particular, guilt ridden.

"Hey Pissass Jr.," Dan said sarcastically. "Now you know how yer fucken brother feels when he pisses the bed."

Some of the guys laughed, and then Billy went over to his locker and changed underwear, then got dressed.

While he was doing that, Dan was making smart remarks, and he warned Billy about keeping his mouth shut. My brother never said a word.

I wondered where Billy thought he was going. It was the middle of February. He was going to freeze his balls off. Dad lived too far away to go there.

I thought about trying to talk him out of leaving, but he was gone before I could say anything.

Afterward, I laid there, and kicked myself for being such a pansy-ass, and letting this bully piss in my brother's bed. Some brother I was. I didn't like it when people fucked with Billy, but I hadn't lifted a finger to stop this creep. I was such a yellow-bellied jerk.

These kinds of thoughts raced through my mind that night, and I worried about Billy, so I didn't go to sleep until late, and low, and behold, my bed was dry when I awoke.

But I didn't feel very good about it, because Billy was sleeping between our bunks on the floor with his blankets. He looked so pathetic, it brought a tear to my eye.

Any good feelings I had about not wetting the bed were quickly dispelled when Dan walked up, and punched me, then as usual, left. Never uttering a word. I let it roll off my back, because he couldn't hit hard anyway and I was feeling too good about not wetting the bed.

I just wished I'd done something the night before. Maybe one of these days he'd piss me off, and I'd really let him have it.

But I knew the chances of that happening were pretty slim.

Billy never told me where he was heading that night. He'd been picked up by the cops, and had gotten a whipping from the Old Man. Dad was really disappointed in him, but Billy never explained why he ran off.

I told him how sorry I was that I hadn't tried to stop Dan, or at least warn him, but he told me not to worry. He could handle things just fine.

That was typical of him to say that to me.

Dan continued to torment me, and I wished there was a way I could get him to stop. I prayed to the Lord to do something to help me, but he didn't seem to be listening.

Then in March, my prayers were finally answered.

Dan was caught shoplifting, which violated his parole, and he was sent back to the Hill. I'd never been so glad to see someone leave the home since Dusty. It was such a relief not to have to worry about him anymore.

After that, things were pretty much returned to normal. If you could call living there as normal.

Then that same month, an event occurred, that was the most exciting thing that had ever happened to me. Even more than finding the Plane.

My dad and Bert got married, and Billy, and I were told that when school let out, we were going to come live with them. We would be a real family.

At last! We'd be rid of this dump! I could hardly wait! Come on, end of school!

Billy was as excited as I was, although of course, he didn't say a whole lot to me. But I could tell he felt he same way.

With the knowledge that I was going to be leaving there, I adopted a happy go lucky attitude, and I didn't let things bother me as much.

But one night in the first week of May, I lost my temper, and got in trouble … We were at supper, and I mouthed off to Kelly, and he got up, walked over, and slapped me on the back of the head. I came up out of my chair, and faced him. I was really mad.

"You son of a bitch!" I screamed "Don't be fucking hitt'en me!"

This time he slapped my face, and I forgot all about getting my ass kicked before and tried to hit him. But he grabbed my arm, then with both hands, threw me to the floor. I was kicking and screaming, and he knelt down on my chest with one knee, and held my arms down.

"Git off me, you fat, son-of-a-bitch!" I yelled, squirming around.

"Shut up!" he told me. "I've about had it with you, you little bastard."

"I'm with you, Kelly," the Old Man said. "I've had it with him too. I'm going to call his father, and tell to come, and get this punk. I don't want him staying here any longer."

"Whut're you doen? Trying to cheer me up?" I told him sarcastically.

"Shut your big mouth, you little creep," Kelly ordered.

He let me up off the floor, and I was escorted to Uncle Harry's office, where I sat on the bench, while the Old Man called my dad, and explained the situation to him.

As Uncle Harry talked, my anger began to subside, and I started to worry about what my father would do. He had told me enough times that I'd better straighten up my act, or else it was Juvenile Hall. Take my pick. That threat usually worked, and I'd be good for awhile, but then I'd blow up in anger, and be in hot water again.

If people would just leave me alone, I'd do just fine. But, somebody was always fucking with me. Like Jake, and his company, or the counselors. I had to do something. Nobody else would stick up for me, and take my side. It sucked.

I sat there dejectedly until the Old Man was through talking to dad, then he told Kelly to take me to the basement, and get my suitcase so I could get my things packed. I was leaving.

When we walked through the dining room, everyone seemed to be looking at me, but I just stared straight ahead. I was feeling kind of numb.

On the way to the basement, Kelly didn't say anything. After we got my bag, he finally spoke and told me to go up, and clean out my locker.

As I walked back up the stairs, I was overcome by a sudden wave of mixed emotions. I felt excited, but, also kind of sad.

Allright! At last, I was getting out of this son-of-a-bitch! I could hardly wait. That is of course, unless I was going to Juvie Hall. I sure hoped not. Then, a wave of sorrow washed over my senses, which surprised me, although it shouldn't have. This had been my home for over four years now, and I'd had some good times here, and made some good friends like Ronny Collins.

I would never forget him. I remembered the rude reception I'd received from him that first day, and how he'd become my biggest tormentor.

And then how that had all changed, and how great a relationship we had built up in the too short a time that we'd become friends, before his tragic death. I really missed the guy.

As I packed my suitcase, I knew the only thing I was going to feel any loss over, was the Camp I had loved the ability to just get away from everyone, and enjoy the peace, and quiet there.

And I had really liked the colorful names given the places like Queens Chair, the Old Mill Pond, etc. And then of course, the beauty, and splendor of the Mountain, and Twin Peaks, and the story of the plane wreck up there, and how it had gripped my imagination.

I remembered the feeling I had whenever I thought about it, and how involved, and enchanted I'd become with it. How magical, and special it would be to finally find out where the Plane had crashed.

Then Herman showed up last year, and made it the best summer of them all, and it had been topped off by our discovery of the storied plane. It had really been exciting to have finally found it's final resting place.

But there had been some disappointment because it wasn't the way I had pictured it would be, and there was the realization about the loss of life. But the search up to then had been fun, and I would never forget it. Then, just before going back to the Home, Herman had quit, and that had really pissed me off. He was the best counselor we'd ever had, and then Uncle Harry hired that stinking Kelly. Things had gone from good to worst, and now I was facing an uncertain, scary future. Just because of him. That fat pig.

I finished packing, and then went over to one of the open windows, and lit up a smoke, then unlatched the screen, so I could flick out my ashes. This wasn't something I would normally do, because of the smell, and I wouldn't want to get caught by one of the counselors. But of course, I didn't give a rat's ass now.

I was really nervous about facing my father. I'd royally screwed things up this time. I hoped he wouldn't come down on me too hard, and put me in Juvenile Hall. I shuddered at the thought.

Outside the window, dusk had began to take over the day, and it was cloudy, and gray. With the way I felt, it was amazing that I wasn't feeling a real mood swing, because of the melancholy thoughts running through my head. But I didn't feel too bad, considering.

I tried not to dwell on the future, and fear of the unknown but that was hard to do given the current circumstances.

I puffed away anxiously at my cigarette for a time, until it started to burn my fingers. Then I opened the screen wider, and flicked the butt over the roof of the porch, and then re-latched it.

Suddenly, I could hear voices, and footsteps coming down the hall, and I knew supper was over. I hoped Jake and his boys weren't making an appearance, and I was relieved when I saw it was my brother, along with Tommy, Darren, and Toby, and Benny.

"So are ya really leav'en?" Tommy asked when they walked in.

"Yea," I answered. "I've got my shit packed. I'm outta this son-of-a-bitch."

"Hey man," he said. "I know yer glad to be leav'en, but I'm … uh … I'm gonna miss ya Tommy. Write me when ya git settled."

"Yea, I will, Buddy," I told him. (I never did)

There was a moment of awkward silence, and then Darren stuck out his hand, and we shook.

"Hey," he said. "Take it easy man."

"Yea, you too," I told him, and then shook Toby's and Benny's.

"See ya," they said.

"As long as it ain't in jail," I replied, then turned to Billy.

"Well, I hate leav'en ya here little brother," I told him. "But I'll see ya when school lets out."

"Yea, well, you better hope dad doesn't throw you in Juvenile Hall for getting kicked out of here," he said.

"Man, don't say that!" I snapped. "I don't even wanna think about it!"

"Okay," he said, and shrugged his shoulders indifferently.

About that time George Kelso walked in, and came up to me. Ever since we had our tussles, we'd respected each others space. Now, he shook my hand, and told me good luck, and then I grabbed my suitcase, and me, and my friends left the dorm. As we went down the stairs, some of the younger guys came up, and paid their respects.

When we walked into the tv room, Jake, Ray, and Scott were there, and of course they mouthed off to me.

"See ya, Pissass," Ray sneered.

"Yea, good riddance," Scott added on.

Jake, as usual, didn't say anything, but just stared at me with those cold, dark eyes of his.

It was really going to be nice not to have to put up with their crap anymore, and I just ignored them as we made our way to Uncle Harry's office.

Billy, and I sat on the bench, and talked to our friends while we waited for our father to show up.

I was really going to miss these guys, and of course Tommy most of all. He'd been there from the get-go, and I don't know how I would've made it if he hadn't been there to make me laugh, and just be my friend. He'd helped me through some tough times.

When dad showed up, Tommy, Darren, Toby, and Benny left. As they were going out of the door, Tommy looked back at me.

"See ya, Tommy," he said.

I waved at him, then turned to dad. He really looked pissed, and a bolt of fear hit my stomach. I just knew I was in for it.

"Hi Dad," I said meekly. "Sorry about this mess I caused."

"Don't give me that shit!" he retorted. "Who the hell do you think you are? A tough guy or something?"

"No," I replied.

"Well, you could've fooled me," he said. "I can send you to a place where they've got a lot of tough guys if that's what you want."

"No, dad," I pleaded, close to tears. "Please don't do that. I'm not a tough guy."

"Well, I should throw your ass in jail anyway," he threatened. "You just keep getting into more, and more trouble. Why can't you be like your brother?"

"I dunno," I said miserably. I wished I was.

About that time, Uncle Harry came out of his quarters, and he, and my father talked about what a problem I'd become. Then finally dad turned to me.

"I think you owe this man an apology for being such a pain in the ass," he said.

"I'm sorry for the way I've acted, Uncle Harry," I told him, trying to drum up as much sincerity as I could. "I know I've caused a lot of problems."

"Well, apology accepted," he said, and a thought ran across my mind that he was probably just as glad to see me go, as I was to leave.

"You know," he continued, "when you want to, you can be a pretty, good kid. You just need to work on that temper, and attitude of yours."

"Yea, I know," I said. "I will," and thought what a phony bastard he was.

Then it was time to go. We said goodbye to Billy, and then I grabbed my suitcase and we walked out on to the front porch.

The darkening sky had opened up, and a gentle, spring rain was falling. Cars passing by on the street made soft, hissing sounds as their tires rolled across the wet pavement.

We walked down the steps to the sidewalk, and over to dad's car. He had me put my suitcase in the backseat, and then we got in. He looked over at me with a scowl on his face.

"I'm going to warn you right now," he said. "If you pull any shit on me or Bert, you're going to learn to regret it."

"I won't, dad," I told him, and meant it. "I promise."

"Well, you just remember what I said," he threatened.

"I will," I replied.

Whew! I'd dodged another bullet, and I felt relieved, and settled back in the seat.

Dad turned on the ignition, and the radio kicked in, and then he switched on the windshield wipers. The sound they made as they swished across the glass, and the patter of the rain on the rooftop, had a soothing effect on me.

A sad, mournful country song was playing, and I wanted to turn it to my favorite rock and roll station, but I knew dad wouldn't allow it.

He turned on the head lights, put the car in gear, then pulled away from the curb. I looked over at the Home, and saw someone waving at me from one of the windows in the front dorm It must've been Tommy, but I couldn't tell because of the light in the background, but I waved back anyway.

When we came to the intersection up the street, dad turned, and we passed the place where Ronny had died.

He had been gone long enough now, that there were days I could walk past it, and not think of him. But, such was not the case tonight. After we'd gone by, I continued to look back over my shoulder and I felt like I was deserting his memory, which left twinge of sadness. He had been such a good friend, and I vowed that I would never forget him.

Dad noticed what I was doing, and he glanced over at me with a scowl.

"What the hell're you looking at?" he asked irritably.

"Nuthen," I muttered, and faced forward.

All of the mixed emotion I'd been feeling all night, were trying to break through, and I felt like crying, but I didn't want my father to see me doing that.

But my eyes still misted over with tears, although I didn't cry as we drove away into the gloomy, rainy night.

Epilogue

Many, many years later, I went to Aunt Marge, and Uncle George's fiftieth wedding anniversary, and family reunion at their old homestead. I lived in a neighboring state then, and I went by myself. My wife had to work, and I was disappointed that she couldn't make the trip with me.

I loved going back to the old farm. It holds a lot of pleasant memories for me, from my childhood visits. And, of course, there's always that, old pleasant feeling that I got, whenever I thought of how Billy, and I had been robbed of the chance to live there. But, that was in the past, and there wasn't anything that could be done about it now.

I joined in the festivities, and really enjoyed visiting with my relatives, some of whom I hadn't seen in a long time.

Billy was there, and I was surprised to see him, although Aunt Marge had told me he might show up. He doesn't socialize a lot with people anymore, and I don't get to visit with him very often. We never keep in touch, but it's always been like that between us. He kind of goes his way and I go mine.

Basically, he's the same, old Billy. Just as he was when we were kids. Quiet, rarely got into trouble, and unlike me, always seemed to do the right thing. He didn't appear to be affected by all the garbage we went through. "But there's a bitterness about him now, that wasn't there before, and I knew most of it had to do with his stint in the Army). After we left the Home, Billy continued to stay out of trouble, went on to graduate from high school, (where he was a jock) got a steady job, did some drinking, and raced cars. Then he met a pretty girl, and wound up getting married. Just like most normal, young adults do.

Of course, I was just the opposite. My attitude, and my temper kept getting me into trouble, and sadly, I never learned anything from my mistakes, and I would keep doing the same things over and over.

It was that way in school. I would disrupt the class, and make smart remarks to the teachers. To my way of thinking, I was just having fun. Why was everybody getting all bent out of shape? I just liked to show off.

Finally, when I was sixteen, I got kicked out of school, for good, but I could've cared less. It was boring, except for the girls.

Dad was really pissed at me, and he said that if I wanted to stay with him, I'd better go find a job.

Well, that was easier said than done. With no diploma or any type of skill, I didn't stand much of a chance of finding someone who would employ me. But I wasn't very keen on working anyway.

I liked to just lay around the house all day, watching tv, or listening to music on the radio. Then at night, I'd go look up some friends, and we'd just hang around, talking, and joking. I didn't indulge in petty thievery, or vandalism, or fight like I had in the Home. I flirted with girls at the local skating rink, and it seemed like I always had a pretty girl on my arm back then.

The years 1960, and 61, were the best ones of my life, and I really was nostalgic when I think about them. During that time, I never got into any real, serious trouble. (Well maybe once, but I don't count that because a couple of guys I knew caused it, not me. I was just there). I wish I could go back to that innocent time in my life.

But my dad was really getting fed up with me setting on my ass, and not doing anything. I wouldn't even clean the house like I should have.

And I couldn't understand what he expected of me. I wasn't hurting anyone. It was nice to just exist, and not have to worry about assholes giving me shit, and that's when I found out how really cold, and uncaring the world could be.

I began to hang out in 3.2 bars (whatever happened to them, and 3.2 beer?) and drink, and fight a lot. I became a real pain in societies' butt. And it got worse when I turned twenty-one, and could drink hard liquor.

A lot of my relatives didn't want me around when I was boozing, especially my brother. I don't know how many times he warned me about coming over to his place drunk, because I was usually upset over something real, or imagined, and I scared his wife.

Of course, I didn't always listen to him, and I'd show up anyway.

But I'll say this for my brother. He never called the cops on me, or tried to kick my ass. I don't know if he could've done that or not. We were about the same size. (Six-feet, two-hundred pounds).

I didn't want to find out anyway. He was my brother, and I really cared about him. But when I was full of alcohol, I was a real Dr. Jekyl, and Mr. Hyde. One minute, I was your buddy, and then the next, a sworn enemy. I could be a mean drunk, especially when the cops would arrest me. I'd fight, and cuss all the way to the drunk tank. I have more than one scar on my head to prove that.

My dad felt the same way as my brother did about my drinking, and lifestyle. I used to see him in a bar, which was owned by a relative of ours, and I'd tense up when he'd start lecturing me.

I liked to drink in there because people were always nice, and treated me with respect. That's because I was my father's son.

My dad was well thought of, but he sure didn't think much of me. Especially when he saw me lapping up the liquor. He'd get on my ass right away, and tell me I needed to get a job, and make something of myself, instead of bumming off people all the time.

I was between the age's of twenty-two, and twenty-three then, and I always figured it wasn't any of his dammed business. As long as I wasn't bothering him or anyone else, I saw no harm in what I was doing, and I wanted to tell him:

"Whut the hell's it to ya? You never gave a shit about me when I was being abused, and molested. Where were ya then? And after I tried to tell ya how I was gitten my ass kicked at the Home, instead of sticking up for me, you told them to go right on ahead. So whut're ya worried about me for now? If I wanna drink, I'll drink. Git outta my face!"

But I never did, and I'd just take off, and find some place else to drink in peace. I liked to just sit there in the warm glow of intoxication and feel good about myself for awhile.

Unfortunately, somewhere along the way, more often than not, I'd get into an argument with someone, which usually led to fisticuffs, and the cops would show up, and throw my ass in jail.

That's why most of my relatives didn't want to have much to do with me, and I guess I couldn't blame them. I was a self-centered S.O.B.

During this time, in 1966, Billy, and his wife had a baby boy, and I remembered how proud I felt. I was an uncle now. Uncle Tommy. It sounded good. I'd like to say that I was there to share in the happy event with my brother.

But, as usual, I was away in jail. I didn't even find out about it until a week later.

Then shortly after his son's birth, something occurred that would change my brother's life forever.

He was drafted into the Army. Then, after getting out of boot camp, he decided to go to Officer Candidate School, where he also took Ranger Training, and came out a Second Lieutenant. Billy was stationed stateside for a couple of years, but then in 1969, he was finally sent to Vietnam, where he served with distinction.

He received a Silver Star, two Bronze Stars, and two Purple Hearts, and several commendations. But they didn't mean that much to him.

What mattered the most, was that in the six months he served in-country, he only lost two men out of his platoon, both of whom were wounded. Billy saw a lot of combat.

His tour in the Army ran out while he was over there, and his commanding officer tried to get him to re-up with a promotion, but Billy had already made First lieutenant, and he wasn't interested. He said that he'd put in his time, and all he wanted to do now, was go home.

When he returned to his wife, and kids, Billy seemed to be okay. But a couple of years later, he got divorced, and moved up into the mountains and became something of a hermit. The only people he'd really have anything to do with were his children, and a few friends.

He did keep in touch with Aunt Marge, and granny though, and that's where I got all of my information about him from. They'd call me once in awhile, and sometimes I'd return the favor. I always enjoyed hearing their voices, even though talking on the phone isn't one of my favorite pastimes.

It was good to see Billy. I love my brother, but unfortunately, I don't know how to show it. I always feel self-conscious around him, and it seems like I'm doing or saying the wrong thing whenever we're together for very long.

So our rare, short visits go pretty well, at first.

As you can tell, I'm proud of my brother. He's everything I'm not. And

I'm especially proud of what he was able to accomplish in those stinking, rice paddies half a world away, when he was called upon.

I look up to all those veterans of all wars who put their lives on hold, and then went off to defend our way of life. And especially for the ones who didn't come back.

I don't know what Billy thought or felt when he was asked to take up arms for his country, but he went ahead, and did his duty. He fought with honor, and bravery on that hallowed, bloodied ground where 58,000 of our men, and women made the ultimate sacrifice, and lost their lives, which hit close to home for me.

There is something about the Vietnam War, that tugs sadly at my senses almost non-stop whenever I watch a movie, or a documentary about that tragic conflict. It was such a brutal, senseless, thankless war, and my heart goes out to all of those men like my brother who had to go through that living hell.

Cowards like myself didn't have to worry about it.

The battle scars I carry about came as a result of my own drunken stupidity. My battle fields were urine splattered alleys, dirty, skidrow streets, and low dives. My commendations for service, can be found in police, and prison files. I feel inferior around Billy, and I guess it's always been like that. We're as different as night, and day, as dad used to say.

Billy had brought his kids with him to the reunion, and that really made me feel good. I rarely see them, just like their dad, and me.

There's my two nephews, Tommy, and Steve, and my niece Carol. Of course, being such a low-life in the sixties, and seventies, I never got to see or have much to do with them when they were small, so I don't know anything about them. But, now with them being pretty well grown, and all, they're nice to me, and that means a lot.

I haven't experienced the closeness of family over the years, but a lot of that had to do with my anti-social behavior, and drinking, and brawling. Nobody wanted to have much to do with me, and I couldn't really blame them.

There were only a couple of smart decisions I made back in those crazy, chaotic days that I could point to, and feel good about. I didn't have much to be proud of back then.

One of them had to do with drinking, and driving, which I didn't do a lot of, thank God. I don't know what I'd have done if I I'd hurt or killed someone in an accident. I wrecked a couple of cars, and was injured myself.

For that reason, I never got my first driver's license until I was twenty-five, but I lost my wallet the first night I had it in a drunken brawl. I didn't even try to have it renewed, because I figured I was better off without one. Back then, if I wanted to get somewhere, I'd depend on buses, or taxis, my feet, or thumb. Or else one of my buddies, who hadn't wrecked his car yet, or have it die of old age.

The other good thing I did back then, was move clear out of the state so I didn't have to be such a burden to granny, or any of my relatives. I stayed out of sight and touch for a while. I thought the change might do me some good, but of course all of the baggage that contained my problems followed close behind, and I continued to screw up.

Finally, though, I did quit drinking, thanks to the sweet, Lord Jesus. I enjoy life now. And it feels good whenever a relative takes an interest in, or shows some attention towards me.

That's what was making this trip so special as I talked, and joked, and laughed with family, and friends.

Billy, and I were talking, and he mentioned something that really piqued my interest. He told me that a couple of years ago, he'd gone to see if the old Camp from our childhood still existed, and it did. Billy said the place hadn't really changed a whole lot, and I thought I'd take a ride up there to see for myself before I had to go back home.

While we were on the subject, I told him about an old acquaintance of ours from the Home who'd I'd run into, and he wanted to drop Billy a line. I wasn't sure how he'd react upon hearing that, but my brother said he'd like to hear from him. I'm like Billy in a lot of ways, because I'm kind of a loner, and I don't like crowds and there were quite a few people at the reunion. But they were blood, and I was made to feel that I belonged with them, and I was comfortable.

I saw my cousin Judy, and her husband David, who's a pilot for a major airline. She's just as sweet, and friendly as ever. I really enjoyed visiting with them, but there was a tinge of sadness in our meeting.

They had been blessed with three, beautiful children, Allen, Timothy, and Angela Dawn. Their oldest son, Allan, wanted to grow up, and be a pilot just like his dad, and that's what he became. He was a co-pilot for a commercial airline that flew out of the city to different ports of call.

Tragically, last December, he, and the pilot of the plane they were flying, crashed short of an airport in some rugged terrain. The lone passenger survived, but Allen, and the pilot perished. Allan's dear, sweet wife, Madge, was waiting for him at the terminal when it happened.

I felt so bad for them. They were still having a hard time dealing with his loss. Allan had really been a neat guy.

After the big get together, I stayed with my aunt, and uncle for a couple of days, and during that time, Aunt Marge, and I took our time, and just talked. It had been pretty hectic up to then.

I love Aunt Marge so. She always make me feel special, and cared about, and genuinely seems to be interested whenever I tell her about what's going on in my life.

Even though she's got her own troubles, (one of which is she's getting up there in years) Aunt Marge always seems to have time for me. It's good to know there's at least one member of my bloodline who cares about whether I live or die. It had been that way with granny, but she had passed away at the ripe, old age of ninety-four the year before Allan's death. Aunt Marge was still grieving over their deaths.

Granny, like Aunt Marge, had been very important in my life. She had never given up on me back in my drinking days, even after everyone else had seemed to. They told her I was no good, and I'd never amount to anything.

But even she seemed to have doubts back then that I would ever quit the slow, painful, dance of death that I was going through in regards to my alcoholic lifestyle. I sensed that Aunt Marge felt that way too.

Poor granny. First, she'd lost grandpa, then a few years later, Uncle Melvin had died from a heart attack due to his drinking. He was only forty-two, but really overweight. Then I showed up four or five years after that.

I'm sure a lot of my relatives were concerned when they learned that I was staying with her. To most of them, I was just white trash, a low-life, drunk, bar-room, brawler, and a waste of time, and effort.

But granny didn't care what other people thought. She had a soft-spot in her heart for me, and she never turned me away. And she sure as hell wasn't afraid to have me there. Granny was a tough, little old lady, and although she didn't look or act like it, she could be mean. For example, one night, shortly after grandpa Brewer died, Uncle Melvin came home drunk. Aunt Marge was there, and she, and her brother got into an argument, and he reached out, and started choking her, and her face turned red.

When granny saw that, she grabbed her big, old cast iron skillet off the stove, and walked up behind her son, and hit him smack in the back of the head with the pan, and cold-cocked him. She could be pretty wicked when you pissed her off. I was like a little boy around her whenever I showed up drunk at her house. I didn't want her getting mad at me. She'd chew me out, and cuss like a sailor, but I never gave her any lip. I really loved, and respected granny.

Of course when I stayed with her, she'd never give me any money, because she knew I'd go out, and spend it on booze. But I had enough drinking buddies who would come, and pick me up, and provide the liquor I craved.

Poor granny. When that happened, she never knew when she'd see or hear from me after I took off with a friend. She'd worry about me, and sometimes I'd call her from jail, and then there was the time I wound up in prison, and that really upset her.

That was one of the things that gave me comfort after I sobered up, and I'd go see granny. She was so happy for me, and in her final years it made me feel good to know that she wasn't worrying about me anymore.

I missed her a lot.

While Aunt Marge, and I sat, and talked, we looked through her photo albums, and I enjoyed looking at all the old pictures. Especially the ones of my mother, Geneva, and us boys. They filled me with the bittersweet memories of years ago, when life had been so new, and the future seemed so promising, and bright.

Although I remember my mom, I didn't know a lot about her, but Aunt Marge has helped fill in the blanks. I liked hearing about my mother's favorite games, and songs as a child, and then the experiences they had shared as adults.

She told me one particular, sad story that made me feel really bad for mom. When she was about eighteen, or nineteen, she had a Jack Russell Terrier named Jip, that she loved so.

One day, she was backing out of the driveway, and she didn't know that her dog was loose, and she ran over and killed him. I could imagine how terrible she must've felt. Aunt Marge said it took mom a long time to get over losing Jip.

Through the years, though, there's a few things that I've learned and recalled about my mother, that make me wish I hadn't. They really upset me.

I've been diagnosed as being bi-polar, and I take medication for depression. I also see a therapist, who helps me deal with all of the issues going on in my life. There's a lot of anger within me because of my past, but I've pretty much got it under control. And it helps that I no longer drink.

My counselor, and I were talking about my mom one time, and he asked me if I ever remembered being hugged or kissed by her when I was a child before her death, and I thought back to those years which had become fuzzy with age. I was surprised to find out I couldn't remember one single time, and that bothered me immensely. Surely she must've, but if she did, I had no memory of that ever happening. I couldn't even recall her smiling at me.

When I really think about those days, I've come to realize that my mom was kind of cool around me. I don't remember any real signs of outward affection. I guess I couldn't blame her. I was always causing problems, and getting into things, and showing up bloodied, and hurt from some accident. I was rather rambunctious.

I told Aunt Marge about that, but she said it couldn't be true, because mom really loved us boys, especially me. I don't dispute her because that what she believes.

But the thing that bothers me the most, regarding my mother, is the way she died, and the fact that I was never told anything about it until I was seventeen. And then it was Billy who let me know.

Where he got the news from, I never asked. But all I know is, I was pretty upset. Somebody could've said something to me before then.

Especially dad. Why hadn't he ever said anything? I really started to get resentful towards him as I got older. It seemed like I was always finding out stuff my father had neglected to tell me. And it didn't help my attitude any, because I blamed him for the way I'd turned out. Don't get me wrong,

I loved my dad, but I hated some of the shit he pulled on Billy, and me. Granny, and Aunt Marge didn't care for him at all. When he first started dating mom, they weren't exactly thrilled, because he liked to party, and drink. So you can imagine how they felt when Frank, and Geneva got married. They were worried about mom.

My parent's marriage seemed okay to me back then, and I don't remember them fighting, or arguing that much, except for one time.

Dad came home drunk one night, and I don't know what it was over, but they got into a knockdown, drag out fight. They were screaming and slapping each other, and I was scared, and crying.

Finally, they wrestled around, and fell on the couch. Then mom began to cry, and dad tried to comfort her. I just stood there, and cried too.

That's the only time I recall anything like that happening.

When dad went off to Korea, things really went to hell for Billy, and me. That was when mom put us with the Bryans.

She would come over to their house to take us out for visits, and she'd have this guy with her. I didn't understand what he was doing there with mom. She was married to dad, not this clown. I resented him.

During that time, she moved out of the apartment that we'd lived in, and had rented a small, two bedroom house. I was excited because that meant when dad got back, we wouldn't have to stay with the Bryans anymore.

So I had a hard time wondering what she was doing with this crud.

I guess she had filed for divorce from dad, and wanted to marry this guy (Another little detail my father forgot to tell me).

They went together for several months, and then he wound up leaving her for another woman. Mom really loved him, and she was devastated.

One night, drunk, and despondent, she went out to the garage of the house she was living in, and stuck one end of a garden hose in the muffler of her car. Then she put the other one inside the driver's side window, got in, started the engine, and then laid her head back, and waited to die.

That's how she was found.

Aunt Marge thinks someone had a hand in mom's death and there is some truth to that. I guess a male friend of hers came over to pay her a visit and found mom in the garage, with the engine running. But instead of doing anything to save her, he just called the cops, and waited for them to show up. I guess they threw him in jail overnight for suspicion in her death, but they turned him loose the next day for lack of evidence.

I don't know how many times Aunt Marge has told me that she wished she had talked dad into letting us live with them when Mr. Bryan, and mom died. If only that could've happened. But I was so screwed up from living with the Bryans, I don't know if I'd have turned out any different than I did. It's hard to say.

The very next day, I drove up to the mountains to go, and see the Camp for myself. Despite some cloudy skies, the scenery was just as pretty as ever.

Along the way, I thought about the Home, which had been torn down in the early 70s (I've often wondered where the spirit who'd haunted me had gone, and if someone else had been aware of it).

Ronny Collins came to mind. I still thought about him once in awhile, and the bond we had formed after getting off to such a rocky start. He had been a special friend, and his tragic death had really affected me.

I was told Uncle Harry had died of a heart attack back in the 1960's, and the memories of those by-gone days began to wash harshly over me.

Billy, and I lost dad to pancreatic cancer in 1968. At his funeral I broke down, and sobbed loudly for all of the pain, and anguish I'd caused him in the last few years of his life. He was only fifty-two at the time of his death.

I'd been filled with so much guilt, and remorse. His passing, left a huge hole in my psyche, which made me feel lost, and alone. First mom, now dad.

I'm sure a lot of the relatives on my father's side of the family who were at the service, thought I was being a phony S.O.B, and they didn't feel any sympathy towards me at all. But as far as I was concered, they could all kiss my rosy, red heinie, and I knew they were smart enough not to say anything to me at the time. They didn't know what I knew anyway. I'd really loved my dad. There were times when my father would let me stay with him as long as I was working, (usually a menial job like washing dishes at some cafe) and not drink.

Dad always seemed to be happy for me, and we'd kid around, and laugh, and that was when I really felt close to him. I wished I could live my life over again, and go back to that time, and sit down with him, and really talk things out between us. There were some issues we needed to resolve.

But we never dealt with the underlying current of lies, and resentments that lurked just below the surface, and after awhile, I'd get bored, and usually blow it by getting pissed with someone at work. I'd quit and go out on a drinking binge, and be in dad's doghouse again. I couldn't seem to get my act together.

Even though we argued, and fought more than once, through it all I never stopped loving him, and as mentioned his death had really hit me hard.

Driving here had brought back somethings that I hadn't thought of in awhile, and I tried to clear my mind, and fill it with the beautiful scenery and look forward to what lay ahead that helped.

Over the years, Ive had several dreams about the mountain and they've been rather vivid. I could hardly wait to see the place that I'd enjoyed so much as a child.

Finally, I came to a curve in the highway, and once I was around it, I saw Mt. Baldwin and Twin Peaks for the first time since I was fourteen. They looked so pretty, and were just like I remembered them.

I wanted to gaze at them for awhile, but I had to keep my eyes ahead for oncoming traffic. I'd have plenty of time to admire them later.

Then I came to the bluff overlooking the highway where the Camp was, and I really started to get worked up. This was going to be fun.

I approached the entrance, and the gate, then slowed down, and made a u-turn, and parked on the side of the road. Because of the coudy conditions, I rolled up the windows, and then got out.

When I went over to the gate, It was locked with a chain, I looked around for a No Trespassing sign, but there wasn't one to be seen, and I went on up, and over the gate to the other side.

As I walked up the fairly steep, old rutted road, memories of summer's past began to wash over me. The Jungle looked as lush, and green as ever.

When I reached the top, I wandered over to where the Old Mill Pond was. I had a camera with me, and I thought I'd get a picture.

But when I got there, I found an inpenetrable wall of dozens of tall, thin aspens that had taken over. Evidently, the dam had disintegrated, and the pond was no more. I could hear the rushing sound of the stream as it made it's way through the trees.

I was disappointed. It had been a pretty spot. I wondered if Indian

Trail had changed any, and I was so frustrated about the situation, I forgot to go over, and check out Queen's Chair.

Instead, I went back to the road, and came to the place where it split, and I looked at the Old Sawmill Road, and thought about the fort, and if it was still standing. I knew if I went up there, I'd never be able to find the trail that led down to the beautiful glade.

I continued to walk up the incline, and when I reached the top, I stopped, and took in the view.

There, for the first time in over thirty years, I saw the Camp. It looked exactly the same way I remembered, and it was like stepping back in time. All of the buildings were still there.

Old memories flooded my mind as I stood there, and stared. Then, I snapped a couple of pictures with my camera, and then began to walk down the slope. As I got closer, I went between the buildings, and Uncle Harry's house. Now that I was near them, there were signs that the passing years had slowly taken a toll on them. There were loose boards, and missing shingles. They all had that same pale, green shade of paint that I recalled.

Everything was locked up tight. It looked like someone had been there recently judging from some tire tracks. I wondered if they'd been made by Uncle Harry's family. He'd had a son, and daughter, who used to come visit every summer for a week or two back then.

As I walked between the chow hall, and the big bunkhouse, peering in the windows, an eerie feeling came over me. It seemed as if the ghosts of Ronny, and the others, were walking with me. I could almost hear their voices, and laughter in the sounds of my footsteps, as they echoed off the buildings.

After I came out on the other side, I quickly forgot about the sensation as I looked up at the Mountain, and the Peaks. It was just like seeing old friends again. I stood there for a moment gazing upwards, and then snapped some pictures.

I wandered down to the joaner holes, but they'd been removed.

All that remained of them were the concrete foundations. The holes had long since been filled in with dirt. The memory of the way they used to smell almost made my nose twinge in disgust.

I looked at where the big joaner had stood, and thought of that summer day when Tommy Madsen, and I had peeked at the graffiti on the wooden walls, and I smiled. But it was a sad smile.

Over the years, I've ran into some guys from the Home. Most of the time, it was in jail, but that's not always been the case.

A couple of years ago, my wife, and I were having some plumbing problems, and my wife said a friend of hers highly recommended an independent plumber she knew. So I let Deb take care of it.

When this guy showed up, the name on his van looked familiar, but I couldn't place it at first. Then it dawned on me.

Shunkwiler! Now that was a moniker I hadn't heard in a long time. I wondered if it was my old friend Darren, but I doubted that. Probably some distant relative. It was just a name you didn't see or hear everyday.

When he came to the door, I peered at the name tag on his work shirt, and I got excited when I saw it read "Darren." Maybe it really was him, because I thought I could see my old buddies face. A little heavier, and age lined, but the eyes were the same.

"How're you doing?" I asked. "My name's Tommy, Tommy Janicek."

I hoped that would get a response from him, but all he did was stick out his hand to shake, and smile at me.

"I'm Darren Shunkwiler," he said. "I understand you've got a leak going on down in the basement."

After he said that, I decided to quit toying around, and just ask him flat out.

"I used to run around with a kid with the same name as yours back in the fifties," I told him. "That wouldn't by chance be you, would it?"

Suddenly his face broke out in a big grin.

"Tommy Janicek!" he exclaimed. "Son-of-a-bitch! I thought that was you when you told me you're name. how the hell are you?"

"Okay," I told him. "How've you been? I see you got your own business."

"Yea," he replied. "It keeps me busy and out of trouble."

The town we live in now is pretty fair sized (50,000 pop) but I couldn't get over how both of us had wound up living here. Talk about a small world.

Darren's grandparents had been residents, and after they both went to a rest home, they'd given him their house, and that's what brought him, and his wife here.

As for myself, this town just happened to be where my drinking days had ended, and although I'd moved away a couple of times, something always drew me back. And this is where I'd met my wife.

And now, one of my old, childhood friends.

It was pure coincidence that we'd met one state over, same town, almost thirty years later.

We talked, while he worked, about the old times at the Home, and what had gone on in our lives since then.

I found out Darren's life had pretty much paralleled Billy's after he left the Home. Despite his childhood problems, he'd stayed out of trouble, graduated from high school, got a job, then married, and then been drafted and sent over to Nam in 1970.

But Darren hadn't been a "grunt," and I think that bothers him for some reason. I just got that feeling when I praised him for having the guts to go over there in the first Place. He'd lost some friends while there, and I sensed that it was a delicate subject around him.

He was however, impressed when I told him about Billy's service record, and some of the stories that my brother had related to me.

Although he was quiet, Billy had no problem talking about his combat experiences, which I enjoyed hearing. Just as I had when my dad used to do that.

Even though I went through a lot of violence. I still get a kick out of hearing someone talk about warfare. I guess that's because I never had to go through anything like that, thankfully.

Billy had taken good care of the men who served under him, and he spent more of his off-duty hours with them, instead of with the other officers, who he said seemed to resent him. He wore his battlefield fatigues most of the time, and he looked pretty scruffy compared to them.

He pulled some stunts out in the field that might have gotten some other officer in trouble, but being as it was Billy, it was kind of overlooked.

That was due to his success in rooting out the V.C. in the Mekong Delta area, with only minimal losses on his side. So he was tolerated.

After Billy had been back home awhile, a couple of men from his unit, paid him a visit, and let him know the officer who had replaced him, had gotten a bunch of the platoon shot up, and killed.

I didn't mention that part to Darren.

We talked about Tommy and Toby Garcia, and what they might be doing now.

"I don't know about Toby," he said. "But Tommy got killed a long time ago."

"What? What happened?" I asked, shocked.

He told me that Tommy had died in a car wreck in 1964. Darren had seen his picture, and name in the obituary column of a paper.

I really hated hearing that, and I was saddened by the news. Tommy had been my buddy ever since that first day at the Home! I don't know what I'd have done sometimes if he hadn't been there to make me laugh. Like Ronny, he'd been special.

When Darren was done with the plumbing, we exchanged phone numbers, and made plans to get together with our wives, and have dinner.

Right after that, I got to meet his lovely wife, Rebeka, and they are the nicest couple. We get together once in awhile, and play cards, and have a few laughs.

The funniest thing about them though, is that they're bike riders. And I'm not talking bicycles. Im talking Harley's.

They go to Stursis, South Dakota every year for the bike rally. I get the biggest kick out of them. From just looking at and talking to them, you'd never guess that was their hobby. It was nice to have him living there.

Now, as I walked back towards the Camp, I passed by the place where we'd had our bonfires. I'd enjoyed them, and the fun we had being scared by Elmer Lehr. I wondered what had happened to him, knowing Elmer, he was probably dead by now, killed in some dare devilish act.

Then I went by the area where Herman Rhinehardt had us box, and Jake Spangler came to mind. Mean Jake.

When I was in prison in 1965, I had a guy tatoo the words "hate" on one hand, and "love" on the other. I thought they would make me look cool, and tough, but nobody seemed impressed. Just me.

Now I wish I hadn't done it. They're ugly, and a reminder of Jake, who was shot, and killed in a bar fight back in 1973.

When I reached the gully, the thought of my wild ride in the wagon came to mind. It was a wonder that I hadn't wound up with a broken neck that day.

I went down the steep slope until I reached the bottom. Then I looked up the at the huge, pine tree where the rope had been, and thought of Jimmy Marcus, who'd gotten so banged up when the rope snapped in two.

Poor Jimmy. He had left the home after the summer of '56, and had missed out on us finally finding the plane. His prediction about being the next one to die after Ronny, sadly, turned out to be true.

In 1959, he, and one of his cousins were playing with a loaded gun, when it went off accidently. The bullet struck him in the head and he died instantly.

Another good friend gone.

I started to ascend the hill on the other side, and pretty soon, was huffing like a steam engine. I remember how easily I used to go up this slope as kid. Not anymore, man.

I was forty-five, weighed two hundred, and fifty pounds, and smoked. I figured I'd better take it easy before I had a heart attack. After finding a big rock, I sat down to rest for a minute or two, then I got up, and resumed my climb.

Finally, I reached Crow's Nest, and rested on the outcropping of rock, and waited to catch a breath. Then I took in my surroundings.

The sky was clouded over, but it still didn't take away from the pretty view. The different hues of green trees, and rancher's pastures, and the hills, and forest that worked their way up to the edges of the mountain, were just as majestic as ever.

The cool air felt good on my skin, and I lit a smoke, and relaxed I could see the tops of the buildings below, and there were a lot of memories running through my mind. Some of them were pleasant.

I gazed up at the mountain, and her twin sisters again, and thought about the Plane. I wondered what the crash site looked like now. It was probably so over grown with bushes, and trees, it would be difficult to find the engines and propellers.

Thoughts of my obsession filled my mind. The dreams I had about finding it, and the wondrous feeling I got whenever I did. I just knew it would be magical and special.

I recollected the first summer I was old enough to go on the hike, and how disappointed I'd been when I sprained my ankle right before the climb. But that didn't lessen my enthusiasm any.

Then came the next trek, and the difficulty of spotting the wreckage in all of the trees. And there had been the bad storm. But, I remained confident that we could find it if the weather left us alone.

And then how on my final climb, the sun had shown us the location of the ill-fated bomber. I remembered the excitement, and the thrill of finally finding it, and reaching my goal.

Although the plane wreck hadn't exactly been the way I thought it would be, it had still been pretty neat. I'd been thrilled at first, but then the reality of the deaths of the men who had crashed into the peak hit me, and then, my perception of the Mountain began to change. When we got back to the Camp. I recalled the empty feelings I started to have. And Herman's departure hadn't helped the situation any.

The magical spell that was The Legend of the Plane had been broken, and I was beginning to learn that life was like that. The search was almost always better than the actual find. After the discovery, I learned that I'd left a part of myself in the wreckage. A part that would never return, no matter how hard I tried to regain it.

An innocence was forever lost, and that was sad.

I remembered my cousin, Dougie, and how I'd promised to bring back a piece of the Plane for him when we found it. He had really liked the souvenir I got him. Now he was also gone. He had been killed in Vietnam in 1969, shortly before Billy arrived there. Dougie was gone, but he would never be forgotten, and his name, Douglas F. Menard, is carved on the wall in Washington, D.C.

I liken the search for the Plane, as being a metaphor of our journey through life's trials and tribulations.

We struggle up the mountain, and slip, and slide, before we reach the top, and attain our goal in life. Some don't make it, and fall. Others just quit.

And once we reach the summit, we aren't always rewarded for our efforts, and our viewpoint changes. We see that there are more mountains to climb.

That's the way it was for me.

A lot of crap has flowed through my life, and I went through some situations where I very easily could've died. But the Good Lord above, sent down a Guardian Angel to watch over and allow me to live.

Some of the guys I ran around with later on after I left the Home, didn't make it. So I'm grateful to be alive. Looking back now, I can truly say I'm a survivor.

I wanted to be a badass, and have people be afraid of me when I grew up. But after I got older, I found out that in order to be one, you have to pay a painful price, both physically, and psychologically.

For one thing, it was a lonely existence, because nobody liked to be around you, except for low-lifes who wanted to watch, and have you fight their battles for them. (I was full of false bravado when I drank).

And you had to be willing to take some lumps, because you quickly learn that there are a hell of a lot of guys out there, who are badder, faster, and stronger than you ever thought of being. And some of them would just as soon shoot or stab you, rather than have you beat on them.

Of course, I got to know law enforcement personnel pretty well. I was on a first name basis with a lot of them.

I was a good poster child for the old adage: Learned about Life from "The School of Hard Knocks." I was sent to institutions of lower education, for my efforts.

Like Reform School, reformity, and penitentiary.

While attending them, I found out I wasn't very tough. I could fight, but in places like that, being good with your fists didn't mean anything because you never knew how someone you thumped on would retaliate. So I chickened out more often than not. I just didn't have what it took to be a real badass.

I could only go so far when it came to fighting someone. All I wanted to do was punch them out so they would leave me alone. I didn't want to hurt them badly or God forbid, kill them like some of the guys I knew back then.

I saw a couple of cons get murdered when I was in prison, and they were terrible events that haunt me to this day.

So many deaths in my life.

But the worst one of them all, occurred when Billy, and I were living with the Bryan family.

During our stay there, they took in two little brothers. There was two year old Alex, and his baby brother, Tommy. They were cute little guys, especially little Tommy. I don't know how old he was, but all he could do

271

was crawl. He hadn't learned to walk yet, and I liked to play with him as he crawled around on the floor, getting into things.

One night, after they'd been with us awhile, Old Man Bryan came home half-drunk and in a bad mood. He was sitting in the kitchen, drinking a beer, while Eunice prepared supper. We kids were in the living room listening to the radio.

Baby Tommy decided to go into the kitchen and investigate. When he got under Eunice's feet, she picked him up and took him out and sat him on the rug. Then she walked back out to the stove. As soon as she was gone, he crawled back in, and again she picked him up, and again, placed him on the rug. The third time he repeated this, she brought him out and really sat him down hard. As she walked away, he began to cry loudly.

This went on for a couple of minutes and Eunice finally yelled at him to stop. But of course, he just continued.

Suddenly Old Man Bryan loomed in the doorway, and I got scared, because I knew how mean he could get, especially when he was drinking. He walked up in front of the crying baby.

"Shaddup!" he roared.

Baby Tommy jumped in fright and then he really cried. Great, big wails of sound.

"Gawdammit!" the Old Man roared again. "I said shaddup!"

Then he bent over and slapped the baby across the face and there was a loud smack. Baby Tommy quit crying, and Old Man Bryan went back out to the kitchen.

The baby had stopped, because he was building up for a loud scream. He rocked back and forth a couple of time, taking in great, gasps of air.

Suddenly, he toppled over backwards and hit his head on the leg of a table behind him. There was a loud thump and his body went limp. Baby Tommy didn't move or make a sound. He just laid there with his head turned to one side. I was stunned.

Eunice rushed out of the kitchen and picked him up. She gently shook him and called his name, but got no response. Old Man Bryan came out and together they tried to wake him up. They were unsuccessful, and finally, they decided to call an ambulance.

I remember how white-faced Eunice was, and how her hands shook after she laid the baby on the couch. The Old Man walked over after making the call, and he looked concerned.

Then he saw Billy, and I watching. I was in a state of shock over what had happened. He gave us a mean look, and I cringed in fear.

"When the ambulance gets here, you little bastards keep your gawdammed mouths shut! You got that?"

We both nodded our heads. There was no way we were going to say anything. He frightened us.

When the medics arrived, the Old Man told them it was an accident, and they took baby Tommy to the hospital.

After we went to bed that night, I prayed little Tommy would be okay, and I had a hard time going to sleep. Thoughts about what had happened kept going through my mind. I hoped he'd come back to us, safe, and sound.

But the next day, I was shocked, and horrified to learn that during the night, Baby Tommy had died from a blood clot to the brain.

After hearing this, I found a place where I could be alone, and I cried. I had felt like doing that the night before, but I hadn't. now, I just let go.

One night, not long after that, I had a terrible nightmare.

I dreamed that I was in a hole in the ground, and Old Man Bryan was rolling big rocks on top of me. I was screaming in terror, and then I woke up, and Eunice was there, trying to settle me down, but I continued to scream, because the image was still etched vividly in my mind.

She asked me what was wrong, and I told her that her husband was trying to kill me. Eunice told me not to be silly, because he was out in the kitchen.

I finally calmed down, and she left. I went back to sleep, and the next morning, the Bryan boys got on me about faking my dream, but I just ignored them.

I never told anyone about what really happened to Baby Tommy.

That incident with him is so traumatic. I try not to think about it. All it does is bum me out, and lust for revenge. But Old Man Bryan is dead, and there's nothing I can do about it now.

I can't remember if the incident with Baby Tommy occurred before mom's death or not. But it eats at me whenever I wonder what would've happened, if I'd just had the balls to tell someone about what that bastard was doing to me. Who knows? Maybe both of them might still be alive now. I like to think that if Billy, and I had been staying with my mother, perhaps she wouldn't have done what she did.

But, I'll never know because I'm gutless, and kept my mouth shut when I should've spoken up.

The shocking events that I went through, and the stigma of the bedwetting stayed with me for a long time. I tried to forget all that bullshit after I got older, but when I was in a bad mood, all it took was for someone to say the wrong thing or put their hands on me, and it was off to the races.

Especially when I was drinking, and I came across some crud from my past. Then I'd try to get some payback.

But whenever I did that, somehow it always left a bad taste in my mouth afterwards. Just as my drinking did.

I remember the first time I felt the full effect that alcohol had on me. I was seventeen, and this wonderful, warm, sense of well-being came over me, and I loved it. However, I didn't get drunk, just high, and I couldn't wait to try it again.

After that, every chance I got, I would seek out the guys who I knew could buy some alcohol. And after I became of age, my life really began to turn into a mess, and I was constantly getting into trouble. I just didn't grasp that maybe what I was doing was bad for me.

I was having too much fun. (When I wasn't being thrown in jail). I liked having people think I was trouble, and a bad guy. (Which as you know, I wasn't) It was more of an act, although I could be loud, and scary when I was mad.

But the older I got, the worse my life became. I began to have blackouts, and I'd wake up in jail, all beat to shit, and have no idea what I was in there for. I was always afraid to ask what I'd done.

But even worse were the alcohol withdrawals. I swear they got to the point where I thought I was going to die. They'd last for two or three days, and after I got out of jail, and felt better, I'd swear that was it. I didn't want to go through all that again, and I'd be okay for awhile. But then invariably, somebody would piss me off, and I'd go charging back into the battle I had with alcohol, and of course, it always kicked my ass. Over, and over, I'd repeat the same crapola.

I did some terrible things back in those days. Things that I have a hard time forgetting, and forgiving myself for. But, I have to let go of that stuff, or else, I might as well go out, and drink again.

I hurt a lot of people back then, both physically, and emotionally, and for that I am truly sorry. Especially for the ones who were close to me.

So it is important that I learn to like, and forgive myself, even if others won't. Just like my dad's side of the family. I can't do anything about those people who still hold a grudge against me.

I finally entered a drug, and alcohol treatment center in 1978. I was at the point where I was desperate to get out of the vicious cycle of alcoholism that I was caught up in.

But I had to go through there three times. I would stay there for thirty days, and go through indoctrination on how to stay sober, and I'd get out willing, and able to take on the world sober, and sane.

Unfortunately, every time I left, the significant other in my life at that time, would pull some shit on me, and I would wind up getting drunk the first night I was out. And then of course, I'd be in the same, sad shape I'd been in before. There seemed to be no end to this living hell I was going through.

But, then finally, in June of 1979, I went to treatment for the last time. With the help of some fans of Bill W.'s, I've stayed sober: since my final drink was in June, I celebrate two birthdays. My own, and my sobriety date.

It's odd, but my life seems to run in threes, and hence it's my lucky number. Take, for instance my trips through treatment. The "third time was a charm."

Going back to my childhood, I had three chances to find the Plane even though I only went up there twice, but I still count it as three.

Another one has to do with my faith in The Father, The Son, and The Holy Ghost I know they exist, because I've felt The Holy Spirit within me at times, and it is the most wonderous feeling I've ever had. (Better than any high I got off drugs, or alcohol.)

And then there's my wife, and how she fits into the equation of number three.

While I was going through treatment for the third, and last time, I met a pretty, sandy-blond haired girl named Deborah. We hit it off right from the start, and we used to sneak off, and make out (which wasn't allowed).

After we both left treatment, she moved to one town, and went to another. We kept in touch, and finally, we got together, and then married in March (another three) of 1980. This was the second marriage for both of us. Two recovering alcoholics, living under one roof isn't supposed to work, but we've got around that.

Evidently, we are meant to be. Deb's mom, Bev, was born on August 23, 1933. Mine, of course is June 23, 1943, and my wife's is April 23, 1953.

All I know is, I'm happy now. I was so lonely before.

My only regret is that we cant have any children. I've never had any as far as I know. I lived with a couple of gals who got pregnant, but then they miscarried. My first wife couldn't have any.

Given all of my problems, I guess not having a child is for the best. I don't think I would've made a very good parent anyway. For one thing, I'm too impatient.

Deb, and I tried, and she got pregnant, but then miscarried, and almost bled to death, and had to have a hysterectomy.

So I've never got to know what it feels like to be a father. Deb had four babies with her first husband, who was an abusive son-of-a-bitch (I can't brag cause I was the same way with the other gals I lived with).

She lost her kids because of her drinking, and drugging. Now, her children won't have much to do with her, and I know she's heartbroken, but she never says much about it.

Dear, sweet, funny Deb. I love her dearly, and I don't know what I'd do without her. She's my rock. We're complete opposites in a lot of ways, and we argue at times.

Whenever I get angry at her or someone else, she tells me to knock it off. She says I need to work on my temper, and quit using my lousy childhood as an excuse to blame people, and take my frustrations out on. That I'm not that important, and nobody owes me anything just because of it and to quit feeling sorry for "poor Tommy" and to get on with my life. She tells me I should have been a proctologist, because I'm a real pain in the ass, and that I just need to sit there, and try to look intelligent. Don't say anything.

Seriously though, I make an effort to listen to her because I know she's right. When we first married, we had a hard time finding good jobs, but without an education, they weren't easy to come by.

Because of my indifference towards school, I'd never made it past the ninth grade. The only reason I'd gotten that far was because I'd attended classes in Reform School. They weren't that hard for me to learn, and I graduated from the eighth grade.

Deb had dropped out in her senior year in high school, and now I understood what my dad had said about how important it was to get a good education.

We struggled along, and we needed to do something.

Finally, in 1981, she talked me into taking A.G.E.D. test with her, and lo, and behold, I passed, along with her, and we had our high school diplomas.

Then she wanted us to go to college, but I didn't think I could do it. After we enrolled though, I surprised myself. Deb prompted me, and I found out I was smarter than I'd previously thought.

I wanted to become an art teacher, and I came close, but I wasn't able to reach my goal. The only thing that held me back was math. I just couldn't fathom algebra, and no amount of tutoring helped. I had to settle for a degree in Fine Arts.

Deb now, was a completely different story. She graduated suma-cum-laude, with a degree in Vocational Rehabilitation.

She worked as a substance abuse counselor then, at a treatment center where I'd been employed as an aide. Deb was boss over me there, just as she was at home. Kind of line Rebekah with Darren.

I wished that Deb would've been there to share this with me, but the picture's would have to suffice. I know Darren would like them at least, I hoped he would.

Suddenly, I was rudely brought out of my musing, by a brilliant flash of light and then a loud clap thunder of as it crackled from the clouds above. I'd been so wrapped up in my thoughts, that I hadn't paid any attention to all of the grumbling overhead, and the brief flickers of brightness in the clouds.

Now, it began to sprinkle.

I was reminded of that summer day in 1954, when I'd been up here, cursing at the Camp below. How I'd heard the rumbling clouds, and thought I'd better get off that hill before I was struck by lightning. Then I'd decided that nobody would care anyway and how sorry I felt for myself.

But then came the deafening crash of sound that convinced me that I'd better get the hell out of there. I smiled in remembrance.

Some drops of rain began to come down and I decided I'd better head for my car. I stood up, snapped a couple of more pictures of the Mountain, then took off.

After reaching the gully, I went up the steep slope, then took one last stroll through the Camp. As I walked, the rain started to pick up.

By the time I reached the entrance, it had really started to pour. When I climbed over the gate, and stepped down, I slipped, and just about fell on my ass.

I hurried to the car, and jumped in, and was glad that I'd decided to roll up the windows. I grabbed the strap that held my camera, and took it from around my neck, and laid it on the seat beside me. I hoped the rain hadn't harmed the film. Then I took the pack of smokes from my shirt pocket, and put them on the dashboard.

After that, as the rain pattered loudly on the roof, I shed my wet, pullover shirt, and tried to dry myself off with it, as best I could. After that, I turned, and threw it on the back seat, and got a clean, dry one from my bag on the floor board, and turned back around, and slipped it on.

Then I got out my car keys, and started the engine. The country western cassette that I'd been listening to earlier, blared forth, loudly at me, and I lowered the volume. I'd forgotten to eject it when I first got here, because I was in such a haste to see the Camp. I swear, I was slowly going deaf.

The rain was continuing to come down hard, and I turned on the windshield wipers, then put the car in gear. I checked to make sure there wasn't any traffic coming, and then pulled out on to the wet asphalt.

After I passed by the bluff upon which the Camp sat, I settled in, and concentrated on the rain-slickened highway straight ahead of me.

I never looked back.

Lightning Source UK Ltd.
Milton Keynes UK
UKHW010830271221
396165UK00001B/8